BUDDHIST POSITIVENESS

BUDDHIST POSITIVENESS

Studies on the Lotus Sūtra

FERNANDO TOLA
CARMEN DRAGONETTI

MOTILAL BANARSIDASS PUBLISHERS
PRIVATE LIMITED • DELHI

First Edition : Delhi, 2009

ISBN: 978-81-208-3191-9 (Cloth)
ISBN: 978-81-208-3406-4 (Paper)

MOTILAL BANARSIDASS
41 U.A. Bungalow Road, Jawahar Nagar, Delhi 110 007
8 Mahalaxmi Chamber, 22 Bhulabhai Desai Road, Mumbai 400 026
203 Royapettah High Road, Mylapore, Chennai 600 004
236, 9th Main III Block, Jayanagar, Bangalore 560 011
Sanas Plaza, 1302 Baji Rao Road, Pune 411 002
8 Camac Street, Kolkata 700 017
Ashok Rajpath, Patna 800 004
Chowk, Varanasi 221 001

Printed in India
By Jainendra Prakash Jain at Shri Jainendra Press,
A-45 Naraina, Phase-I, New Delhi 110 028
and Published by Narendra Prakash Jain for
Motilal Banarsidass Publishers Private Limited,
Bungalow Road, Delhi 110 007

To the beloved memory of
our brother Jimmy Zeballos.

CONTENTS

PREFACE

This book contains some of the results of the research work we carried out in the *Fundación Instituto de Estudios Budistas FIEB*, of Buenos Aires, Argentina, thanks to the support of a subsidy received, during the years 1998 and 1999, from the *Agencia Nacional de Promoción Científica y Tecnológica* of Argentina, for the *Project PICT 04-00000-01611*: *El Sūtra del Loto (Saddharmapuṇḍarīkasūtra): Doctrinas, Problemas, Actualidad* ("The Lotus Sūtra (Saddharmapuṇḍarīkasūtra): Doctrines, Problems, Actuality").

It is also thanks to the *Agency* that we could finish the ten years Project of translating from Sanskrit into Spanish the *Lotus Sūtra*, translation that appeared in Mexico, in May 1999, published by *El Colegio de México* and by the *Asociación Latinoamericana de Estudios Budistas.* We began this Project in Tokyo in 1989, and it had the generous support of Dr. Tsugunari Kubo, President of *The Reiyukai.* This Project is tightly connected with the book that now we present, since it was in the course of the translation of the *Lotus Sūtra* that the ideas, problems and interpretations that gave rise to these studies reunited in this book evolved.

It is also thanks to the same support of the *Agency* that the translation into Spanish from Chinese (with Introduction and Notes) of the *Sūtra of the Infinite Meanings* could be done, and was published in Spain by Desclée de Brouwer editors in the year 2000. This *sūtra* is also very much related to the *Lotus Sūtra* and to the religious doctrines, philosophical theories and/or Buddhist themes, which are developed in this book.

In the frame of the same Project our *Foundation* invited the well-known Peruvian scholar Dr. Santiago Erik Antúnez de Mayolo, Honorary President of the *Sociedad Geográfica del Perú* ("Geographic Society of Peru"), to attend the *Simposio sobre el Alimento* ("Symposium on Food") that he presided in our institution, the *Fundación Instituto de Estudios Budistas FIEB*, on 25th June, 1999. His important communication on *El alimento en el Incanato* ("Food in the Inca Empire") was accompanied by other two papers on *The Attitudes in face of Food in Ancient India:* Fernando Tola's on *Vedism, Brahmanism, Hinduism*, and Carmen Dragonetti's on *Buddhism and the Lotus Sūtra*, both included in their English version in this book united in a sole essay.

The studies included in this book are enumerated in the following paragraphs with Roman numbers from I to XIII. We point out the academic journals where some of them were published for the first time or the congresses or academic meetings in which some of them were presented as papers by both authors; we give also the indication about the language in which they were originally published (Spanish or English or both). They appear now with some modifications as for instance the inclusion of the original texts Sanskrit, Pāli or Tibetan:

I: **in English**, in *Cahiers d'Extrême-Asie,* Kyoto, 9, 1996-1997, **The conflict of change in Buddhism. The Hīnayānist Reaction***; **in Spanish,*** in *'Ilu, Revista de Ciencias de las Religiones*, Madrid (Spain), número 4, 1999, pp. 303-326, **El conflicto del cambio en el Budismo. La reacción hīnayānista**.

II: **in English**, in *Hokke-Bunka Kenkyū* or *Journal of the Institute for the Comprehensive Study of the Lotus Sutra* (Hokekyō Bunka Kenkyūjo), Rissho University, Tokyo (Japan), N° 24, 1998, ***The conflict of change in the Lotus Sūtra. The Hīnayānist Reaction***; **in Spanish**, in *'Ilu, Revista de Ciencias de las Religiones*, Madrid (Spain), número 5, 2000, pp. 179-198, ***El conflicto del cambio en el Sūtra del Loto. La reacción hīnayānista***.

III: **in English**, in *Indologica Taurinensia*, Torino, Italia, Vol. XXV-XXVI, 1999-2000 (paper read in the *XIth World Sanskrit Conference*, Torino, 2000) (a first brief version), ***The Lotus Sūtra as an apologetic work***; in English, in an enlarged version,

Hokke-Bunka Kenkyū or *Journal of the Institute for the Comprehensive Study of the Lotus Sutra* (Hokekyō Bunka Kenkyūjo), Rissho University, Tokyo, N° 29, 2003, ***Apologetics and Harmony in the Lotus Sūtra and in Bhavya***; **in Spanish**, in *Congreso Nacional de la Asociación Latinoamericana de Estudios de Asia y Africa ALADAA* (paper read as *Opening Conference*, La Plata / Buenos Aires, Argentina, 2004), ***Apologética y armonía en el Budismo: el Sutra del Loto y Bhavya.***

IV: **in English**, in *Hokke-Bunka Kenkyū* or *Journal of the Institute for the Comprehensive Study of the Lotus Sutra* (Hokekyō Bunka Kenkyūjo), Rissho University, Tokyo (Japan), N° 26, 2000, pp. 63-84, ***Śūnyatā in the Lotus Sūtra.***

V: **in English**, in *Aspects of Buddhist Sanskrit (Proceedings of the International Symposium on the Language of Sanskrit Buddhist Texts, 1991)*, Central Institute of Higher Tibetan Studies, Sarnath, Varanasi, India, 1993, Kameshwar Nath Mishra editor (paper read *in absentia*), pp. 483-508, ***On translating into Spanish the Saddharmapuṇḍarīkasūtra: A. The Language of the Lotus Sūtra B. Problems of Translation and Communication in the Lotus Sūtra***; **in Spanish**, in *Volumen de Homenaje a Adolfo Prieto*, Instituto de Filología Clásica, Facultad de Filosofía y Letras, Universidad de Buenos Aires, 2000, pp. 1-10, ***El idioma del Sūtra del Loto. El Sánscrito budista híbrido.***

VI: **in English**, in *Indo-Iranian Journal*, Vol. 42, 1999, pp. 53-55. ***Ekaṃ samayam.***

VII: **in English**, in *Hokke-Bunka Kenkyū* or *Journal of the Institute for the Comprehensive Study of the Lotus Sutra* (Hokekyō Bunka Kenkyūjo), Rissho University, Tokyo (Japan), N° 17, 1991, pp. 107-116, ***The meaning of the infinite numbers in the Lotus Sūtra***; **in Spanish**, in *Revista de Estudios Budistas REB*, México-Buenos Aires, N° 5, 1993, pp. 67-82, ***El significado de los números infinitos en el*** Sūtra del Loto (Saddharmapuṇḍarīkasūtra).

VIII: **in English**, in *Tōhō (The East)*, *The Eastern Institute*, Tokyo (Japan), N° 9, 1993, pp. 243-250, ***Beginninglessness of the Veda and the Dharma***; **in Spanish**, in *Revista de Estudios Budistas REB*, México-Buenos Aires, N° 11, 1996, pp. 28-36, ***Eternidad del Dharma en el Sūtra del Loto***.

IX: **in English**, in *Tōhō (The East)*, *The Eastern Institute*, Tokyo (Japan), 11, 1995, pp. 225-245; and in *Hokke-Bunka Kenkyū* or *Journal of the Institute for the Comprehensive Study of the Lotus Sutra* (Hokekyō Bunka Kenkyūjo), Rissho University, Tokyo, N° 22, 1996, pp. 107-116, ***On the Names of Bhikṣus and Bodhisattvas in the Lotus Sūtra***; **in Spanish**, in *Revista de Estudios Budistas REB*, Mexico-Buenos Aires, 10, 1996, pp. 41-85, ***Los nombres de Bhikshus y Bodhisattvas en el* Sūtra del Loto**.

X: **in English**, in *Hokke-Bunka Kenkyū* or *Journal of the Institute for the Comprehensive Study of the Lotus Sutra* (Hokekyō Bunka Kenkyūjo), Rissho University, Tokyo (Japan), N° 26, 2000, pp. 35-62, ***Positiveness in the Lotus Sūtra***.

XI: **in Spanish**, paper read in the panel "Religión y Familia" ("Religion and Family") of the *Congreso Internacional de Familia, Terapia Familiar, Siglo XX, Siglo XXI* ("International Congress of Family, Family Therapy, 20eth century, 21st century", Fundación CEFYP, Buenos Aires, 1999.

XII: **in Spanish**, in *Actitudes frente al Alimento en la India Antigua: Vedismo-Brahmanismo-Hinduismo. Budismo y Sūtra del Loto*, Buenos Aires: Fundación Instituto de Estudios Budistas FIEB, 1999.

XIII: ***Reviews on some publications concerning the Lotus Sūtra*, in Spanish**:

In *Revista de Estudios Budistas,* México-Buenos Aires:

- N° 5, 1993, pp. 176-177, *The* Lotus Sūtra *Written in* kana *Characters Kept in the* Myōichi Memorial Hall *of the* Reiyukai, Tokyo, edited by Norio Nakada (1988) in 3 Volumes (ix-724, 725-1346 pp.; iv, iii pp., 1341 col.; vi, ix, iii, 615, xii pp.

- N° 6, 1993, pp. 164-166, *The Lotus Sūtra, The White Lotus of Marvelous Law, Translated from the Chinese of Kumārajīva, by Tsugunari Kubo and Akira Yuyama,* Tokyo, The Reiyukai, 1991, xiii- 332 pp.

In *Boletín de la Asociación Española de Orientalistas*, Madrid, Universidad Autónoma:

- Año XXXIII, 1997, pp. 423-424, *Tao-sheng's commentary on the Lotus Sūtra*, by Young-ho KIM, Albany N.Y.: State University of New York Press, 1990, ix-374 pp.

In *'Ilu, Revista de ciencias de las Religiones*, Madrid, Universidad Complutense:

- N° 5, 2000, pp. 282-284, *The Lotus Sūtra*, translated by Burton Watson, New York: Columbia University Press, 1993;
- *Le Sūtra du Lotus, suivi du Livre des sens innombrables et du Livre de la contemplation de Sage-Universel*, traduit du chinois par Jean-Noël Robert, Paris: Fayard, 1997, 480 p.;
- *Sūtra von der Lotosblume des wunderbaren Gesetzes, nach dem chinesischen Text von Kumārajīva ins Deutsche übersetzt und eingeleitet von Margareta Borsig*, Darmstadt: Wissenschaftliche Buchgesellschaft, 1993, 415p.;
- Seishi Karashima, *A Glossary of Dharmaraksha's Translation of the Lotus Sūtra*, Tokyo: The International Research Institute for Advanced Buddhology, Soka University, 1998, 696 p.

***

We have chosen as title of this book *Buddhist Possitiveness : Studies on the Lotus Sūtra*, because "Buddhist Possitiveness" is the most representative essay of those we have gathered here, because the Lotus Sūtra is one of the Buddhist texts which can give a real idea of the force, originality, influence, and value of the Buddhist Possitiveness, and finally, because every one of these studies is on and around the Lotus Sūtra. This essay on Buddhist Positiveness was originally written (1994) by Fernando Tola as an answer to the Catholic Pope's criticism of Buddhism, according to which Buddhism is a 'negative' religion; and this essay was presented afterwards, in an abridged version, as a paper, in *The International Conference* of *The International Association of Buddhist Studies* held in Lausanne, Swiss (in 1999).*

Fernando Tola and Carmen Dragonetti
Fundación Instituto de Estudios Budistas FIEB
cldragon@mail.retina.ar
Buenos Aires, June 20, 2005

* In this book the titles of the Chinese texts are given according to the transcription of the *Répertoire du Canon Bouddhique Sino-Japonais. Fascicule Annexe du Hōbōgirin. Édition révisée et augmentée. Édition de Taishō (Taishō Shinshū Daizōkyō)*, compilé par Paul Demiéville, Hubert Durt, Anna Seidel, Paris-Tōkyō: Librairie d'Amerique et d'Orient Adrien-Maisonneuve-Maison Franco-Japonaise, 1978.

I

The Conflict of Change in Buddhism: The Hīnayānist Reaction

Reactions and conflict provoked by the arising of Mahāyāna

Whatever may be the sect or sects out of which Mahāyāna developed, whatever may be the causes that produced that development, and whatever may be the form assumed by the development, it is obvious that the new doctrines that were to constitute the Mahāyāna had necessarily to produce reactions on both sides: in those who were introducing the new doctrines, in regard to those who kept adhering to the traditional ideas; and in those who were attached to tradition, in regard to those who were promoting the change.

As the development of Mahāyāna Buddhism was gradual, the number of the new doctrines increased over the course of time, their opposition to the traditional doctrines became stronger, and they spread gaining new adherents, it was natural that the reactions they provoked had to be different. These reactions many times adopted very aggressive forms, contrary to what is generally admitted. These reactions were the manifestation of the *conflict of change* that was taking place inside the Buddhist community.

The history of the councils and sects in Hīnayāna Buddhism offers good instances of the reactions and conflicts originated by the proposal of new doctrinal or disciplinary positions. What distinguishes the reactions and conflicts provoked by the Mahāyāna is the importance of the differences between the opposed positions, and of the consequences that followed.

The aim of this article.

In this article we shall refer only to the reactions that the new Mahāyānist ideas caused in those Buddhists who adhered to the ancient tradition (whom we shall call for convenience 'Hīnayānists' although this name is not appropriate at all). These reactions show the different aspects assumed by the conflict.

It is easy to find in the Mahāyānist texts references to the harsh attitudes adopted against the Hīnayānists by the supporters of the new form of Buddhism. What is not so easy to encounter are descriptions of how the old Buddhists reacted in the face of the great changes that were being introduced in the Buddhist Doctrine by the Mahāyānists. In what follows we give specially testimonies offered by the Mahāyāna texts on the reactions of the Hīnayānists, which show the diverse aspects and the intensity of the conflict.

Testimonies in Mahāyāna texts

1. *Saṃdhinirmocanasūtra*

The *Saṃdhinirmocanasūtra* VII, 11-23 (*Ḥphags pa dgoṅs pa ṅes par grel patheg pa chen po'i mdo= Āryasaṃdhinirmocana-mahāyānasūtra, Tōhoku* 106. Lamotte's edition) exposes the different kind of reactions of beings (*sems can, sattva*) when they hear the doctrine of inexistence of an own being (*ṅo bo ñid med pva ñid, ni'svabhāvatā)* that the Sūtra attributes to Buddha (*ṅa'ī chos)* and that is a characteristic doctrine of Mahāyāna Buddhism. From the context it is clear that this text is referring to "beings" belonging to the Buddhist community. It presents a "scale of adhesions" (*mos pa'i rim pa, adhimuktyanukrama),* i.e., different kinds of reactions. In paragraphs 11-21 positive reactions to the indicated new teaching are mentioned, but in paragraphs 22 and 23 negative reactions are described: there were people who openly rejected the doctrine asserting that it was not "the word of Buddha" (*saṅs rgyas kyi bka' ma yin, buddhavacana*), but "the word of Māra" (*bdud kyis smras pa yin, Māravacana*):

Tibetan text

22./ gaṅ dag lta ba la dga' bar mi byed pa de dag ni de dag las chos rnams kyi ṅo bo ñid med pa ñid thos çiṅ chos rnams kyi skye ba med pa daṅ / 'gag pa med pa daṅ/ gzod ma nas zhi ba daṅ raṅ bzhin gyis yoṅs su mya ṅan las 'das pa thos nas skrag ciṅ dṅaṅ la kun tu dṅaṅ bar 'gyur zhiṅ 'di skad ces 'di ni saṅs rgyas kyi bka' ma yin gyi / 'di ni bdud kyis smras pa yin no zhes kyaṅ zer zhiṅ de ltar rig nas mdo sde de dag la skur pa 'debs par byed / spoṅ bar byed / mi bsṅags pa brjod par byed / ṅan du brjod par byed / gzhi des na phoṅs pa chen po 'thob par 'gyur zhiṅ las kyi sgrib pa chen pos kyaṅ reg par 'gyur ro // gzhi des kyaṅ gaṅ dag skye bo phal po che la las kyi sgrib pa chen po 'thob pas slu bar byed pa / mtshan ñid thams cad med par lta zhiṅ don ma yin pa don du ston par byed pa de dag ni las kyi sgrib pa chen po daṅ ldan par ṅa smra'o /

23. / don dam yaṅ dag 'phags de la sems can gaṅ dag dge ba'i rtsa ba ma bskyed / sgrib pa yoṅs su ma dag / rgyud yoṅs su ma smin / mos pa mi maṅ / bsod nams daṅ ye çes kyi tshogs yaṅ dag par ma grub ciṅ / draṅ po daṅ draṅ po'i raṅ bzhin can ma yin la rtog pa daṅ sel <mi> nus la / raṅ gi lta ba mchog tu 'dsin par gnas pa de dag gis ni chos de thos na / ṅa'i dgoṅs te bçad pa 'aṅ yaṅ dag pa ji lta ba bzhin du rab tu mi çes çiṅ chos de la mos par yaṅ mi 'gyur la / de dag chos la chos ma yin par 'du çes çiṅ / don la don ma yin par 'du çes la / chos la 'aṅ chos ma yin pa daṅ / don la 'aṅ don ma yin par mṅon par zhen nas 'di skad ces 'di ni saṅs rgyas kyi bka' ma yin gyi / 'di ni bdud kyis smras pa yin no zhes kyaṅ zer zhiṅ de ltar rig nas mdo sde dag la skur pa 'debs par byed / spoṅ bar byed / mi bsṅags pa brjod par byed / ṅan du brjod par byed ciṅ lhad kyaṅ 'jug par byed de / rnam graṅs du mar mdo sde de dag spaṅ ba daṅ / chud gzan pa daṅ / rnam par gzhig pa'i phyir zhugs çiṅ de la mos pa'i gaṅ zag rnams la 'aṅ dgrar 'du çes par 'gyur ro // de dag ni daṅ po ñid nas kyaṅ las kyi sgrib pas sgribs pa yin la / gzhi des kyaṅ yaṅ las kyi sgrib pa de lta bus sgrib par byed de / las kyi sgrib pa de'i daṅ po ni gdags par sla'i / bskal pa bye ba khrag khrig 'bum phrag 'di sñed kyi bar gyis 'byuṅ bar 'gyur ro zhes gdags par ni dka'o // don dam yaṅ dag 'phags de ltar na ṅa'i chos 'dul ba legs par gsuṅs pa / çin tu gya nom pa / bsam pa çin tu rnam par dag pa ston pa chos legs par bstan pa la sems can rnams kyi mos pa'i rim pa de lta bu dag kyaṅ snaṅ ṅo /

Translation

"22. Those who do not like this theory, on hearing from others that things do not possess an own being, that things do not arise, do not cease, on hearing that (things) are calm from the beginning and completely nirvānized by nature, they are afraid, they are frightened, they are terrified. They say: "This is not the word of Buddha; this has been said by Māra." Saying so, thinking thus, they speak impiously of the *sūtras*, they reject them, they criticize them, they revile them. From this reason, they get a great misfortune and they are also affected by the great hindrance due to past actions. For this reason, I say: "Those who, because of having got the great hindrance due to past actions, deceive the great mass of beings, and, thinking that all the characteristics do not exist, teach what is not truth as truth- they are enchained to the great hindrance due to past actions."

23. O Paramārthasamudgata, those beings who have not caused roots of merit to grow, who have not compeltely purified the hindrances, who have not completely ripened the series, who have not multiplied the adhesions, who have not done the accumulation of merits and knowledge, who are not honest nor possess an honest nature, who are (not) able to reason and to refute, who persevere in taking for the best their own view, they, on hearing this doctrine, do not understand correctly and according to truth my intentional language, they do not adhere to this doctrine either. They consider that this doctrine is not the doctrine, they consider that this truth is not the truth. Owing to their attachment to the idea that this doctrine is not the doctrine, that this truth is not the truth, they say: "This is not the word of the Buddha; this has been said by Māra." Saying so, thinking thus, they speak impiously of the *sūtras*, they reject them, they criticize them, they revile them. They also adulterate them. In many ways they apply themselves to eliminate, to destroy, to annihilate these *sūtras*. They consider as enemies those persons who adhere to them (= these *sūtras*). From the very beginning they are hindered by the hindrance due to past actions and for this reason they hinder (others) with a similar hindrance due to past actions. It is easy to know the beginning of this hindrance due to past actions; it is difficult to know after how many hundreds of thousands of *nayutas* of *koṭis* of cosmic periods it has come forth. O Paramārthasamudgata, such is the scale of adhesions of beings to the discipline of my Doctrine, which has been well explained, is most excellent, and has been preached (by me) with extremely pure intention – to (my) well-taught Doctrine."

2. *Mahāprajñāpāramitopadeśa* (I)

In the *Mahāprajñāpāramitopadeśa* or *Mahāprajñāpāramitāśāstra* (*Ta tche tou louen, Taishō* 1509, p. 506a, line 13-15) attributed to Nāgārjuna is found a passage which expresses a similar idea:

Translation of the Chinese text

"... The disciples, reciting and repeating what Buddha had said, composed and wrote the books of the *sūtras*. Ignorant people slander (the *sūtras*) saying that they are not the Buddha's word, that they have been composed by Māra or by Māra's people and also that they have been written by people adhering to the false view of *ucchedavāda* (annihilation)."

3. *Adhyāśāyasaṃcodana* (?)

The sūtra *Adhyāśāyasaṃcodana* (?) (*Fa cheng tche lo houei*, 25th of *Mahāratnakūṭasūtra* = *Ta pao tsi king, Taishō* 310, p. 528b, lines 10-14), introduces Māra himself, disguising himself as a *Bhikṣu* and trying to deceive people in regard to the origin of Mahāyāna *sūtras.* Of course, Māra represents in this text the opinion of real Hīnayānist monks:

Translation of the Chinese text

"At that time, Māra the Evil, having seen that, in order to deceive (people), assumed the appearance of a *Bhikṣu,* and arriving at that place said such words: "All these *sūtras* have been composed all of them by ordinary people of skilful language. They are not the word declared by the Tathāgata. Why? Because by means of what is said in this *sūtras,* you will not obtain any merit, any benefit"."

4. *Pañcaviṃśatisāhasrikāprajñāpāramitāsūtra*

The *Pañcaviṃśatisāhasrikāprajñāpāramitāsūtra* (*Mo ho pan jo po lo mi king, Taishō* 223, p. 340 b lines 6-14) depicts a scene similar to that of the previous text with more details:

Translation of the Chinese text

"Evil Māra transforming himself into a *Bhikṣu,* wearing the (Buddhist) robes, went to the place where the Bodhisattvas were, and said these words to the Bodhisattvas: 'You have heard before that you must practise with purity the six Pāramitās, etc. up to: you must obtain, after practising them, with purity, the *anuttarasamyak-saṃbodhi.* But you (should) detest, reject, repudiate these things. Under the Buddhas of the past, the future and the present, from the moment you formed your initial resolution (*prathamacitta-utpādāt*) until the realization of the Dharma, in the meantime, you produce roots of merit. You find pleasure in the earnest application directed towards (*ābhoga*) the *anuttarasamyaksaṃbodhi.* You (should) also detest, discard, repudiate these things. If you detest and repudiate (them), I will tell you the True Doctrine of the Buddha. All you have heard before is not at all the Doctrine of the Buddha, is not the teaching of the Buddha. All this (teaching as contained in the *sūtras*) is only an adulterated compilation. What I say is the True Doctrine of the Buddha'."

In relation to the four preceding texts it should be noted that in the first and the second the Hīnayānists affirm that some doctrines of the *sūtras* of the Mahāyāna are 'the word of Māra', while in the third and the fourth the Hīnayānist monk who rejects the Mahāyāna *sūtras* as not being composed by the Buddha, and the doctrines they contain as not being the true doctrine of the Buddha, is in reality Māra the Evil disguised as a monk. It is interesting that Hīnayānists and Mahāyānists identify their opponents with Māra, the Enemy of the Buddha. This reveals the strength of the conflict that pitted the two major forms of Buddhism against each other.

5. *Mahāprajñāpāramitopadeśa* (II)

The *Mahāprajñāpāramitopadeśa* preserves a curious episode concerning Śāriputra, p. 145a, lines 12-25:

Translation of the Chinese text

"Thus Śāriputra during sixty *kalpas* followed the Way of the Bodhisattva. He wished to cross the river of *dāna* (giving). Then a beggar came to beg for his (=Śāriputra's) eye. Śāriputra said: 'My eye is of no use to you. Why do you demand it? If you need my body or my propoerty, then I will give them to assist you.' The beggar replied: 'I do not need your body or your property, I only wish to get your eye. If you truly practised *dāna* (giving), you would give your eye to me.' Then Śāriputra taking out one of his eyes gave it to him. The beggar takes the eye, and in the presence of Śāriputra smells it, spits on it with disgust at its bad smell, throws it on the ground and crushes it with his foot. Śāriputra pondering said: 'Persons of such evil practices are difficult to save! My eye was really useless for him, but he demanded it in a compulsory way. When he got the eye, he threw it away and crushed it with his foot. What evil practice is worse than this? Men like that cannot be saved. It is better to train oneself to escape as soon as posible from *sāṃsara.*' Having pondered thus, he retired from the Way of the Bodhisattva and returned to Hīnayāna. This is called 'Not to reach the other shore'."

This episode of Śāriputra comes after an explanation of the meaning of the word *pāramitā.* It is given as an example of a failure concerning the practise of the *dānapāramitā* or 'Perfection in Giving': Śāriputra, who has converted to Mahāyāna and is following the Bodhisattva's discipline, performs an act of 'heroic' *dāna* in giving his eye to a beggar, but, on seeing the recipient's violent reaction, he repents and turns back to Hīnayāna. From the Mahāyānist point of view Śāriputra has failed. As noted by Lamotte, *Le Traité de la Grande Vertu de Sagesse*, II, p. 701, note 2, the encyclopaedia *King liu yi siang* (*Taishō* 2121, p. 69b, lines 6-12), "Different aspects of the Sūtras and the Vinaya", by Pao-ch'ang (502-557 A.D.) gives a resumé of this same episode.

It is possible to trace in Śāriputra's words and thoughts a Hīnayānist criticism of an extreme kind of *dāna,* highly extolled in Mahāyāna, including the donation of the head, the eyes, the marrow, the brain (cf. in this same treatise p. 73a, lines 26-27, p. 143c, line 14, p. 146a, lines 3-4, p. 146b, lines 3-4; other references in Lamotte's translation, p. 143, note 1), and of the idea that all persons, the wicked and the righteous, friends or enemies, the deserving and the undeserving, may be recipients of a gift that produces merit (cf. in this same treatise pp. 145c, line 25 – 146a, line 1, and Asaṅga's *Mahāyāna-sūtrālaṅkāra*, p. 112, lines 4-5, S. Lévi edition, and *Bodhisattvabhūmi*, p. 135, lines 16-17, and p. 132, line 25, Woghihara's edition). Śāriputra considers this kind of donation as useless and criticizes the beggar as unworthy of that donation because of his compulsory demand and violent behaviour. As a result of this experience Śāriputra returns to Hīnayāna, thinking that it is better to apply oneself to *one's own* training in order to obtain liberation from *saṃsāra* than to perform such deeds of exaggerated generosity. Very probably Śāriputra's attitude reflects the attitude of many Hīnayānists of that time.

Testimonies from Hsüan-tsang

The testimonies of the preceding texts are corroborated by the information given in the biography of Hsüan-tsang written by Hui-li and revised and annotated by Yen-ts'ung, *Ta t'ang ta ts'eu ngen sseu san tsang fa che tchouan* ("Biography by the Master of the Law of Tripiṭaka, [who lived] in the Monastery of the Great Compassion, [made] under the Great T'ang", *Taishō* 2053), and in Hsüan-tsang, *Ta t'ang si yu ki* ("Records of the Western Lands

[made] under the Great T'ang", *Taishō* 2087): four testimonies are from the *Biography* and two from the *Records.*

6. *Biography of Hsüan-tsang* (I)

The *Biography* (p. 226c, lines 21-22; p. 226c, lines 22-25; p. 226c, lines 27-29) mentions a monk, Mokṣagupta by name, who stayed in a Monastery in Kucha, in Central Asia. Mokṣagupta was a very learned and respected monk. He was an adherent of the Hīnayāna and in his dialogue with Hsüan-tsang reveals his negative opinion of the Mahāyāna:

Translation of the Chinese text

"(Then) he (Mokṣagupta) adressed the Master of the Law saying: 'In this country we have all (the books) such as the *Saṃyuktahṛdayakośa*, the *Vibhāsā* and so on...' The Master of the Law asked him: 'Do you have the *Yogācārabhūmiśāstra* here or not?' Mokṣagupta replied: "What is the purpose of inquiring after a book that contains only erroneous views? The true disciples of the Buddha do not study it all'.

At first the Master of the Law felt a profound respect for him: but when he heard these words he considered him a vulgar person, and said: '... The *Yogācārabhūmi(śāstra)* has been revealed by Maitreya Bodhisattva in his last body. Calling it now an erroneous book, how are you not afraid of falling into a bottomless abyss?'."

7. *Biography of Hsüan-tsang* (II)

The *Biography* (p. 244c, lines 14-25; p. 244c, lines 28-29; p. 244c, lines 29 - p. 245a, line 3; p. 245c, lines 2-3) narrates a story concerning the great King Harśa (Śīlāditya), that besides showing that in Hsüan-tsang's epoch there were Hīnayānists who considered the Mahāyāna doctrine as contrary to the true teaching of the Buddha and the Mahāyānists as heretics, also reveals the bitter animosity that marked, at times, the relations of the two great forms of Buddhism with one another:

Translation of the Chinese text

"Before (the monk) Siṃharaśmi departed King Śīlāditya had built a *vihāra* covered with brass plates, by the side of the Nālandā monastery, higher than ten *chang* (1 *chang* = 10 feet). It was known in all countries by everybody. The King, after having personally reduced to submission Koñyodha (modern Ganjam, in the East coast of India), came to the country of Uch'a (modern Orissa). All the Buddhist priests of this country study the Hīnayāna and do not have faith in the Mahāyāna. They consider that it is (a doctrine only) of the 'sky–flower' heretics, not the word of the Buddha.

When they saw the King after his arrival, making fun of him, they said: 'We have heard that the King has made by the side of the Nālandā (monastery) a *vihāra* covered with brass plates, an extremely imposing and admirable work. Why did you not construct it in the monastery of the Kāpālika heretics or in some other (place like that)?'

The King answered: 'Why such words?'

In reply, they said: 'Because the Monastery of Nālānda with its 'sky-flower' heretics is not different from those Kāpālikas.'

Prior to this an old Brāhman whose name was Prajñagupta, *ācārya* of a consecrated king of South India and well versed in the teachings of the Saṃmatīya School, composed a treatise in 700 *ślokas* to destroy the Mahāyāna. All the teachers of the Hīnayāna admired and esteemed it. For this reason (the Buddhist priests of Orissa) taking (a copy of that book) showed it to the king and said: 'Thus is our school. Is there a man of the Mahāyāna able to refute and destroy one single word of it?'...

If the King has any doubt, 'why does he not assemble a conference and compare (the doctrines) and decide in order to fix what is right and what is wrong?'...

Then on that (same) day (the King) wrote a letter and send it to the Nālānda monastery of Śīlabhadra, the Master of the Law, 'The Treasure of the True Doctrine', saying: 'Your disciple, on coming to Uch'a (Orissa), saw some teachers of the Hīnayāna who trust to a *Śāstra* composed on the basis of inferior views, which slanders and defames the Mahāyāna. They accuse (the Mahāyānists) of earnestly harming the fundamental principles (of Buddhism) and of being outside the common (Buddhist) beliefs'...

At that time the Master of the Law wished to go to Uch'a (Orissa), and inquired about getting the (treatise) composed by the Hīnayāna in 700 *ślokas* in order to destroy the teachings of the Mahāyāna."

8. *Biography of Hsüan-tsang* (III)

The *Biography* (p. 247b, line 2) refers to the same King Śīlāditya as having said about a certain Master of the Hīnayāna, called Devasena:

Translation of the Chinese text

"(This religious) leader (=Devasena), promoting heterodox theories, incessantly defamed the Mahāyāna."

9. *Biography of Hsüan-tsang* (IV)

What happened after the conference, as narrated in the *Biography* (p. 247c, lines 18-19, lines 23-24, and lines 24-25), in which Hsüan-tsang and the Masters of Hīnayāna debate on points of doctrine, shows the bitterness of the theoretical conflict that opposed Hīnayānists and Mahāyānist doctors:

Translation of the Chinese text

"After five days had passed the heretics of the Hīnayāna, on seeing that (Hsüan-tsang) had defeated their school, united full of hate wishing to plot to injure (him).

The King, on hearing about it, issued a proclamation saying: '... The followers of extravagant and false (doctrines) (i.e., the Hīnayānists) do not know shame and remorse; they plot sedition to overturn everything and to cause (him) harm intentionally ... If there is only one of all these that injures or touches the Master of the Law, I shall cut off his head; and if he reviles (him) I shall cut out his tongue'."

10. *Records of the Western Lands* (I)

In the *Records of the Western Lands* there are also references to the attitude of the Buddhists belonging to the Hīnayāna. Hsüan-tsang, p. 891c, lines 1-12, tells about Guṇaprabha, a Master of *śātras,* who lived in old times in Matiputra (Mo-ti-pu-lo) (=Madāwar or Mandāwar or Mundore, a large town in Western Rohilkhand near Bijnor). Originally he belonged to the Great Vehicle but afterwards attached himself to the Little Vehicle. Two facts are to be noted in the text that follows: on the one hand, that Guṇaprabha composed several treatises to overthrow the Great Vehicle, and on the other, he considered himself, as a fully ordained Bhikṣu, superior to Maitreya as a Bodhisattva, since he was dedicated to ascetism while Maitreya was enjoying heavenly beatitude:

Translation of the Chinese text

"At first he (Guṇaprabha) studied (the doctrines of) the Mahāyāna, but, not having yet thoroughly investigated its profound and subtle (principles), in consequence of having read the *Vibhāṣāśāstra,* he gave up his (former) work (in Mahāyāna) and learned the (doctrines of) Hīnayāna. He composed several tens of volumes of treatises in order to refute the principles of the Mahāyāna and devoted himself entirely to the Hīnayāna. Moreover, he composed more than several tens of volumes of secular books, criticizing and blaming the authoritative treatises done by his predecesors. He comprehensively studied the *sūtras* of the Buddha, but he had some ten doubts (concerning their doctrines), and although he thoroughly investigated them for a long time, he could not remove his feeling of doubt.

At the time there was an Arhant Devasena — in the Chinese Language T'ien Chün ('Army of the Gods)—who visited now and again the Tuṣita Heaven. Guṇaprabha was desirous to see Maitreya to ask him for further information in order to solve his doubts. Devasena, by means of his ubiquitous supernatural power, took him up to the dwelling (of Maitreya) in Heaven. When (Guṇaprabha) saw Maitreya, he slowly bowed low to him, but he did not worship him. Devasena said: 'Maitreya Bodhisattva is the next in order to reach the rank of the Buddha. Why are you so self-conceited as to dare not to worship (Maitreya). A moment ago you wished to receive a benefit (from him); why do you not humble yourself (before him)?' Guṇaprabha replied saying: 'Venerable sir! these words are honest, intended to guide and admonish me. But I am a *Bhikṣu* who keeps all the rules, I entered ascetic life as a disciple; Maitreya Bodhisattva receives the happiness and the joy of Heaven; he is not a companion for one who has entered ascetic life. Nevertheless I wished to offer him worship, but I feared it would not be proper'."

11. *Records of the Western Lands* (II)

In the same country of Matipura, according to the *Records* of Hsüang-tsang, p. 892b, lines 12-14, there was a *stūpa* containing the relics of Vimalamitra, another Master of *śāstras*, from Kashmir, attached to the Sarvāstivāda school. Vimalamitra had been a renowned Master who decided to write treatises in order to lead people away from the Great Vehicle, but his design could not be fulfilled because he lost his mind and died:

Translation of the Chinese text

"With that which I perfectly know, I will compose treatises to cause the learned people of Jambudvīpa to interrupt their praise of the Mahāyāna and to destroy the fame of Vasubandhu: this will be my imperishable task and will fulfill my long-cherished ambition."

Three testimonies from Vasubandhu's biographies:

12. *Biography by Paramārtha* (I)

Paramārtha in his *Biography of Vasubandhu* (*P'o seou p'an teou fa che tchouan*, *Taishō* 2049, p. 190 c lines 12-13, 19-20, 27-

28, p. 191a lines 1-5) describes the opposition of Vasubandhu to the Mahāyāna before his conversion to it:

Translation of the Chinese text

"When the Master of the Law (=Vasubandhu) wholly understood the principles of the eighteen schools (of Hīnayāna), he admirably explained the Hīnayāna. He firmly adhered to Hīnayāna as being the right (Buddhist doctrine); he had no faith in the Mahāyāna, thinking that the Mahāyāna was not what the Buddha had said ...

(Words of Asaṅga to Vasubandhu:) The brother (=Asaṅga) said: 'You do not have faith in the Mahāyāna, and you are always defaming it to an extreme...'

Since he (=Vasubandhu) formerly defamed the Mahāyāna and had not the luck to have faith in it, he (=Asaṅga) feared that, as a consequence of this wrong conduct, he would necessarily enter an evil destiny...

(Words of Vasubandhu to Asaṅga:) 'I formerly defamed in an intense way (the Mahāyāna) by means of my tongue; now I will cut out my tongue in order to atone for this evil action.' His brother said: 'Even if you cut out a thousand of your tongues, you could not do away with that evil action. If you wish to do away with that evil action, you must employ another means.' Then the Master of the Law requested his brother to tell him the means to do away with that evil action. The brother said: 'Your tongue was able and skilful to defame the Mahāyāna. If you wish to do away with that evil action, be equally skilful in expounding the Mahāyāna'."

13. *Biography by Bu-ston* (II)

The same attitude against the Mahāyāna is attributed to Vasubandhu, before his conversion, by Bu-ston in his history of Buddhism, *Chos-'byuṅ* (second part: *History of Buddhism in India and Tibet*), 842, 7-843, 5. Bu-ston contains some details of the life of Vasubandhu, which are not in Paramārtha's Biography:

Tibetan text

(842,7) ...*(Dbyig gñen) Nālandār byon pa daṅ / gcen gyis bstan bcos maṅ du brtsams pa 'aṅ gsan nas /*

kye ma thogs med nags su lo /
bcu gñis bar du tiṅ 'dsin bsgrubs /
tiṅ 'dsin ma grub glaṅ chen gyi /
rgyab khal loṅs pa 'i grub (843,1) *mtha ' brtsmas /*

źes theg chen gyi gaṅ zag daṅ chos la bstiṅ pa ... (843,5) *khyod so so 'i skye bo yin ciṅ daṅ por theg chen la skur pa btab pas tshe 'di la mthoṅ ba 'i skal ba med kyi sgrib pa sbyaṅ bar bya ba 'i phyir theg chen gyi mdo 'grel maṅ du rtsoms /*

Translation

"...(Vasubandhu) came to Nālandā and, having heard (the exposition of) numerous treatises composed by his elder brother (Asaṅga), abused the people and the Doctrine of the Mahāyāna, saying:

'Alas! Asaṅga, in the forest,
for twelve years
has performed profound meditation;
he did not succeed in his meditation;
he has created a philosofical theory,
which is (as heavy) as the burden
carried on the back of an elephant!'

...(Words of Asaṅga:) 'You (=Vasubandhu) must compose numerous commentaries to the *sūtras* of the Mahāyāna in order to remove the sin of not being worthy of seeing (Maitreya) in the present life, because you, as an ordinary person, have formerly abused the Mahāyāna'."

14. *Biography by Tāranātha* (III)

In regard to this matter the narrative of the life of Vasubandhu in Tāranātha's history of Buddhism in India, *Rgya gar chos-'byuṅ*, p. 92, line 19-p. 94, line 21, Schiefner's edition, is similar to that of Bu-ston and Paramārtha.

15. *Tāranātha's History of Buddhism* (I)

In Tāranātha's *Rgya gar chos-'byuṅ*, already quoted, p. 51, lines 6-8, there is a reference to the negative reaction of the Śrāvakas to the spread of the Mahāyāna:

Tibetan text

...theg pa chen po'i sñan pa'ī grags pas phyogs thams cad du khyab pa na / ñan thos rnams kyi blor ma śoṅ nas / theg pa chen po saṅs rgyas kyi bka' ma yin no źes skur pa btab bo /

Translation

"...when the fame of the Mahāyāna spread through all the regions, there was no room for it in the mind of the Śrāvakas, and so they abused the Mahāyāna saying: 'It is the not word of Buddha'."

16. *Tāranātha's History of Buddhism* (II)

In another passage, p. 57, lines 4-6, Tāranātha mentions a *Bhikṣu* named Śaṅkara (Bde byed) who composed a treatise in which he attacked the Mahāyāna. According to Tibetan tradition – Tāranātha reports – this treatise had an extension of 1200000 *ślokas*, but according to Indian sources it had in fact 12000 *ślokas:*

Tibetan text

...dge sloṅ bde byed ces bya bas rig pa'i rgyan źes bya ba'i bstan bcos theg chen sun 'byin pa'i phyir brtsams pa...

Translation

"A treatise called *Nyāyālaṅkara* was composed by a *Bhikṣu* named Śaṅkara in order to refute Mahāyāna."

17. *Bu-ston's History of Buddhism*

Bu-ston, *Chos-'byuṅ* (second part: *The History of Buddhism in India and Tibet*), in the section corresponding to the life of Nāgārjuna, also refers to the same monk. According to him the *Bhikṣu* Śaṅkara in this treatise refuted "*every one (who chanced) to dispute with him.*"

18. *Asaṅga*

Asaṅga, *Mahāyānasūtralāṅkāra*, introduces *śloka* I, 7 (where he enumerates in a concise way the reasons why the Mahāyāna must be considered as the word of the Buddha) with the following words which express the point of view of the Hīnayānists in regard to the praise of the Mahāyāna made by Asaṅga:

Sanskrit text

naivedaṃ mahāyānaṃ buddhavacanaṃ, kutas tasyāyam anuśaṃso bhaviṣyatīty atra vipratipannās tasya buddhavacanatvaprasādhanārthaṃ kāraṇavibhājyam ārabhya ślokaḥ (= *śloka* I,7)

Translation

"There are people who dissent in regard to this saying: 'This Mahāyāna is not at all the word of the Buddha. How (then) will there be such a praise of it?' In order to establish that is the word of the Buddha, there is the following *śloka* having to do with the analysis of the reasons."

19. *Sāramati* (I)

In the classification of beings, *Ratnagotravibhāga ad* I, 32-33 (p. 53), Sāramati points out that among the Buddhists "attached to existence" there were some who hated the doctrine of the Mahāyāna:

Sanskrit text

tatra (= sattvarāśau) bhavābhilāṣiṇo dvividhā veditavyāḥ. mokṣamārgapratihatāśā aparinirvāṇagotrakāḥ sattvā ye saṃsāram evecchanti na nirvāṇaṃ tanniyatipatitāś cehadhārmikā eva. tadekatyā mahāyānadharmavidviṣo.

Translation

"Among them (beings), those who desire existence (*bhavābhilaṣin*) should be seen as of two types: (1) those beings whose wishes are against the path of Liberation, who do not belong to the family of (those who look for) the *parinirvāṇa*: they only desire the *saṃsāra,* not the *nirvāṇa*; (2) And those who (although) belonging to Buddhism have fallen into that destiny (of being *bhavābhilāṣin*). Some of these (latter) are enemies of the Doctrine of the Mahāyāna."

20. *Sāramati* (II)

The *ślokas* 21 and 22 of the fifth chapter, p. 217, of Sāramati's *Ratnagotravibhāga* contain a description of the Hīnayānists who abuse the Doctrine of the Mahāyāna, and explains the reasons thereof:

Sanskrit text

āryāṃś cāpavadanti tannigaditaṃ dharmaṃ ca garhanti yat sarvaḥ 'so 'bhiniveśadarśanakṛtaḥ kleśo vimūḍhātmanām / ... (21) dhīmānyād adhimuktiśuklavirahān mithyābhimānāśrayāt sadharmavyasanāvṛtātmakatayā neyārthatattvagrahāt / lobhagredhatayā ca darśanavaśād dharmadviṣāṃ sevanād ārād dharmabhṛtāṃ ca hīnarucayo dharmān kṣipanty arhatām (22).

Translation

"The fact that (people) revile the Noble ones and blame the Doctrine preached by them, all this is the impurity produced by the false views caused by strong attachment proper to foolish-minded ones... (21). Because of weakness of intelligence, of lack of pure faith, of being endowed with false pride, of being filled with (the evil of) throwing away the true Doctrine, of holding as truth the meaning which has to be determined owing to their nature, and on account of their false views owing to their greed and covetousness, and because of their honouring the enemies of the Doctrine and being far from those bearing the Doctrine – those taking pleasure in the *hīna* (the inferior or little or lesser Vehicle, Hīnayāna), abuse the Doctrine of the Arhants (22) ..."

Let us note that in the *śloka* 22 the Chinese translation interprets *hīna* as *Hīnayāna*, translates *kṣipanti* by *pang* (to speak ill of, to slander, to villify), understands *arhatām* as *of the Buddhas,* and adds "the lack of faith in the Mahāyāna" as another cause of the wrong behaviour of the kind of people described in the text.

Two Indirect Testimonies

In many Mahāyāna texts there are harsh attacks against the Hīnayāna and criticism of their doctrines accompanied with a scornful attitude. All this could be considered as a *reaction* provoked by the hostility of the Hīnayānists; or, if this Mahāyanist behaviour was not a reaction produced by the Hīnayāna, it had necessarily to be a *cause* of violent responses on the part of the Hīnayāna. In any event, the *conflict* was there.

There was a vast Mahāyāna literature aimed at establishing the authenticity of the *sūtras,* trying to prove by means of different kinds of arguments that they had been preached by the Buddha, that they were the words of the Master. Lamotte, *Le Traité de la Grand Vertu de Sagesse* II, pp. 939-942, note 1, indicates a good number of texts that expound the defence made by the Mahāyāna of the authenticity of the *sūtras.* This allows us to infer that among

Hīnāyanists it was common to consider the Mahāyāna *sūtras* as apocryphal. In the texts previously quoted there are many examples of this Hīnāyanist position.

Extension of the Conflict to China and Japan

This conflict between Mahāyāna and Hīnāyana began in the Northwest India (where Hīnāyana as the first preached form of Buddhism had firm roots) at the beginning of the Christian Era; then it accompanied the spread of Buddhism northward, through the Silk Road, into the countries of Central Asia, and then China and afterwards Japan, and southward into Sri Lanka and South-east Asia. The testimonies contained in the preceding pages concern India, with the exception of testimony number 6, which has to do with Central Asia.

References to this conflict in China can be found in Zenryū Tsukamoto, *A History of Early Chinese Buddhism*, for instance in pp. 446 and 449 (letter of Fan-t'ai to Tao-sheng and Hui-kuan), p. 447 (Fa tu), etc., and in Kōgen Mizuno, *Buddhist Sūtras*, pp. 124-125.

The same Mizuno, *The Eastern Buddhist* 1997, 1, pp. 79-80, gives interesting information about the controversy on the authenticity of the *sūtras* in Japan up to the recent years, pp. 125-133 (Tominaga Nakamoto, Hattori Ten'yū, Hirata Atsutane, Murakami Senshō).

The Conflict in Sri Lanka

The conflict between Hīnayāna and Mahāyāna tendencies also reached Sri Lanka. The principal protagonists were the monks of the Mahāvihāra monastery, who adhered to the (Hīnayānist) Theravāda tradition and were most orthodox and opposed to the Mahāyāna, and the monks of the Abhayagiri monastery who were open to the Mahāyānist ideas and were therefore considered by the monks of the Mahāvihāra as heretics.

Vetullavāda and Vītaṇḍavāda as designations of Mahāyāna

The Mahāyānist ideas were referred to by name of *Vetullavāda* (or *Vetulyavāda)* in Pāli (*Vaitulyavāda* in Sanskrit), and people adhering to these ideas by the name of *Vetullavādins.* The identification of Vetullavāda with Mahāyāna and of Vetullavādins with Mahāyānists is generally accepted. Asaṅga, *Abhidharmasamuccaya*, p. 79, lines 1-2, P. Pradhan edition, says that the words *vaipulya, vaidalya*, and *vaitulya* designate what has been said by the Buddha and is contained in the *Bodhisattvapiṭaka* (*vaipulyaṃ katamat / bodhisattvapiṭakasaṃyuktaṃ bhāṣitam / yad ucyate vaipulyaṃ tad vaidalyam apy ucyate vaitulyam apy ucyate*) and in lines 14-15, says that *Vaitulya* is in the *Sūtrapiṭaka* of the *Bodhisattvapiṭaka* (*vaitulyam abhutadharmaś ca ete dve bodhisattvapiṭakasya sūtrapiṭake saṃgṛhite bhavataḥ*). Buddhaghosa in his *Kathāvatthu-Aṭṭhakathā* XVII, 6, says that the *Vetullakas* are also called *Mahāsuññatāvādins* (*mahāsuññatāvādisaṇkhātānaṃ vetullakānaṃ*).

Sometimes the Mahāyāna was also called *Vitaṇḍavāda* as is clearly seen in *Dīpavaṃsa* XXII, 43-45 (reign of King Vohārika Tissa):

Pāli text

tassa rañño tu vijite dīpanti akappiyaṃ bahuṃ /
vitaṅḍavāde dīpetvā dūsesuṃ jinasāsanaṃ //
disvā rājā pāpabhikkhū dūsente jinasāsānaṃ /
Kapilāmaccam ādāya akāsi pāpaniggahaṃ //
Vitaṇḍavādaṃ madditvā jotayitvāna sāsanam ...

Translation

"In the kingdom of that king (Tissa)
they proclaim many improper things.
Proclaiming the *Vitaṇḍavāda*
they spoiled the Teaching of the Conqueror.
The king, seeing the evil *bhikkhus*
spoiling the Teaching of the Conqueror,
together with his minister Kapila punished the evil (*bhikkhus*),
crushing *Vitaṇḍavāda*, and making the (Conqueror's) Teaching shine."

Cf. the text of the *Mahāvaṃsa*, 36, 41, quoted afterwards. Thus the Mahāyānists were also called *Vitaṇḍāvādins*. But the term *Vitaṇḍāvāda* was used also to designate doctrines dissenting from the *Theravāda*, and not neccesarily Mahāyānist doctrines. So it is not possible to refer all that is said about the *Vitaṇḍāvādins* to the Mahāyāna and the Mahāyānists. References to *Vitaṇḍāvādins* who are not Mahāyānists can be found for instance in Buddhaghosa's Commentary on *Vībhaṅga*, pp. 9, 51, 319, 459, PTS edition, and in *Aṭṭhasālinī*, pp. 3, 90, 92, PTS edition.

King Vohārika Tissa and King Goṭhābhaya

The conflict became violent during the reigns of Vohārika Tissa (269-291 A.D.) and Gothābhaya (309-322 A.D.). During these reigns the Vetulyavādins were supressed or banished. *Mahāvaṃsa* 36, verse 41:

Pāli text

vetulyavādaṃ madditvā kāretvā pāpaniggahaṃ /
Kapilena amaccena sāsanaṃ jotayī ca so.

Translation

"Crushing the Vetulya-doctrine
and punishing the wrong-doers ("heretics," according to Geiger),
with his minister Kapila he (Tissa) made the Doctrine shine,"

and 36, verses 110-112

Pāli text

... pāpakānaṃ niggahena sodhento sāsanaṃ tu so //
Vetulyavādino bhikkhū Abhayagirivāsino /
gāhayitvā saṭṭhimate jinasāsanakaṇṭake //
katvāna niggahaṃ tesam paratīre khipāpayi ...

Translation

"By means of the punishment of the wrong-doers
purifying the Doctrine, he (Goṭhābhaya),
seizing sixty *bhikkhus* Vetulyavādins who dwelt in Abhayagiri,
who were (like) thorns in the Doctrine of the Conqueror,
punishing them, banished them to the farther coast."

In Walpola Rahula's *History of Buddhism in Ceylon*, p. 89, there is an interesting commentary in relation to this matter, drawn from *Nikāyasaṅgraha*, a later Sinhalese chronicle (ed. Simon de Silva and others, Ceylon Government Press, 1907, p. 11):

> "Referring to the Vaitulyans who came to Ceylon in the days of Vohārika Tissa the *Nikāya-saṅgraha* says that the monks of the Abhayagiri, who were known as Dhammarucikas, accepted and proclaimed as the teaching of the Buddha the *Vaitulyapiṭaka* composed by the heretic brāhamaṇas who had assumed the garb of bhikkhus in order to ruin Buddhism during the time of Asoka; and that the monks of the Theriya-nikāya, having compared their doctrine with the dharma and the vinaya, rejected it as false teaching. The reference to the brāhmaṇas here suggests that the *Vaitulya-piṭaka* that was brought to Ceylon was composed in Sanskrit, and we know that Mahāyāna sūtras are all in Sanskrit."

Buddhaghoṣa

Buddhaghoṣa is in *Samantapāsādikā*, Commentary to the *Vinaya* (*Pācittiya* IV), pp. 742-743, PTS edition, enumerates several works outside the Theravāda tradition, among which the *Vedaḷhapiṭaka* (var. *Vedalla*°), and declares them to be *abuddhavacana*: not the word of the Buddha. The same statement appears in his *Sāratthappakāsinī*, Commentary on the *Saṃyuttanikāya* (XVI, 13), Vol. II, pp. 201-201, PTS edition, where instead of *Vedaḷhapiṭaka* the text has *Vetullapiṭaka* (var. *Vedalla*°).

The fact that the conflict between Hīnayānā and Mahāyāna concerning the authenticity of the *sūtras*, and consequently of the Mahāyānists doctrines they contain, occurs also in China, Japan and Sri Lanka contributes another proof of the existence of that conflict from the very moment of the arising of the Mahāyāna in India.

Existence and Acuteness of the Conflict

The previous texts and remarks leave no doubt about the *existence of the conflict* between the adherents to the ancient form of Buddhism and those who were propounding the new doctrines. The fact that, as is well known, in many monasteries

Hīnayānist and Mahāyānist monks did live together does not destroy the evidence offered by the texts on the existence of the conflict. Cf. Hubert Durt, "Daijō", in *Hōbōgirin*, Vol. 7 (1994), pp. 767-801.

This conflict was of course *theoretical*, as it implied the confrontation of two doctrinal systems, different in their principles and in their effects. But it was not limited to the theoretical level; it acquired a practical dimension, as it resulted in arduous discussions and controversies in which the Masters of both tendencies tried to defeat each other and to show the lack of validity of the contrary position, and as it also resulted in a missionary rivalry in which the Hīnayānist and Mahāyānist monks attacked and deprecated each other in order to gain new adherents to their own thesis, more proselytes for their Liberation path.

This opposition between the two forms of Buddhism adopted at times an *aggressive character*. In the *sūtras*, as we have said, there are numerous examples of the severe and harsh attitude adopted by Mahāyānists against the adherents to the ancient teachings of the Buddha. The very name of 'Hinayāna' (Little, Lesser, Inferior Vehicle), given to them by the Mahāyāna, is the best evidence of such a deprecatory attitude. As A. Hirakawa says, *A History of Indian Buddhism*, p. 256: "*No Buddhist groups ever referred to themselves as Hīnayānists.*" According to the texts that we have quoted, the Hīnayānists in their own turn were no less aggressive in their opinion of the Mahāyāna and its followers, and in their behaviour towards them. Concerning the information that comes from the Mahāyāna side, it is very probable that it is trustworthy, taking into account what has previously been said in *Two indirect testimonies*, and also the agreement between the Mahāyānist and the Hīnayānist sources. Through the Mahāyānist texts it is known that the Hinayānists labelled the Mahāyānists as 'enemies', 'heretics', 'men of a different religion', 'similar to Kāpālika', '*ucchedavādins*'; and the Hīnayānist texts apply to them the qualifications of 'heretics', 'sophists', 'wrong-doers', 'thorns in the Doctrine'.

Charges of the Hīnayānists against the Mahāyāna

Another important aspect of the violence of the conflict is shown by the contents of the serious accusations directed against the Mahāyāna by the Hinayānists, as found in the texts we have examined:

- the Mahāyāna *sūtras* are not the word of Buddha;

- the *sūtras* have been composed by Māra, the Evil or by ordinary people of skilful language or by people adhering to false views; they are only adulterated compilations;

- the doctrines of the *sūtras* are not the Teaching of the Buddha: doctrines such as the non-existence of an own being, theses like those that affirm the non-arising and non-ceasing of things, that things are calm since the beginning and nirvānized by nature; the absence of essential characteristics; the six *pāramitās*; the *anuttarasamyaksaṃbodhi* as the final goal; the exaggerated heroic *dāna*; the possibility for all beings to be saved under any circumstances; the 'sky-flower doctrine', i.e., the idealistic philosophy of the Yogācāra school as taught in Nālandā and expounded in many Mahāyāna treatises; the worship rendered to Bodhisattvas;

- the *śāstras* of the Mahāyāna (as the *Yogācārabhūmi*) contain erroneous views, are difficult and burdensome

- the inferiority of the Mahāyānist ideal, as embodied in the figure of the Bodhisattva enjoying a happy existence in his heavenly beatitude, in face of the Hinayānist ideal of the Bhikṣu dedicated to the ascetic life, having self-training as his first duty, and imbued by the will to escape from *saṃsāra* as soon as posible.

REFERENCES

We leave for another article the analysis of the numerous testimonies of the conflict produced in the Buddhist Community by the preaching of the new Mahāyānistic doctrine that are also found in the *Lotūs Sūtra*. (See the next part of this book).

We thank Professor Kōgen Mizuno for having the kindness to indicate to us, in a personal letter, two interesting references related to the subject-matter of this article: *Taishō* 310, p. 528b 10-14 and 1509, p. 506a 13-15.

Asaṅga, *Abhidarmasamuccaya*, P. Pradhan ed., Santiniketan, Visva-Bharati, 1950.

—, *Bodhisattvabhūmi,* U. Wogihara ed., Tokyo, Sankibo Buddhist Book Store, 1971.

—, *Mahāyānasūtralaṅkara,* S. Lévi ed., Paris, Honoré Champion, 1907.

Bu-ston, *Chos-'byuṅ* in *The Collected Works of Bu-ston.* Part 24 (Ya), edited by Prof. Dr. Lokesh Chandra, New Delhi, International Academy of Indian Culture, 1971.

—, *Chos-'byung (History of Buddhism) II. The History of Buddhism in India and Tibet*, trans. From Tibetan by E. Obermiller, Harrassowitz, Leipzig, 1932, Reprint Series 5: Suzuki Research Foundation, 1964.

Hirakawa, A., *A History of Indian Buddhism*, trans. from Japanese by P. Groner, Hawaii, University of Hawaii Press, 1990.

Hiuan Tsang, *Ta t'ang Si yu ki (Records of the Western Lands)*, Taipei, The Horizon Publishing Co., 1978.

Lamotte, E., *Le Traité de la Grande Vertu de Sagesse*, Louvain, Institut Orientaliste, 1944-1980.

Mizuno, Kōgen, *Buddhist Sūtras*, Tokyo, Kosei Publishing Co., 1982.

PTS = Pali Text Society

Saṃdhinirmocanasūtra, É. Lamotte ed., Louvain-Paris, Université de Louvain, 1935.

Sāramati, *Ratnagotravibhāga*, Z. Nakamura ed., Tōkyō, Sankibō Buddhist Book Store, 1961.

Sasaki Shizuka, *A study on the Origin of Mahāyāna Buddhism, in The Eastern Buddhist*, 1997, 1, pp. 79-113.

Taishō = *The Taishō Shinshū Daizōkyō*, Tōkyō, Taishō shinshū daizōkyō kankō kai, 1924-1935.

Tōhoku = *A complete Catalogue of the Tibetan Buddhist Canons*, ed. By H. Ui and others, Sendai, Tōhoku Imperial University, 1934.

Tārānātha's *History of Buddhism* = *Tārānāthae de Doctrinae Buddhicae in India Propagatione Narratio*, ed. A. Schiefner, Petropoli, 1868, Reprint Series 2: Suzuki Research Foundation, 1963.

Tsukamoto, Zenryū, *A History of Early Chinese Buddhism*, trans. from Japanese by L. Hurvitz, 2 Vol., Tōkyō-New York-San Francisco, Kōdansha International Ltd., 1979.

Walpola Rahula, *History of Buddhism in Ceylon*, Dehiwala, The Buddhist Cultural Centre, 1993.

II

The Conflict of Change in the *Lotus Sūtra* : The Hīnayānist Reaction

The aim of this article

This article is the second part of a previous one, "The Conflict of Change in Buddhism: The Hīnayānist Reaction", published in *Cahiers d'Extrême-Asie* 9, Kyōto, 1996-1997, pp. 233-254, included in this book as Part I. In that article we examined the reactions that the new Mahāyānist ideas caused in those Buddhists who adhered to the ancient tradition (whom we call for facility's sake 'Hīnayānists') through the testimonies offered by several Mahāyāna texts, not taking into account the numerous testimonies coming from the *Lotus Sūtra*. We considered that these testimonies deserved treatment in a separate study.

As we said in the previous article, it is easy to find in the Mahāyānist texts references to the harsh attitudes adopted by the supporters of the new form of Buddhism against the Hīnayānists. What is not so easy is to meet with are descriptions of how the old Buddhists reacted in face of the great changes that were being introduced in the Buddhist Doctrine by the Mahāyānists.

In the *Lotus Sūtra* are found many testimonies of the conflict produced in the Buddhist Community by the preaching of the new Mahāyānist doctrine. The following episodes of the *Lotus Sūtra*, that we pass to examine, give us information about that conflict. They will show that, besides the doctrinal value and interest of the *Lotus Sūtra*, in it is found a rich information about the history and evolution of Buddhism.

I

Reactions of the 5000 members of the Assembly before their withdrawal

After the exposition made by Śākyamuni in the beginning of the Second Chapter (KN = Kern-Nanjio ed. pp. 29-33 line 4), a reaction occurs in the Śrāvakas and Pratyekabuddhas attending the Assembly, including Śāriputra himself (KN p. 33 line 5 - p. 38 line 11). What they all feel, think and say can be considered to represent a widespread attitude among Hīnayānists in face of the new teachings of the Mahāyāna. And as such it constitutes an interesting testimony in relation to the conflict between Hīnayāna and Mahāyāna.

The Hīnayānist members of the Assembly are perplexed (*na jānīma*) by Śākyamuni's praises of his *upāyakauśalya* and of the deepness of his teaching and by the affirmation that his teaching is difficult or even impossible to be understood by his Hīnayānist disciples.

We must have in mind that the *upāyakauśalya* is the ability the Buddha possess to transmit to each audience that teaching in a way adequate to the audience. The *upāyakauśalya* implies that there is a hierarchy among the doctrines taught by the Buddha and in this hierarchy the Hīnayānist teaching, which was first imparted, occupies a level inferior to that of the Supreme Truth that the Buddha is about to reveal and which constitutes the Great Vehicle. If the Buddha was obliged to preach Śrāvakas and Pratyekabuddhas a provisional doctrine that would have to be superseded by another definitive one, it was due - the Mahāyānists said - to their deficient intellectual, psychological and spiritual condition.

Moreover, the Hīnayānists were sure that they had received the *True Doctrine* of the Buddha, that they had mastered it, that they have followed the True Path, and that they have attained the True Goal, *Nirvāṇa.* Now they are said that it is not so, and that it is only now that the Buddha will preach his True Doctrine, and that this is inaccessible to Śrāvakas and Pratyekabuddhas.

This explains, makes understandable and founded the perplexity of the Hīnayānist members of the Assembly.

Sanskrit text (KN p. 33 lines 5-11)

atha khalu ye tatra parṣatsaṃnipāte mahāśrāvakā ājñātakauṇḍinyapramukhā arhantaḥ kṣīṇāsravā dvādaśavaśībhūtaśatāni ye cānye śrāvakayānikā bhikṣubhikṣuṇyupāsakopāsikā ye ca pratyekabuddhayānasaṃprasthitāḥ teṣāṃ sarveṣāṃ etad abhavat / ko nu hetuḥ kiṃ kāraṇaṃ yad bhagavān adhimātram upāyakauśalyaṃ tathāgatānāṃ saṃvarṇayati / gambhīraś cāyaṃ mayā dharmo 'bhisaṃbuddha iti saṃvarṇayati / durvijñeyaś ca sarvaśrāvakapratyekabuddhair iti saṃvarṇayati / yathā tāvad bhagavatā ekaiva vimuktir ākhyātā vayam api buddhadharmāṇām lābhino nirvāṇaprāptāḥ / asya ca vayaṃ bhagavato bhāṣitasyārthaṃ na jānīmaḥ //

Translation

"And then the Great Śrāvakas headed by jñātakauṇḍinya, the twelve hundred Arhants whose impurities had been destroyed and who were self-controlled, and other monks and nuns, laymen and laywomen belonging to the Vehicle of the Śrāvakas and those who had entered the Vehicle of the Pratyekabuddhas, who were in that Assembly, all of them thought: Which is the cause, which is the reason why the Bhagavant so extremely praises the skilfulness (in the use) of the means proper of the Tathāgatas? He praises it by saying: 'Profound is this Doctrine discovered by me.' He praises it by saying: 'It is difficult to be understood by all the Śrāvakas and Pratyekabuddhas.' But as by the Bhagavant only one Liberation has been announced, so we also are in possession of the Principles of the Buddhas, we have attained Nirvāṇa. So we do not understand the meaning of what has been said by the Bhagavant."

Reaction of Śāriputra before the withdrawal of the 5000 members of the Assembly

The reaction of Śāriputra is similar to that of the other Hīnayānist members of the Assembly, but more complex, since in his question directed to the Buddha he mentions as being praised by Śākyamuni more subjects than those referred to by the other members.

Among these subjects the most important is *saṃdhābhāṣya* ('intentional language'). This constitutes a powerful instrument for the introduction of the new Mahāyānist doctrines, it is tightly connected with *upāyakauśalya* ('hability in the use of means') and is also closely related to the idea that living beings have different intellectual, psychological and spiritual development. Many sayings of the Buddha have, on one side, a first, *prima facie*, obvious, direct, provisional meaning, accessible to persons whose nature allows them to grasp *only* that meaning; and, on the other side, they have a second, definitive, true, authentic meaning, to which have access *only* persons rich in faith, intellectual receptivity, keen insight, and other such attributes. The sayings of the Buddhas have thus various levels appropriate to the different nature of their followers. The *saṃdhābhāṣya*, as well as the *upāyakauśalya*, presupposes a hierarchy among living beings, and in this hierarchy the Hīnayānists are located in the inferior level.

An important remark on Śāriputra's questioning is that he, one of the most important disciples of the Buddha, has never heard from the Buddha such an exposition of the Dharma. This is a reference to the novelty of the teachings expounded by the *sūtras*.

Sanskrit text (KN p. 34 lines 1-3)

ko bhagavan hetuḥ kaḥ pratyayo yad bhagavān adhimātraṃ punaḥ punas tathāgatānām upāyakauśalyajñānadarśanadharmadeśanāṃ saṃvarṇayati / gambhīraś ca me dharmo 'bhisaṃbuddha iti / durvijñeyaṃ ca saṃdhābhāṣyam iti punaḥ punaḥ saṃvarṇayati / na ca me bhagavato 'ntikād evaṃrūpo dharmaparyāya'ḥ śrutapūrvaḥ.

Translation

"Which is the cause, O Bhagavant, which is the reason why the Bhagavant so extremely, so repeatedly praises the skilfulness (in the use) of the means, the exhibition of knowledge and the teaching of the Dharma proper of the Tathāgatas, saying: 'Profound is the Dharma discovered by me'? He repeatedly praises them saying: 'Difficult to be understood is the intentional language'. And I have not heard before from the Bhagavant such a way of teaching the Dharma."

Then Śāriputra expresses that the members of the Assembly as well as himself are full of doubt and uncertainty (*imāśca ... catasraḥ parṣado vicikitsākathaṃkathāprāptās* KN p. 34 line 4; *adyeme saṃśayaprāptā* KN p. 34 v. 25 a; *mamāpi saṃśayo hyatra sveke sthane ...* KN p. 35 v. 29 a-b).

The withdrawal of the 5000 members of the Assembly

For three times Śāriputra asks Śākyamuni to explain the meaning of his words, and to teach his Doctrine. Twice Śākyamuni refuses. In his second refusal he indicates the reason of his negative response: *abhimānaprāptā bahu santi bālā nirdiṣṭadharmasmi kṣipe ajānakāḥ* (KN p. 37 line 5): "there are many stupid men, full of pride; in their ignorance they would throw away (insult, revile, abuse, disdain, destroy) the Dharma revealed by me". At the third request of Śāriputra Śākyamuni accepts to speak.

But just in that moment 5000 monks and nuns, laymen and laywomen rose from their seats and respectfully saluting the Bhagavant (though without doing the *pradakṣiṇa* and the *añjali*), withdrew from the Assembly - an extremely violent action on the part of the disciples in regard to their Master, the Buddha.

Sanskrit text (KN p. 38 line 12 - p. 39 line 2)

samanantarabhāṣitā ceyaṃ bhagavatā vag atha khalu tataḥ parṣada ābhimānikānāṃ bhikṣūṇāṃ bhikṣuṇīnām upāsakānām upāsikānāṃ pañcamātrāṇi sahasrāṇy utthāyāsanebhyo bhagavataḥ pādau śirasābhivanditvā tataḥ parṣado 'pakrāmanti sma / yathāpīdam abhimānākuśalamūlenāprāpte prāptasaṃjñino 'nadhigate 'dhigatasaṃjñinaḥ / ta ātmāṇaṃ savraṇaṃ jñātvā tataḥ parṣado 'pakrāntāḥ.

Translation

"Immediately after this speech was uttered by the Bhagavant, from that Assembly five thousand proud monks and nuns, laymen and laywomen, rising from their seats, respectfully saluting with their head the feet of the Bhagavant, retired from that Assembly, because, owing to the root of demerit that was their pride, they imagined having obtained what they had not obtained, they imagined having understood what they had not understood. They, knowing themselves to be at fault, retired from that Assembly."

The members of the Assembly that went away from it are said to be *ābhimānika*, 'proud' (KN p. 38 line 12); and (in KN p. 43 lines 11-13) the *sūtra* explains that any *Bhikṣu* or *Bhikṣuṇī*, who pretends to be an Arhant not having taken the vow of the Supreme Perfect

Enlightenment, thinking that he or she has nothing to do with the Great Vehicle, because he or she is in his or her last incarnation and about to enter into *Parinirvāṇa*, is to be considered 'proud'. So we may think that the members of the Assembly that went away from it had they also these ideas, characteristic of Hīnayānists not liable to be converted.

Remarks on the kinds of reactions shown in the episode of the withdrawal of members of the Assembly

The foregoing episode concerning the reactions of the members of the Assembly and of Śāriputra, and the withdrawal of 5000 of them in the very moment Śākyamuni is going to preach his true Dharma, reveals different attitudes in regard to the change that the new Mahāyānist doctrines were introducing in the Buddhist Community.

Many Buddhists had a feeling of perplexity and doubt: they did not understand why, after having heard a teaching that was presented to them by the Buddha himself as *his* own true teaching, now they are said not to be in possession of the true teaching of the Buddha and that the true teaching is only now about to be revealed. They did not understand either why the reason for not having received the *true* teaching before was their deficient, inferior condition, notwithstanding their faith and the fact that they have followed the method preached by the Buddha to reach the goal. Śāriputra partakes in these feelings of incertitude and doubt.

Among the Buddhists that heard the new teachings, many rejected them, as is shown by the 5000 that move away from the Assembly, i.e. they did not believe the Mahāyāna assertions, because of the difficulties they involved and which provoked their perplexity and doubt. They are even not desirous to hear the new preaching and have a quite aggressive attitude.

Other Buddhists, including Śāriputra, even having the same doubts as those who went away from the Assembly, remain in the Assembly and are ready to listen to the new preaching, to which they will finally adhere, revealing in this way an attitude of openness and acceptance.

II

Śāriputra

In the Second Chapter Śāriputra has heard the preaching that Śākyamuni has delivered to him and to the other members of the Assembly who remained in it (KN p. 39 line 7 - p. 44, line 4, and pp. 45-59).

The Third Chapter begins describing the joy and happiness of Śāriputra after having heard the new message of the Buddha. This joy and happiness are the proof that Śāriputra has been *converted* and adheres to the new teaching, i.e., that he has abandoned the Hīnayāna and has entered the Mahāyāna. In fact in KN page 65 line 3 ff. Śākyamuni himself pre-announces Śāriputra that he will be the Tathāgata Padmaprabha (*Śāriputra bhaviṣyasi ... Padmaprabho nāma tathāgato...*).

Śāriputra's crisis of conscience

Śāriputra explains to the Bhagavant (KN pp. 60 - 64, verse 22) the feelings his has experienced after hearing the exposition of the new doctrines by Śākyamuni and before giving his adhesion to these doctrines - in an interval of time that we must suppose has elapsed between the end of Chapter Two (*the preaching*) and the beginning of Chapter Three (*the conversion*).

We shall point out the texts where the principal sentiments that took possession of Śāriputra during the process of his inner transformation are expressed: *surprise* in face of the novelty of the new (Mahāyānist) teaching of the Buddha; *frustration*, accompanied by deep suffering, on the idea that he has been deprived of the benefits that the Mahāyāna bestows on its followers; *resentment* against the Bhagavant for having been provided by him with an inferior Vehicle; *acknowledgement* that this happened owing to his own fault and *self-reproach* thereon; *culpability* for having been unable to grasp the true essence of the Buddha's Teaching; *deceit* by his own mind dominated by erroneous thoughts; *doubts*; *consciousness* of having adhered to false theories; *terror* that the new (Mahāyānist) teachings were Māra's product; *freedom* from doubts and *certitude* about his destiny as a future Buddha in terms of the Mahāyānist doctrines.

Sanskrit text (KN p. 60 lines 4-6, p. 60 line 8 - p. 61 line 1, p. 61 stanza 4 - p. 64 stanza 21)

aśrutvaiva tāvad ahaṃ bhagavann idam evaṃrūpaṃ bhagavato 'ntikād dharmaṃ tadanyān bodhisattvān dṛṣṭvā bodhisattvānāṃ cānāgate 'dhvani buddhanāma śrutvātīva śocāmy atīva saṃtapye bhraṣṭo 'smy evaṃrūpāt tathāgatajñāna(gocarāj jñāna) darśanāt / (p. 60 lines 4-6);

tulyanāmadharmadhātupraveśe vayaṃ bhagavatā hīnena yānena niryātitāḥ / evaṃ ca me bhagavaṃs tasmin samaye bhavaty asmākam evaiṣo 'parādho naiva bhagavato 'parādhaḥ / tat kasya hetoḥ / saced bhagavān asmābhi' pratīkṣitaḥ syāt sāmutkarṣikīṃ dharmadeśanāṃ kathayamāno yadidam anuttarāṃ samyaksaṃbodhim ārabhya teṣv eva vayaṃ bhagavan dharmeṣu niryātāḥ syāma / yat punar bhagavann asmābhir anupasthiteṣu bodhisattveṣu saṃdhābhāṣyaṃ bhagavato 'jānamānais tvaramāṇaiḥ prathamabhāṣitaive tathāgatasya dharmadeśanā śrutvodgṛhītā dhāritā bhāvitā cintitā manasikṛtā so 'haṃ bhagavann ātmaparibhāṣaṇayaiva bhūyiṣṭhena rātriṃ divāny atināmayāmi / (p. 60 line 8 - p. 61 line 1);

aho 'smi parivañcitu pāpacittais tulyeṣu dharmeṣu nāsraveṣu /
yan nāma traidhātuki agradharmaṃ na deśayiṣyāmi anāgate 'dhve //4//

dvātriṃśatīlakṣaṇa mahya bhraṣṭā suvarṇavarṇacchavitā ca bhraṣṭā /
balā vimokṣāś cimi sarvi riñcitā tulyeṣu dharmeṣu aho 'smi mūḍhaḥ //5//

anuvyañjanā ye ca mahāmunīnām aśītipūrṇāḥ pravarā viśiṣṭāḥ/
aṣṭādaśāveṇika ye ca dharmās te cāpi bhraṣṭā ahu vañcito 'smi //6//

...

hā vañcito 'smīti vicintayāmi asaṅgajñānātu acintiyātaḥ //7//

...

pṛcchāmi tāvad bhagavantam eva bhraṣṭo 'ham asmīty atha vā na veti //8//

dṛṣṭīvilagno hy aham āsi pūrvaṃ parivrājakas tīrthikasaṃmataś ca /... //11//

balavac ca āsīn mama chambhitatvaṃ prathamaṃ giraṃ śrutva vināyakasya /
mā haiva māro sa bhaved viheṭhako abhinirminitvā bhuvi buddhaveṣam //15//

...

... tato 'smi niṣkāṅkṣu śruṇitva dharmam //16//

yadā ca te ātmana yādṛṣī carī abhiniṣkramitvā prabhṛtīya saṃstutā / buddhaṃ ca te yādṛśu dharmacakraṃ yathā ca te 'vasthita dharmadeśanā //19//

tataś ca jānāmi na eṣa māro bhūtāṃ cariṃ darśayi lokanāthaḥ/ na hy atra mārāṇa gatīha vidyate mamaiva cittaṃ vicikitsaprāptam //20//

yadā tu madhureṇa gabhīravalgunā saṃharṣito uddhasvareṇa cāham / tadā mi vidhvaṃsita sarvasaṃśayā vicikitsa naṣṭā ca sthito 'smi jñāne //21//

Translation

"O Bhagavant, not having heard up to the present on the part of the Bhagavant, such a teaching as this one, on seeing the other Bodhisattvas and on hearing that in a future time the Bodhisattvas will get the name of 'Buddhas', I extremely suffered, I was extremely afflicted (thinking): 'I am deprived from the vision of such a sort of knowledge proper of the Tathāgatas' (p.60 lines 4-6);

(I thought:) Whereas there is an entrance equally available (to all) into the sphere of the Dharma, we have been presented by the Bhagavant with a lesser vehicle. But, at the same time, O Bhagavant, I thought: 'Ours is the fault, not of the Bhagavant is the fault'. Why? If we had paid attention to the Bhagavant, when he was expounding the excellent Teaching of the Dharma, namely that concerning the Supreme Perfect Enlightenment, then, O Bhagavant, we would have become conversant with these Principles. But, O Bhagavant, owing to the fact that the Teaching of the Dharma of the Tathāgata, merely as it was uttered at the first stage (of his preaching), just on hearing it, was caught, kept in the memory, reflected upon, fixed in mind by us, not being present the Bodhisattvas, (by us) who did not understand the intentional language of the Bhagavant and who were in a hurry – (owing to that) I, O Bhagavant, passed the nights and the days mostly with self-reproach (p. 60 line 8 - p. 61 line 1);

O! whereas the pure Principles are equally available (to all),
I have been deluded by evil thoughts:
certainly I shall not preach the highest Doctrine,
in the Three Worlds in a future time.(4)

The thirty-two characteristic marks have been lost for me,
and the golden colour of the skin has also been lost (for me);
all the Powers, the Liberations have perished.
O! I have been confounded in relation to the Principles,
which are equally available (to all).(5)

And also all the excellent peculiar eighty minor marks
of the great sages
and the eighteen special qualities (of a Buddha)
have been lost for me.
O! I have been deluded! (6)

...

'O! I have been deluded' – I thought –
'away from the unobstructed, inconceivable knowledge' .(7)

...

... Now, I ask the Bhagavant: 'Am I lost or not?' (8)

Formerly I was attached to false views (Hīnayānist views),
being a wandering mendicant (a Hīnayānist monk),
highly honoured by the heretics (the Hīnayānists) ... .(11)

And great was my fear
on hearing for the first time the words
(expressing the Mahāyānist ideas) of the Guide,
lest it might be the harmful Māra
having magically assumed on earth
the Buddha's outward form (15).

...

then, on having heard the Doctrine,
I was free from doubt (in regard to it) (16).

And when you praised of what sort!
your own course had been after leaving home,
and of what sort!
was the Wheel of the Dharma discovered by you,
and how was decided by you the teaching of the Doctrine, (19)

then I came to know:
'This is not Māra;
the Lord of the Universe has shown the true course;
it was my mind that was filled with doubt'. (20)

But when I was gladdened
by the sweet, profound and lovely voice of the Buddha,
then all my incertitudes were dispersed
and my doubt was destroyed:
'I am established in Knowledge'."(21)

Remarks on Śāriputra's conversion

Each Buddha has two chief disciples (*aggaṃ sāvakayugam, Dīgha Nikāya*, XIV, paragraph 9). Sāriputta (Śāriputra in Sanskrit) and Moggallāna were the two chief disciples of Śākyamuni (*ibidem*, cf. *Lotus Sūtra* II verse 28). And it is well-known that, as the *Bhagavadgītā* says (III, 21):

yad yad ācarati śreṣṭhas tat tad evetaro janaḥ /
sa yat pramāṇaṃ kurute lokas tad anuvartate

"Whatsoever the noblest does,
Just that in every case other folk (do);
What he makes his standard,
That the world follows."

– Edgerton's translation

Thus Śāriputra's behaviour served as a most important model for the other members of the Buddhist faith. And this is perhaps the reason why the *Lotus Sūtra* presents him overcoming his doubts and converting from Hīnayāna into Mahāyāna, immediately after Śākyamuni preaches the Mahāyāna's true and definitive form of the Dharma: Śāriputra's conversion could induce many other members of the Buddhist community to follow his steps.

What precedes could have been a proselytist intention of the author(s) of the *Lotus Sūtra*, in order to gain followers. Anyhow the (fictitious) case of Śāriputra in the *Lotus Sūtra*, with his doubts, frustration, fears, feelings of deceit, self-reproach, etc., can be considered as a 'condensation' of a great number of real cases that occurred in the period of transformation and change of the Buddhist Doctrine.

From a historical point of view it is obvious that a real 'crisis of conscience' and a conversion on the part of Śāriputra was not possible; but from the religious traditional point of view, which locates the preaching of Hīnayāna and Mahāyāna within the period of life of Śākyamuni and his disciples, that crisis and that conversion are possible facts.

III

The Tathāgata tells no falsehood

In Chapter III Śākyamuni narrates the story of the house set afire and describes how the old man of the story rescued his children from fire, persuading them to go out from the burning house, saying that he had got for them diverse kinds of vehicles according to the likings of each one. When the children were safe outside the house, the father gave each of them a vehicle of the same kind - a magnificent vehicle. Śākyamuni asks Śāriputra whether the man of the parable has lied to his children:

Sanskrit text (KN p. 76, lines 5 - 7)

tat kiṃ manyase Śāriputra mā haiva tasya puruṣasya mṛṣāvādaḥ syād yena teṣāṃ dārakāṇāṃ pūrvaṃ trīṇi yānāny upadarśayitvā paścāt sarveṣāṃ mahāyānāny eva dattāny udārayānāny eva dattāni.

Translation

"O Śāriputra, what do you think about this? Would this man have told a lie by the fact that, he having first promised to the children three vehicles, afterwards great vehicles were given to all of them, magnificent vehicles were given?"

Śāriputra answers that the man is not a liar and expresses the reasons why he thinks so (KN p. 76 line 8 - p. 77 line 3): he saved his children and besides that he gave them much more than what he had promised before.

The parable is applied by Śākyamuni to Himself, his Teaching and his disciples. Śākyamuni concludes that, as the man of the parable did not lie, so also the Tathāgata does not lie either:

Sanskrit text (KN p. 82, lines 6 - 7)

evam eva Śāriputra tathāgato 'py arhan samyaksaṃbuddho na mṛṣāvādī bhavati yena pūrvam upāyakauśalyena trīṇi yānāny upadarśayitvā paścān mahāyānenaiva sattvān parinirvāpayati.

Translation

"... so too. O Śāriputra, the Tathāgata, arhant, perfectly enlightened, tells no lie by the fact that He having first preached three Vehicles, with ability in (the use of) the means, afterwards only by the Great Vehicle He brings beings to complete nirvāṇa."

In verse III, 100 Śākyamuni also affirms that the Tathāgata (*lokanāyaka*) is *ananyathāvādin* ('not a teller of falsehood'). This affirmation appears many times in the *Lotus Sūtra* (Cf. KN p. 32 line 16, p. 39 line 10, p. 49 line 2, p. 92 line 4, p. 308 line 13, p. 312 line 7). See also Chapter XV and in it especially the parable of the good physician which has the same intention that the parable of the father who saved his sons from fire.

Remarks on the accusation of falsehood to Śākyamuni

We think that in the just quoted passages there is a clear intention to free the Buddha from the guilty of falsehood.

We may understand that this attitude of the Mahāyānists was provoked by a possible Hīnayānist reaction in face of the new doctrines, reaction consisting in the accusation that the Buddha could be considered as a liar if, having first preached the Hīnayāna (i.e., the Śrāvakayāna and the Pratyekabuddhayāna) as *his* salvific method, afterwards he had preached the Mahāyāna as his *only* definitive salvific Vehicle, declaring the Hīnayāna, that he first preached, as a provisional teaching, adequate to the deficient intellectual and psychological conditions of his first disciples and that was to be superseded by the Mahāyāna, considered as his *only* Vehicle. And the Hīnayānists were justified in thinking that, as the Tathāgata cannot be accused of falsehood, the new Mahāyānist doctrines could not be attributed to Him.

In many of the texts that we have examined in our previous article on this matter the Mahāyānist doctrines are considered by the Hīnayānists not as the words of the Buddha but as the words of Māra or uttered by ordinary people skilful in the use of language.

For converted Hīnayānists, as for instance Śāriputra in this chapter, Śākyamuni's behaviour is not deceitful, because it can be explained in terms of *upāyakauśalya*: Śākyamuni acted as He acted because that was the only means to save people - in the same way as the father of the parable.

IV

Reaction of the old Great Disciples of the Buddha

In Chapter IV of the *Lotus Sūtra* is described the reaction of the old Great Disciples of the Buddha, Subhūti, Mahākātyāyana, Mahākāśyapa, Mahāmaudgalyāyana. They are very happy on hearing the prediction made by Śākyamuni to Śāriputra that he will be a Buddha and, in a very respectful way, they speak to Śākyamuni. But in their speech, on one side, we can trace the expression of a critical attitude towards the Buddha and the form He has acted, and, on the other side, we find a particular new position in face of the new (Mahāyānist) doctrines and the change they imply.

Reproaches

The old Great Disciples *admit* that they were *hīnādhimuktika*: "provided with an inclination towards what is low", but anyhow a note of reproach resounds in their words. They complain that they were induced (*prayukta*) by the Bhagavant to reflect upon inferior *dharmas*, that they were employed by Him in inferior things, that they were neglected by Him, that He did not pay attention to them and did not tell them the true doctrine, although they exerted themselves and made efforts, and they have long been thoroughly imbued with the notion of void and have carried on the Discipline of the Tathāgata:

Sanskrit text (KN p. 108 line 17 - p. 109 line 7; p. 117 stanza 45)

... vayaṃ... abhūma... saṃsāre ca hīnādhimuktikāḥ/ tato vayaṃ bhagavatā bahūn dharmān praty avarān saṃkāradhānasadṛśān anuvicintayitāḥ / teṣu cāsma prayuktā ghaṭamānā vyāyacchamānā nirvāṇamātraṃ ca vayaṃ bhagavan

divasamudrām iva paryeṣamāṇā mārgāmaḥ/ tena ca vayaṃ bhagavan nirvāṇena pratilabdhena tuṣṭā bhavāmo bahu ca labdham iti manyāmahe tathāgatasyāntikād eṣu dharmeṣv abhiyuktā ghaṭitvā vyāyamitvā / prajānāti ca tathāgato 'smākaṃ hīnādhimuktikatāṃ tataś ca bhagavān asmān upekṣate na saṃbhinatti nācaṣṭe yo 'yaṃ tathāgatasya jñānakośa eṣa eva yuṣmākaṃ bhaviṣyatīti.

nirvāṇaparyanti samucchraye 'smin paribhāvitā śūnyata dīrgharātram / parimukta traidhātukadukhapīḍitāḥ kṛtaṃ ca asmābhi jinasya śāsanam //45//

Translation

"In the *saṃsāra* we were of low aspirations. Then we have been induced by the Bhagavant to reflect upon numerous inferior things (*dharma*), similar to the place where rubbish is heaped. And we applied ourselves to them, exerting ourselves and making efforts, and we were striving to attain only the *nirvāṇa*, searching for it as (the man of the parable) the daily fee. And we were, O Bhagavant, satisfied with that *nirvāṇa* we had obtained. And we thought that we had gained much - employed by the Tathāgata in these (inferior) things (*dharma*) - exerting ourselves and making efforts. And the Tathāgata knew our inclination towards what is low and therefore the Bhagavant neglected us, did not deal with us and did not tell us: 'The Tathāgata's treasure of Knowledge will be yours'.

In this existence, which has as its end the *nirvāṇa* we have long been thoroughly imbued with (the notion of) Voidness; we have been released, after having been tortured by the sufferings of the Three Worlds, and the Discipline of the Conqueror has been accomplished by us" //45//

Feeling of injustice or incongruency

Besides that, it seems that the old Great Disciples of Śākyamuni feel that they have been treated, if not in an injust way, at least in an incongruent way. On one side they haven been accused of being of low inclinations and on the other side they have taught the Bodhisattvas and led them to realise the Perfect Supreme Enlightenment. This feeling is expressed in the following passages:

Sanskrit text (KN p. 101 lines 3 - 4; p. 110 lines 6 - 7; p. 116 verses 38, 39 and 40 (a-c)

tato bhagavann asmābhir apy anye bodhisattvā avavaditā abhūvann anuttarāyāṃ samyaksaṃbodhāv anuśiṣṭāś ca (p. 101) ...

vayaṃ punar bhagavatā dve kārye kārāpitā bodhisattvānāṃ cāgrato hīnādhimuktikā ity uktās te codārāyāṃ buddhabodhau samādāpitāḥ (p. 110).

vayaṃ ca teṣāṃ sugatena preṣitā bahubodhisattvāna mahābalānām / anuttaraṃ mārga pradarśayāma dṛṣṭāntahetūnayutāna koṭibhi ' //38//

śrutvā ca asmāka jinasya putrā bodhāya bhāventi sumārgam agryam / te vyākriyante ca kṣaṇasmi tasmin bhaviṣyathā buddha imasmi loke //39//

etadṛśaṃ karma karoma tāyinaḥ saṃrakṣamāṇā ima dharmakośam / prakāśayantaś ca jinātmajānāṃ ... //40//

Cf. texts of pages 109 and 109-110 quoted afterwards.

Translation

"Hence, O Bhagavant, other Bodhisattvas have been admonished and instructed by us in relation to Supreme Perfect Enlightenment (p. 101).

We have been induced by the Bhagavant to fulfil a double function: in face of the Bodhisattvas we have been called 'of low inclinations', but they have been incited (by us) to the noble Enlightenment proper of the Buddhas. (p. 110)

And, being directed by the Sugata,
we have shown to many Bodhisattvas of great powers
the Supreme Path
by means of millions of millions of examples and arguments. (38)

And, on hearing us,
the sons of the Conqueror realise
the eminent Good Path towards Enlightenment,
and then they are prophesied: 'You will become Buddhas'.(39)

Such a task we did for the Protector
preserving the Treasure of the Doctrine
and explaining it to the sons of the Conqueror ... .(40)"

Lack of aspiration

But, perhaps more important than the reproach and feeling of injustice or incongruency is the fact that the old Great Disciples of Śākyamuni, who have done efforts to reach spiritual perfection according to the first teachings of Śākyamuni, and who have instructed Bodhisattvas to attain Enlightenment, are old, tired, and that they have been without any aspiration or desire or attraction for the benefits offered by the Mahāyāna to its adepts; they have had no faith in it; they have felt no joy in relation to the Buddha's worlds; it was difficult for them to admit that all is Voidness:

Sanskrit text (KN p. 100 line 8 - p. 101 line 5; p. 109 lines 7 - 8; p. 109 line 10 - p. 110 line 2; p. 110 lines 9 - 10; p. 117 stanzas 42 c-d, 43, 45, 46)

vayam hi bhagavañ jīrṇā vṛddhā mahallakā asmin bhikṣusaṃghe sthavirasaṃmatā jarājīrṇībhūtā nirvāṇaprāptāḥ sma iti bhagavan nirudyamā anuttarāyāṃ samyaksaṃbodhāv apratibalāḥ smāprativīryārambhāḥ sma /... tato vayaṃ bhagavan bhagavato dharmaṃ deśayamānasya śūnyatānimittāpraṇihitaṃ sarvam āviṣkurmo nāsmābhir eṣu buddhadharmeṣu buddhakṣetravyūheṣu vā bodhisattvavikrīḍiteṣu vā tathāgatavikrīḍiteṣu vā spṛhotpāditā /... na ca bhagavaṃs tatrāsmabhir ekam api spṛhācittam utpaditam abhūt. (pp. 100-101)

bhagavāṃś cāsmākam upāyakauśalyenāsmiṃs tathāgatajñānakośe dāyādān saṃsthāpayati / ni'spṛhāś ca vayaṃ bhagavaṃs. (p. 109)

te vayaṃ bhagavan bodhisattvānāṃ mahāsattvānāṃ tathāgatajñāna-darśanam ārabhyodārāṃ dharmadeśanāṃ kurmas tathāgatajñānaṃ vivarāmo darśayāma upadarśayāmo vayaṃ bhagavaṃs tato ni'spṛhāḥ samānāḥ. (pp. 109-110)

sahasaivāsmābhir niḥspṛhair anākāṅkṣitam amārgitam aparyeṣitam acintitam aprārthitaṃ sarvajñatāratnaṃ pratilabdhaṃ. (p. 110)

...

nāsmāka harṣo pi kadāci bhoti kṣetreṣu buddhāna śruṇitva vyūhān //42//

śāntāḥ kila sarvimi dharma nāsravā nirodhautpādavivarjitāś ca /
na cātra kaścid bhavatīha dharmo evaṃ tu cintetva na bhoti śraddhā //43//

suniḥspṛhā sma vaya dīrgharātraṃ bauddhasya jñānasya anuttarasya /
praṇidhānam asmāka na jātu tatra ... //44//

yaṃ hi prakāśema jinātmajānāṃ ye prasthitā bhonti ihāgrabodhau /
teṣāṃ ca yatkiṃci vadāma dharmaṃ spṛha tatra asmāka na jātu bhoti //46//

Translation

"O Bhagavant, being old, aged, advanced in years, honoured as the Seniors in the Order of the monks, worn out by old age, we thought that we had attained Nirvāṇa, and so, O Bhagavant, we made no effort for Supreme Perfect Enlightenment, we were not competent, we had no energy sufficient (for any undertaking) ... Hence, O Bhagavant, we made known the Doctrine of the Bhagavant who teaches that all is void, causeless, aimless, but we conceived no desire for these qualities of the Buddhas or for these supernal manifestations of the Buddha-fields or for these exhibitions of supernatural power proper of the Bodhisattvas or for these exhibitions of supernatural power proper of the Tathāgatas ... but, O Bhagavant, not a simple thought of desire for it (the Supreme Perfect Enlightenment) was conceived by us (pp. 100-101).

And the Bhagavant, with skilfulness in the (use of) means, appointed us as heirs to this Treasure of Knowledge proper of the Tathāgata, but we had no desire (for that Treasure), O Bhagavant ... (p. 109).

O Bhagavant, we imparted to the Bodhisattvas Mahāsattvas the noble teaching of the Dharma, referring to the vision of the Knowledge proper of the Tathāgata; we revealed, we showed, we exposed to them the Knowledge proper of the Tathāgata, being ourselves, O Bhagavant, without desire for it (pp. 109-110).

Unexpectedly has been received by us, who were without desire for it, the Jewel of Omniscience, which we did not covet, which we did not look for, which we did not seek, which we did not expect, which we did not beg for (p. 110).

...

We did never rejoice on hearing about the supernal manifestations
in the Fields of the Buddhas (42).

All the *dharmas* are calm, free from impurities,
devoid of cessation and arising;
even more,
there is not in this world any *dharma*
- but, thinking in this way, faith could not originate in us (43).

For a long time we were completely without desire
for the Supreme Knowledge proper of the Buddhas;
never had we aspiration for it ... (44).

For that (Doctrine) which we revealed to the sons of the Conqueror,
who in this world had departed towards the Highest Enlightenment,
for whatever Doctrine we explained to them
- for them we had never a desire (46)."

Conversion and Buddhahood of the old Great Disciples

But the feelings and attitudes of the old Great Disciples, expressed in the previously quoted texts, belong to the past. Now they have just heard the preaching of the new (Mahāyānist) Doctrine by Śākyamuni and, thanks to it, they have come to learn that also the Śrāvakas can attain the Supreme Perfect Enlightenment, so they are full of admiration and joy; they have gained a 'great jewel', the omniscience proper of the Tathāgata, and suddenly and unexpectedly all is perfectly clear to them and they are completely reassured. This reaction of the old Great Disciples marks the moment of their conversion from Hīnayāna to Mahāyāna, according to the *Lotus Sūtra.* In Chapter VI Śākyamuni will preannounce to the old Great Disciples to which Chapter IV is dedicated, their future Buddhahood with all the privileges this condition entails.

Sanskrit text (KN p. 101, lines 5 - 10)

te vayaṃ bhagavann etarhi bhagavato 'ntikācchrāvakāṇām api vyākaraṇam anuttarāyāṃ samyaksaṃbodhau bhavatīti śrutvāścaryādbhutaprāptā mahālābhaprāptāḥ sma bhagavann adya sahasaivemam evaṃrūpam aśrutapūrvaṃ tathāgataghoṣaṃ śrutvā mahāratnapratilabdhāś ca sma bhagavann aprameyaratnapratilabdhāś ca sma / bhagavann amārgitam aparyeṣṭam acintitam aprārthitaṃ cāsmābhir bhagavann idam evaṃrūpaṃ mahāratnaṃ pratilabdham / pratibhāti no bhagavan pratibhāti naḥ sugata.

Cf. verses 1-2 of this same chapter.

Translation

"O Bhagavant, having heard now from the Bhagavant that also for the Śrāvakas there is the prophecy of their (future) Supreme Perfect Enlightenment, we are filled with atonishment and wonder, we have obtained a great gain; O Bhagavant, on hearing now, unexpectedly, such words from the Bhagavant, not heard before, we have gained a great jewel, we have gained an incomparable jewel. O Bhagavant, by us has been gained this great jewel, of such a kind, which we did not covet, which we did not look for, which we did not seek, which we did not beg for! It is perfectly clear to us, O Bhagavant! It is perfectly clear to us, O Sugata!"

Remarks on the previous episode

As Śāriputra in KN p. 34 line 3, the old Great Disciples express that the preaching, they have just heard from the Buddha, is something new (*aśrutapūrva*), which constitutes a reference to the novelty of the Mahāyānist teaching.

As we have said regarding Śāriputra's conversion, we can presume that there was on the part of the author(s) of the *Lotus Sūtra* a proselytist intention in the description of the Great Disciples of the Buddha converting from Hīnayāna to Mahāyāna after having understood the new message expounded by Śākyamuni.

The old Great Disciples may represent the feelings of many Hīnayānists, who had received the first Buddhist message, had followed its precepts, had spread Śākyamuni's Teaching and were sure that they had attained the goal of Nirvāṇa. Thus the new (Mahāyānist) message that declares the first Buddhist message to be provisional and its adepts to be persons of low inclinations (*hīnādhimuktika*), necessarily had to disturb them. Moreover, having been fully immersed in the Hīnayānist tradition, they are not in a state of mind proclivous to a change to a new form of belief. Nevertheless, due to the power of eloquence of the *dharmabhāṇakas* of the Mahāyāna, and being prepared by their Hīnayānist practices, they had the force to open their minds for receiving the new message, to grasp it in an act of *pratibhā* and to adhere to the Great Vehicle.

V

Great number of Śrāvakas who did not accept the Mahāyānist teaching of the Lotus Sūtra as exposed by Mahābhijñājñānābhibhū

In Chapter VII there could be a slight reference to the conflict of change we are dealing with. In face of the preaching of the *Lotus Sūtra*, one of the most representative texts of the Mahāyāna, many Śrāvakas were full of faith, but "many hundreds of thousands of *nayutas* of *koṭis* of beings were filled with doubt" (*bahūni ca prāṇikoṭīnayutaśatasahasrāṇi vicikitsāprāptāny abhūvan*) (KN p. 181 lines 13-14).

With regard to the word *vicikitsāprāptāni* ('filled with doubt') let us remark that it is the reading of Kern-Nanjio's, Wogihara's and Dutt's editions. Kashgar manuscript, p. 175 b line 3, Lokesh Chandra's edition, has *vicikitsā* °. Kumārajīva (*Taishō* 262, Vol. IX, p. 25 b lines 1-3), the Tibetan translator (who has: *the tshom za bar gyur to*, in Z. Nakamura's edition in *Hokke-Bunka Kenkyū*, 8, March 1982, p. 181 line 13), É. Burnouf (p. 111), Gadjin Nagao and others (I, p. 163), Yukio Sakamoto and Yutaka Iwamoto (II, pp. 62 and 63), Bunjiu Nanjio and Oka (according to Bunnō Katō and others, pp. 159-160, note 9), who translate from Sanskrit, adopt this reading. Of course the translators of Kumārajīva's Chinese version also follow this reading, as for instance: Bunnō Katō and others, Murano, Sakamoto and Iwamoto, Tsugunari Kubo and Akira Yuyama.

There is (in 'one manuscript', according to KN p. 181 note 8) a rare variant reading: *nirvicikitsāprāptāni* which Kern adopts in his translation, considering it 'more appropriate': "... and many hundred thousand myriads of *koṭis* of beings acquired perfect certainty". We think that Kern's choice is wrong. We support this opinion in the fact that Kumārajīva's Chinese translation reveals that the Sanskrit text he followed had *vicikitsāprāptāni*.

Kumārajīva's translation of this passage (*Taishō*, Vol. IX, p. 25 b lines 2-3) reads as follows:

Translation of the Chinese text

> "Among the Śrāvakas
> there were also (some) who believed and understood (the Sūtra),
> but the rest of thousands of myriads of koṭis of sentient beings
> (i.e., the other Śrāvakas that were in the Assembly),
> all harboured doubts."

The translators of Kumārajīva's version - especially Murano - have understood the text as we do.

Hurvitz, p. 145: "Among the voice-hearers also were *some* who were inclined to it. But the remainder of the multitudinous beings, in their thousands of myriads of millions of varieties, all evinced doubts".

Bunnō Katō, p. 159: "... and amongst the host of śrāvakas there were also (*those who*) believed and discerned it, but the other living beings of thousands of myriad kois of kinds all cherished doubts and perplexities".

Kubo and Yuyama, p. 129: "There were also *some* among the *śrāvakas* who believed it. But all the other thousands of myriads of *koṭis* of sentient beings became bewildered."

Murano, p. 142: "Some Śrāvakas understood it by faith, but the *other Śrāvakas* and other living beings, thousands of billions in number, doubted it."

The italics are ours. All these translations understand that among Śrāvakas not *all* of them had faith.

The Sanskrit text with the reading *vicikitsāprāptāni* introduces the problem of *who* were those beings (*prāṇin*) who were filled with doubts on hearing the preaching of the *Lotus Sūtra* by Mahābhijñājñānābhibhū. It may be said that these beings could be either Śrāvakas (different from the Śrāvakas of Mahābhijñājñānābhibhū who were full of faith) or non Buddhist *tīrthikas* (heretics) or both Śrāvakas and *tīrthikas*.

We think the text refers to the numerous Śrāvakas who did not adhere to the new Mahāyānist teachings as offered by the *Lotus Sūtra*. Our opinion is based on the context. The Tathāgata Mahābhijñājñānābhibhū is preaching the *Lotus Sūtra* to the Four Assemblies composed of Buddhists according to KN p. 181 lines 6-7, and in the following lines are indicated the reactions of the attendants: the sixteen princes who had become novices grasp the message, keep it in their minds and are full of faith (lines 8-9 and 13), and the Śrāvakas followers *of this* Tathāgata (*tasya*) are also full of faith (line 13). We may suppose that the words *bahūni ca prāṇikoṭīnayutaśatasahasrāṇi* refer also to the reactions of other members of the Four Assemblies, i.e., to other Śrāvakas.

These arguments have to do with the context of the episode. Other arguments, that support our interpretation, derive from a larger context, from the *Sūtra* as a whole. There is no doubt that the interest of the *Sūtra* is centered around the Buddhist Community, does not trancends the limits of what concerns the Buddhist Community. The protagonists of the *Sūtra* are *Buddhas*, *Pratyekabuddhas*, *Śrāvakas*, *Bhikṣus*, *Bhikṣuṇīs*, *upāsakās* and *upāsikas*, and the participation of the Śrāvakas in the Sūtra is very important. A great concern of the Sūtra are the Śrāvakas, their feelings, their behaviour, their destiny. The Sūtra reveals a profund desire to incorporate the Śrāvakas within the Buddhist Community as conceived by the Mahāyāna, even more to make them think and feel that they already belong to or are about to belong to the Mahāyāna. The Sūtra wants to save the unity of the Buddhist world that is being created anew; not to leave any Buddhist outside it. This attitude of the Sūtra is clearly expressed in KN p. 236 stanza 21-22:

Sanskrit Text

yadā tu gambhīram idaṃ śrāvakāṇāṃ viniścayam /
sūtrarājaṃ śruṇiṣyanti cintayiṣyanti vāsakṛt //21//

te bhonti saṃnikṛṣṭā vai budddhajñānasya paṇḍitāḥ /
yathaiva cārdre pāṃsusmin āsannaṃ jalam ucyate // 22//

Translation

"But, when they hear this King of the Sūtras,
profound doctrinal exposition for the benefit of the Śrāvakas,
and often meditate on it,"

"they are near the Knowledge of the Buddha,
they become sages
as it is said when sand is moisten:
'Water is close'."

The passage of Chapter VII, p. 181 lines 13-14 shows the existence of a very great number of Hīnayānists who did not believe and did not understand the new Mahāyanist message, at least as expressed in one of its most important documents, the *Lotus Sūtra.*

VI

Reaction of fear among the Hīnayānists

In Chapter VIII of the *Lotus Sūtra* is narrated the episode of Pūrṇa, known as the Śrāvaka (KN 200 line 13: *śrāvaka iti saṃjñāyate sma*).

Pūrṇa was also, like Śāriputra and the Great Śrāvakas mentioned in the previous chapters, a great personage of the Hīnayāna. The *Lotus Sūtra* depicts Pūrṇa as having been a Bodhisattva acting as a Śrāvaka in all his existences. This could be considered as another proselytist device in order to enhance the prestige of the Mahāyāna and thus to facilitate and promote the conversion from Hīnayāna to Mahāyāna.

The *Sūtra* declares that many times the Bodhisattvas like Pūrṇa, as a method, present themselves as Śrāvakas preaching Hīnayānist doctrines, because there are many persons that are afraid of the Great Vehicle. In this way the Bodhisattvas are able to induce many beings to accept the new message. These *beings* to which this stanza (VIII, 2) refers are *Śrāvakas* as it is indicated in the stanza 5 (*vayaṃ khalu śrāvaka*), and by the use of the word *hīna*° in relation to them.

Sanskrit text (KN p. 203, stanza 2)

hīnādhimuktā ima satva jñātvā udārayāne ca samuttrasanti /
tatu śrāvakā bhontimi bodhisattvāḥ pratyekabodhiṃ ca nidarśayanti //2//

Translation

"Knowing that these beings are of low inclinations
and that they are afraid of the lofty Vehicle,
then the Bodhisattvas become Śrāvakas
and expound the individual Enlightenment".

Stanzas 1-7 of Chapter VIII, of the *Lotus Sūtra* explain, from the Mahāyānist point of view, that the great alarm felt by many Śrāvakas was due to their low inclination (*hīnādhimukti*), or to their lazy nature (*kusīdarūpa*), or to their ignorance (*ajñāna*°), or to their tendency to assume insignificant duties (*alpakṛtya*). From a general point of view, it can be said that the Śrāvakas *were frightened by the mere fact of the change*, the great transformation in the religious practices, in the beliefs, in the ideals to be reached, etc. that the passage or conversion from one form of Buddhism to the other carried with itself.

Remarks on the reaction referred to in this episode

Whatever may have been the cause of the great alarm of the Śrāvakas mentioned by the text, the fact is that there was also among the Śrāvakas a *reaction of fear* in face of the change that the Mahāyānist doctrines (*udārayāna = mahāyāna*) implied.

VII

Joy and repentance of the Five Hundred Great Disciples

In the same Chapter VIII, KN p. 207 lines 1-5, Śākyamuni predicts the Enlightenment of Five Hundred Great Disciples beginning with the brothers Kāśyapa who are in his presence.

On hearing this announcement, the Five Hundred Great Disciples express two kinds of feelings. On one side they are full of an extreme joy, and on the other side they feel remorse for having wrongly understood the Teaching of the Buddha: they had believed that they were in possession of Nirvāṇa, they were contented with a limited kind of knowledge - they who were supposed to aspire to the highest Knowledge of the Tathāgatas. They consider their error as a fault, due to their ignorance and intellectual weakness, and therefore they repent before Śākyamuni.

Sanskrit text (KN p. 209 line 9 - p. 210 line 4)

atha khalu tāni pañcārhacc hatāni bhagavataḥ saṃmukham ātmano vyākaraṇāni śrutvā tuṣṭā udagrā āttamanasaḥ pramuditāḥ prītisaumanasyajātā yena bhagavāṃs tenopasaṃkrāntā upasaṃkramya bhagavataḥ pādayoḥ śirobhir nipatyaivam āhuḥ / atyayaṃ vayaṃ bhagavan deśayāmo yair asmābhir bhagavann evaṃ satatasamitaṃ cittaṃ paribhāvitam idam asmākaṃ parinirvāṇaṃ / parinirvṛtā vayam iti yathāpīdaṃ bhagavann avyaktā akuśalā avidhijñāḥ / tat kasya hetoḥ / yair nāmāsmābhir bhagavaṃs tathāgatajñāne 'bhisaṃboddhavya evaṃrūpeṇa parīttena jñānena paritoṣaṃ gatāḥ sma.

Translation

"Then those Five Hundred Arhants, on hearing from the Bhagavant in person the announcement of their Enlightenment, contented, happy, joyful, cheerful, full of joy and delight, went to the place where the Bhagavant was and, having gone there, falling down with their heads at the feet of the Bhagavant, said thus: "O Bhagavant, we acknowledge our fault, we who, O Bhagavant, constantly had this idea: 'This is our Parinirvāṇa, we have attained the Parinirvāṇa' - obviously, O Bhagavant, because we were ignorant, inept, not knowing the way of things. Why? Because, O Bhagavant, we were satisfied with such a limited knowledge, whereas the knowledge of the Tathāgata was to be obtained'."

Cf. KN p. 211 lines 9 - 11, p. 212 stanza 35, p. 213 stanzas 42-43, p. 214 stanza 45.

The Five Hundred Disciples also regret for not having been aware of the fact that the aspiration (*prāṇidhāna*) to become Buddhas had been given to them in previous existences by Śākyamuni himself. It was a hidden treasure that they possessed - as the jewel that the man of the parable had inside his cloth, given by his good friend. It is this *prāṇidhāna* that will enable the Five Hundred Disciples to reach the Supreme Perfect Enlightenment, and to become Tathāgatas:

Sanskrit text (KN p. 213 stanza 42)

emeva bhagavan vayam evarūpam ajānamānā praṇidhānapūrvakam /
tathāgatenaiva idaṃ hi dattaṃ bhaveṣu pūrveṣv iha dīrgharātram //42//

Translation

"In the same manner, O Bhagavant,
we were not aware of the fact
that this ancient aspiration had been given to us by the Tathāgata
during long time in our previous existences."

Remarks on the reaction of the old Great Disciples

The reaction of these Five Hundred Great Disciples completely differs from the reactions that we have examined till now and which reveal rebelion, doubts, reproaches, etc. These Five Hundred Disciples represent those Hīnayānists who accepted the new Mahāyānist Doctrine with great happiness and considered that it was their own fault not to have understood and accepted it in due time.

The attitude of Bhikṣus/Śrāvakas of Chapter VIII is different: they have adhered to the new Teaching, are possessed of a firm aspiration for Perfect Enlightenment, and are pervaded by a feeling of pure joy and serenity.

VIII

Feelings of fear on the part of the Śrāvakas

We find a direct reference to the feeling of fear that can arise in a member of the Śrāvakayāna on hearing the Mahāyanist Teaching.

Sanskrit Text (KN p. 233 line 14 - p. 234 line 2)

saced punaḥ śrāvakayānīyo 'sya dharmaparyāyasyottraset saṃtraset saṃtrāsam āpadyed adhimānikaḥ sa bhaiṣajyarāja śrāvakayānikaḥ pudgalo veditavyaḥ

Translation

"But if a man belonging to the Vehicle of the Śrāvakas, in regard to this Exposition of the Doctrine, is afraid, is frightened, feels terror, such a person, O Bhaiṣajyarāja, must be considered as a person ensnared in error, belonging to the Vehicle of the Śrāvakas".

The reaction of fear felt by the Śrāvakas has already appeared in section VI of this article.

IX

Violent words and actions

Some passages of Chapter X of the *Lotus Sūtra* reveal that the *Dharmabhāṇakas* or 'Preachers of the Dharma', while preaching, were exposed to harsh words and even to violent attacks.

Sanskrit Texts (K p. 227 lines 5-6; p. 229 stanza 11; p. 236 stanza 25; p. 237 stanza 29)

... yaś ca teṣāṃ tathārūpāṇāṃ dharmabhāṇakānām asya sūtrāntasya dhārakāṇāṃ gṛhasthānāṃ vā pravrajitānāṃ vaikām api vācam apriyāṃ saṃśrāvayed bhūtām vābhūtām...

yaś cāpi sūtrāntadharāṇa teṣāṃ prakāśayantān iha sūtram etat /
avarṇam ākrośa vadeya teṣāṃ ... //11//

loṣṭaṃ daṇḍaṃ vātha śaktī ākrośatarjanātha vā /
bhāṣantasya bhavet tatra ... //25//

loṣṭaṃ daṇḍāṃs tathākrośāṃs tarjanāṃ paribhāṣaṇām /
ye cāpi tasya dāsyanti ... //29//

Translation

"... and he who should say even a single harsh word, founded or unfounded, to such Preachers of the Dharma, Keepers of this Sūtra ...

But he who should say insults and abusive words
to those Keepers of the Sūtra,
when they are preaching this Sūtra here ... (11)

Clods, sticks or swords,
abusive words or threats could be (used) against him,
when he is preaching ... (25)

And those who should use against him
clods, sticks, abusive words, threats, rebukes ... (29)"

Who were those who dare to attack the *Dharmabhāṇakas* with words or blows? We think they were Śrāvakas before converting to Mahāyāna on the basis of: 1. the context of the quoted passages here, 2. the reasons given by us in Section V in relation to a similar situation in which Śrāvakas are not explicitly mentioned, and 3. the violent behaviour explicitly attributed to the Bhikṣus = Śrāvakas in Chapter XII.

X

Difficult acceptance of the new Mahāyānist Teaching

The reaction of the Śrāvakas analyzed in the previous Sections give full reason to Buddha when, in relation to the *Lotus Sūtra* which contains important Mahāyāna teachings, He affirms:

Sanskrit Text (KN p. 230 lines 5-9)

bahavo hi mayā bhaiṣajyarāja dharmaparyāyā bhāṣitā bhāṣāmi bhāṣiṣye ca / sarveṣāṃ ca teṣāṃ bhaiṣajyarāja dharmaparyāyāṇām ayam eva dharmaparyāyaḥ sarvalokavipratyanīkaḥ sarvalokāśraddadhanīyaḥ / ... bahujanapratikṣipto 'yaṃ bhaiṣajyarāja dharmaparyāyas ...

Translation

"... many Expositions of the Doctrine have been said, are said and will be said by me, O Bhaiṣajyarāja, and among all these Expositions of the Doctrine, O Bhaiṣajyarāja, this Exposition of the Doctrine is antipathetic to the whole world, not believable by the whole world, ... this Exposition of the Doctrine O Bhaiṣajyarāja, is rejected by many people."

This text is a right estimate of the situation that the Mahāyāna faced on being introduced in the Buddhist world and at the same time a proof of the negative reaction, in regard to the Mahāyāna, adopted by many of the Buddhists that adhered to the traditional form of Buddhism.

Buddha in Chapter XIII, KN p. 290 line 12 and p. 291 line 3, also declares that his Mahāyānist message as revealed in the *Lotus Sūtra* is 'antipathetic to the whole world' (*sarvalokavipratyanīka*) and 'not believable' (*sarvalokāśraddheya*).

XI

More on violence

In the stanzas of Chapter XII are found diverse aspects of violent behaviour against the Bodhisattvas who preached the *Lotus Sūtra*:

Sanskrit Text (KN pp. 271-274, stanzas 3, 7, 11, 12, 13, 14, 15, 17)

ākrośāṃs tarjanāś caiva daṇḍaudgūraṇāni ca /
... //3//

...

... asmākaṃ parivādakāḥ
//7//

vakṣyanty avarṇam asmākaṃ ...
... //11//

ye cāsmān kutsayiṣyanti ...
... //12//

... ... *asmākaṃ paribhāṣakāḥ*
//13//

... *utsahāma suduṣkaram /*
... //14//

anarthikā sma kāyena jīvitena ca ... /
... //15//

bhṛkuṭī sarva soḍhavyā aprajñaptiḥ punaḥ punaḥ /
niṣkāsanaṃ vihārebhyo bahukuṭī bahūvidhā //17//

Translation

"Abuses, threats, brandishing of sticks
... (3)

...
... reviling us (7)

They will say blames against us ...
... (11)

And those who will offend us ...
... (12)

...
... rebuking us (13)

... we shall support the grave misdeed (done to us)
... (14)

We shall not care for our body and our life ...
... (15)

We shall support threatening frowns,
reiterated disapproval, expulsion from the *vihāras*,
the numerous revilings of every kind (17)

In this case there is not doubt that those who committed the violent acts were Bhikṣus of the Śrāvakayāna. They are described in stanza 4 as *bālādhimāninaḥ* ('ignorant and proud') and *aprāpte prāptasaṃjñī* ("imagining having obtained what they have not obtained"); the same expressions are employed to refer the 5000 thousand Bhikṣus who withdrew from the Assembly in Chapter II (KN p. 38 line 12 and line 14 - p. 39 line 1: *abhimānikānāṃ bhikṣūṇām ... aprāpte prāptasaṃjñino 'nadhigate 'dhigatasaṃjñinaḥ*). See Section I of this article. And stanzas 13 and 16 explicitly designate these evil-doers as Bhikṣus.

XII

The Mahāyānist Sūtras are not authentic

In stanzas 8-9 of the same Chapter XII a most serious accusation raised by the Śrāvakas against the Mahāyānists is mentioned: the Sūtras of the Mahāyāna are inventions of the heretic Bhikṣus of the Mahāyāna.

Sanskrit Text (KN p. 272 stanzas 8-9)

asmākaṃ caiva vakṣyanti lābhasatkāraniśritāḥ/
tīrthikā vatime bhikṣū svāni kāvyāni deśayuḥ//8//
svayaṃ sūtrāṇi granthitvā lābhasatkārahetavaḥ/
parṣāya madhye bhāṣante asmākam anukuṭṭakāḥ//9//

Translation

"And they (= the Śrāvakas), bent on gain and honours,
will say against us:
'These heretic monks allow themselves
to teach their own inventions (8),

composing themselves Sūtras
for the sake of gain and honours,
they preach in the midst of the Assembly'
- slanderously abusing us (9)."

XIII

Sadāparibhūta

The episode of the Bodhisattva Bhikṣu Sadāparibhūta in Chapter XIX of the *Lotus Sūtra* is very interesting for the purpose of this article.

Sadāparibhūta was a Bodhisattva Bhikṣu who 'did not teach nor study' (*nodeśaṃ karoti na svādhyāyaṃ karoti*, KN 378 line 4); the only thing he did was to approach any monk or nun, male or female lay devotee he saw, and say:

Sanskrit Text (KN 378 lines 1-3 and lines 6-7)

nāham āyuṣmanto yuṣmākaṃ paribhavāmi / aparibhūtā yūyam / tat kasya hetoḥ / sarve hi bhavanto bodhisattvacaryāṃ carantu / bhaviṣyatha yūyaṃ tathāgatā arhantaḥ samyaksaṃbuddhā iti / ... nāham bhaginyo yuṣmākaṃ paribhavāmi / aparibhūtā yūyam / tat kasya hetoḥ / sarva yūyaṃ bodhisattvacaryāṃ caradhvam bhaviṣyatha yūyaṃ tathāgatā arhantaḥ samyaksabuddhāḥ/ (Cf. KN 383 stanza 3.)

Translation

"I do not despise you, Sirs; you are not despised. Why? Because you all pursue the course of the Bodhisattvas. You will be Tathāgatas, Arhants, Perfectly Enlightened ... (the same thing is said to the nuns and female lay devotees)."

Reaction of monks, etc. addressed to by Sadāparibhūta

The reaction of the *Bhikṣus, Bhikṣuṇis, upāsakas* and *upāsikas*, addressed to by Sadāparibhūta, was a violent one as shown by the following text:

Sanskrit Text (KN p. 378 lines 9 and 10)

sarve 'sya yadbhūyatvena krudhyanti vyāpadyanty aprasādam utpādayanty ākrośanti paribhāṣante.

Translation

"They all, for the most part, were irritated at him, showed him their displeasure, lost their temper, abused and insulted him."

(Cf. KN p. 382 line 12: *taṃ bodhisattvaṃ mahāsattvam ullāpitavanta uccaghitavanta;* and KN p. 384 stanza 4, *pāda* b: *ākrośaparibhāṣa*).

They harboured a feeling of malevolence against him *(yais tasya bodhisattvasyāntike vyāpādacittam utpāditam abhūt,* KN p. 382 lines 6-7*).* And even they attacked him with stones and sticks:

Sanskrit Text (KN p. 379 lines 2-3)

ye cāsyaivaṃ saṃśrāvayato loṣṭaṃ vā daṇḍaṃ vā kṣipanti sa teṣāṃ dūrata eva uccaiḥsvaraṃ kṛtvā saṃśrāvayati sma ...

Translation

"And to those who threw at him stones and sticks, upraising his voice, from afar, he said ..."

Who were the monks, etc. addressed to by Sadāparibhūta

The monks, nuns and devotees who reacted in this violent way against Sadāparibhūta were undoubtedly Buddhists, members of the Śrāvakayāna. They are referred to as *Bhikṣus*, *Bhikṣuṇis*, *upāsakas* and *upāsikas* (KN p. 377 line 12 - p. 378 line 1, and *passim*), i.e., members of the Buddhist Community. They are said to be *proud* (KN p. 379 line 3: ... *tābhir abhimānikabhikṣubhikṣuṇyupāsakopāsikābhiḥ satatasamitaṃ saṃśrāvyamāṇabhiḥ sadāparibhūta iti nāma kṛtam abhūt,* and KN p. 379 line 13 - p. 380 line 1: *ye ca te 'bhimānikāḥ sattvā bhikṣubhikṣuṇyupāsakopāsikāḥ*), and 'proud' (*abhimānika*) is the epithet given to the members of the Assembly who withdrew from it (KN 38 line 12). Cf. Section I of this article. And finally these monks, etc. become angry when Sadāparibhūta says to them and predicts them what would have gladdened any Buddhist belonging to the Mahāyāna.

Doctrinal position of the monks, etc. addressed to by Sadāparibhūta

Besides their violent attitude towards Sadāparibhūta these monks, etc. express their opinion contrary to the existence of two important doctrines of the Mahāyāna mentioned by Sadāparibhūta: the *bodhisattvacaryā* ('Course of conduct of Bodhisattvas') and the *vyākaraṇa* ('Prophecy' or 'Prediction of the future Enlightenment'). With relation to *vyākaraṇa* Edgerton (*Dictionary sub vyākaroti* (2) says "*vyākaraṇa ... seems to come to be regarded as a regular, perhaps necessary, preliminary to Buddhahood in Mahāyāna*". These monks, etc. consider those doctrines not true (*asanta*), i.e., not authentic, and as such they were not desired (*anākāṅkṣita*) by them (KN p. 378, line 11).

XIV

Chapter XXI: The dhāraṇīs

This Chapter deals with the *dhāraṇīs* given by Bodhisattvas, Mahārājas and Rākṣasīs to the *Dharmabhāṇakas* for their "safeguard, defence and protection" (KN p. 396, line 3: *rakṣāvaraṇaguptaye*) against violence, and declares that all the Buddhas would be offended by any one who would attack such Preachers (KN p. 397, lines 3-4: *te sarve buddhā bhagavantas tena drugdhāḥ syur ya evaṃrūpān dharmabhāṇakān evaṃrūpān sūtrāntadhārakān atikrāmet*). But there is not any hint in this Chapter that the authors of the possible violent acts against the Preachers of the Dharma are Śrāvakas. The text explicitly mentions *Yakṣas, Rākṣasas* and other demoniac beings, as well as diverse illnesses, as the possible causes of the evil that could be inflicted to the *Dharmabhāṇakas*.

Chapter XXVI: Encouragement of Samantabhadra

As in Chapter XXI there are in Chapter XXVI some references to the violent acts to which the *Dharmabhāṇakas* can be exposed (KN p. 474, lines 3-10; p. 476, lines 6-9; p. 482, line 5 - p. 483 line 2), but there is no allusion to Śrāvakas as the authors of those violent acts.

Conclusion

The texts of the *Lotus Sūtra* that we have analyzed in this article show that the appearance of the Mahāyāna gave rise to a conflict within the Buddhist Community, and to violent verbal, physical and mental reactions in the members of the traditional form of Buddhism, i.e., the Hīnayānists. It is convenient to have in mind that such conflicts and reactions have frequently occurred in the history and evolution of religions, and in many cases with a violence that Buddhism did not know.

The doctrinal opposition of the Hīnayānists to the Mahāyāna has more presence in the texts we studied in our previous article (mentioned at the beginning of this one) than in the *Lotus Sūtra.* The principal concern of the Sūtra, in relation to the matter we are dealing with, is for the emotions, feelings, and sentiments of the Śrāvakas in face of the rise of the Mahāyāna. Thus the Sūtra refers to the perplexity, doubt, uncertainty, pride (Section I); joy and happiness after conversion, surprise, frustration, deep suffering, resentment, self-reproach, sense of culpability, feelings of having been previously deceived, consciousness of having adhered to false theories, terror that the new Teaching was Māra´s product, freedom from doubt and certitude about their future Buddhahood after conversion (Section II); reproaches, complaints, feeling of injustice or incongruency in the treatment received, lack of aspiration or desire for the benefits offered by the Mahāyāna, lack of faith, absence of joy in relation to the Worlds of the Buddhas, admiration, joy, confidence, understanding after conversion (Section IV); doubt, lack of faith and understanding (Section V); fear and alarm (Section VI); joy and remorse, acknowledgement of arrogance and intellectual weakness, sense of culpability and repentance, regret for not having been aware of their hidden aspiration for becoming Buddhas, after conversion (Section VII); fear (Section VIII); pride (Section XI). The Sūtra gives in this way a rich and complex description of the experience of the Śrāvakas before, during and after their conversion.

The doctrinal charges adduced by the Hīnayānists against the Mahāyāna as expressed in the *Lotus Sūtra* are the following ones:

- The Mahāyānist doctrine could not be attributed to the Buddha, because, if, after having preached the Śrāvakayāna as his salvific method, He would have preached the Mahāyāna as his *only definitive* salvific Vehicle, He could be accused of deceiving his first Disciples. To defend the Buddha from the accusation of falsehood was a major preoccupation of the Mahāyāna in general and of the *Lotus Sūtra* in particular, and the two great means to solve the problem were the *saṃdhābhāṣa* and the *upāyakauśalya.*

- Consistent with this Hīnayānist position are the reaction of terror of Śāriputra (Section II) thinking that the new Mahāyānist Teaching could be a product of Māra, and the accusations that the 'heretic Bhikṣus' of the Mahāyāna taught 'their own inventions' (*svāni kāvyāni*) (Section XII) and that they have composed themselves the Sūtras.

- The Śrāvakas declared to be untrue (*asanta*) two important doctrines of the Mahāyāna, mentioned by Sadāparibhūta: the *bodhisattvacaryā* and the *vyākaraṇa* (Section XIII).

- For the Śrāvakas it was difficult to admit that all is Void - a central philosophical doctrine of the Mahāyāna (Section IV).

- It is possible to think that the qualities of the Buddha (*buddhadharma*) or the supernal manifestations of the Buddha-Worlds (*buddhakṣetravikrīḍita*) or the exhibition of supernatural power proper of the Tathāgatas (*tathāgatavikrīḍita*) or the Treasure of Knowledge proper of the Tathāgata (*tathāgatajñānakośa*) or the vision of the Knowledge proper of the Tathāgata (*tathāgatajñānadarśana*) or the Jewel of Omniscience (*sarvajñatāratna*) were not desired (*nāsmābhir... spṛhotpāditā, anākāṅṣitam*) by the old Great Disciples of the Buddha mentioned in Section IV, because they considered them not to exist - taking into account the idea expressed in the Sūtra (KN p. 378 line 11) by the Śrāvakas addressed to by Sadāparibhūta that "they did not desire what is untrue" (*asantam anākāṅkṣitam*).

The Hīnayānist reaction due to the conflict of change caused in Buddhism by the rise of the new Mahāyānist doctrines is a historical fact that has to be acknowledged. But the *Lotus Sūtra* provides us not only with testimonies on the conflict, but also reveals the will of harmony and of inclusiveness. Although the Sūtra considers that beings can be in diverse levels in regard to intellectual, psychological, and spiritual development, and in diverse stages of the Path of Liberation, anyhow the Sūtra also emphatically affirms that the Goal is one and the same for all beings, that all beings can reach it, and, still more, that all beings will ineludibly reach it: *sarve yūyaṃ bhaviṣyatha buddhāḥ*. And the Sūtra gives many and important instances of incorporation of Śrāvakas into the Mahāyāna, so as to constitute a single body inspired in the same principles and the same aim.

III

Apologetics and Harmony in the *Lotus Sūtra* and Bhavya

Śrāvakayānist position:
the Sūtras are not the work of the Buddha.
Texts which express this idea

The 'Śrāvakas' (ñan thos) of 'the eighteen sects' (sde pa bco brgyad), as Bhavya names the first Buddhist movement in history (denomination for what was also called "Hīnayāna" by the Mahāyāna) *negated that the Sūtras (i.e., the fundamental texts in which the teaching of the Mahāyāna is exposed) were written or spoken by the Buddha.* The negation of the authenticity of the Mahāyāna Sūtras is frequently expressed in many Śrāvakayānist texts.

In an article, that we published in *Cahiers d'Extrême Asie*, Kyoto, 1996-1997, under the title "The Conflict of Change in Buddhism: The Hīnayānist Reaction", we have analyzed several texts that contain this Theravāda thesis.

We enumerate now these texts with their number of reference or of page in that article. In that article the texts are included in their original language and in English translation. These texts are the following ones:

-1.*Ḥphags pa dgoṅs pa ṅes par 'grel pa theg pa chen po'i mdo* (Tibetan translation of *Saṃdhinirmocanasūtra*) (*Tōhoku* 106), VII, 11-23 É. Lamotte's edition;

-2.*Ta chih tu lun* (Chinese translation of *Mahāprajñāpāramitopadeśa* or °*pāramitāśāstra*), attributed to Nāgārjuna (*Taishō* 1506), p. 506 a, lines 13-15, *Taishō* edition;

-3.*Fa sheng chih le hui* (Chinese translation of *Adhyāśayasaṃcodana* (?), 25th Sūtra of the *Mahāratnakūṭasūtra* = *Ta pao chi ching*) (*Taishō* 310), p. 528 b, lines 10-14 *Taishō* edn.;

-4.*Mo ho pan jo po lo mi ching* (Chinese translation of *Pañcaviṃśatisāhasrikāprajñāpāramitāsūtra*) (*Taishō* 223), p. 340 b, lines 6-14 *Taishō* edn.;

-7.*Ta t'ang ta tz'u en ssu san ts'ang fa shih chuan* (Chinese translation of the *Biography* of Hsüan tsang) (*Taishō* 2053), by Hui li and Yen ts'ung, p. 244 c, lines 14-p. 245 c, line 3 (*Taishō* edn.);

-12.*P'o su p'an tu fa shih chuan* (Chinese translation of the *Biography* of Vasubandhu) (*Taishō* 2049) by Paramārtha, p. 190 c, lines 12-13, *Taishō* edn.;

-15.*Rgya gar chos 'byun* (History of Buddhism in India), by Tāranātha, p. 51, lines 6-8 Schiefner edn.;

-*Text from p. 251. Nikāya-saṅgraha*, p. 11, quoted by Walpola Rahula;

-18.*Mahāyānasūtrālaṃkara* by Asaṅga, st anza 7, and the commentary *ad locum*. Cf. Hsüan tsang, *Tch'eng wei che louen* (*Vijñaptimātratāsiddhi* [from now on: *Siddhi*], *Taishō* 1585, p. 14 c, line 19-p. 15 b, line 18);

-*Text from p. 251 of Cahiers' article, 1996-1997. Samantapāsādikā* (Vinaya Commentary) by Buddhaghosa, section *Pācittiya* IV, pp. 742-743, Pali Text Society edn.;

-*Text from p. 251 of the Cahiers' article, 1996-1997. Sāratthappakāsinī* (Commentary of *Saṃyuttanikāya*) by Buddhaghosa, XVI, 13, Vol. II, p. 201-202, Pali Text Society edn.

In another article, published in *Hokke Bunka Kenkyū*, Tokyo, 1998, pp. 1-30, under the title "The Conflict of Change in the Lotus Sūtra: The Hīnayānist Reaction", we commented two passages of the *Lotus Sūtra* which express the idea that the Sūtras were not composed by Buddha. These two passages are:

- *Lotus Sūtra, Chapter XII, stanzas 8-9* (p. 272 Kern-Nanjio ed.): we find a reference to the Disciples (*Śrāvakas*) who thought that there were the Mahāyānists themselves those who have composed the Sūtras in order to procure for themselves material benefits.

- *Lotus Sūtra, Chapter III*: it is also found an interesting reference to this matter in the passage (pp. 60-64 KN edn.) that describes what we have called the 'crisis' of the Great Disciple of Buddha, Śāriputra. Śāriputra tells how when he heard by the first time the teaching of the Mahāyāna (from the mouth of Buddha himself!) he became full of fear (stanza 15), because he was afraid that it was Māra, the Evil, himself who, assuming the form of the Buddha, imparted that teaching. This was a reaction very common among the 'Śrāvakayānists', according to the texts quoted in previous paragraphs. Śāriputra makes clear afterwards (stanza 20) that he later recognized that it was not Māra but the Buddha himself who was preaching.

To the cited texts may be added others not mentioned in our already quoted two articles:

-*Aṣṭasāhasrikāprajñāpāramitā*, p. 163, lines 26-30 Vaidya ed. (= p. 674 Wogihara ed.);

-Fragment of the *Commentary* (today lost) *by Paramārtha* (Vth century A.D.) to the *Treatise on the sects* by Vasumitra – fragment quoted by the monk Chūkan (XIIIth century A.D.) in his commentary to the work of Ki-tsang (549-623 A.D.) entitled *San lun hsüan i (Profound Sense of the Three Treatises)*, *Taishō* ed., p. 459, lines 10-22, and

-*Madhyamakahṛdayavṛttitarkajvālā* by Bhavya,[1] Chapter IV,especially folios 155 b line 7-156 a line 6, Sde-dge edition. This work by Bhavya has as aim precisely to demonstrate that the Mahāyāna is a work of the Buddha, contrarily to what is said by the 'Śrāvakas' (*ñan thos*) of the eighteen sects (*sde pa*

[1] On Bhavya, named also Bhāvaviveka and Bhāviveka (*circa* 500-570 ? A.D.) see David Seyfort Ruegg, *The Literature of the Madhyamaka School of Philosophy in India*, Wiesbaden: Otto Harrassowitz, 1981, pp.61-66; Donald S. Lopez, *A Study of Svātantrika*, New York: Snow Lion Publications, 1987; A.L. Heitmann, "Bibliographie zur Bhavya-Literatur", in K.N. Mishra (ed.), *Glimpses of the Sanskrit Buddhist Literature*, Sarnath, Varanasi: Central Institute of Higher Tibetan Studies, 1997, pp. 106-154. Concerning Bhavya's works *Madhyamakahṛdaya* (*kārikās*) and its commentary *Madhyamakahṛdayavṛttitarkajvālā* let us say that the first one has been preserved in Sanskrit (Chr. Lindtner's edition in The Adyar Library and Research Centre, India, 2001), and that the second one is preserved only in its Tibetan version that of course contains the text of the *kārikas*.

bco brgyad) (folio 144 b line 7) (*theg po chen po saṅs rgyas kyi gsuṅ ñid du sgrub paḥi phyir rab tu byed pa bźi pa rtsom par byed de*).

Śrāvakayānist argument in support of their thesis: the Mahāyānist doctrines are not Buddhist doctrines. Texts that point out which are these doctrines

In support of their thesis that denied the authenticity of the Mahāyāna Sūtras, *the Śrāvakayānists maintained that these Sūtras contained doctrines which either were openly different from the fundamental Buddhist doctrines preached by the Buddha and reunited in the Canons of the Theravāda sects or schools, or which even contradicted them.* What is more probable is that, while the new Mahāyānist doctrines were arising, they were being criticized by the Śrāvakayānists as they went away from the traditional Buddhist teachings or they were opposed to them, and thereby they were considered as a proof that the Mahāyāna had not been preached by the Buddha.[2]

We point out some of these *Mahāyānist doctrines* (mentioned in some of the texts enumerated in section I. of this article, or in our articles in *Cahiers* and in *Hokke Bunka*, also already cited in that section) *not accepted by the Śrāvakayānists*:

-Text 1 *(Saṃdhinirmocanasūtra.* The Mahāyānist theory expressed in the *Prajñāpāramitā Sūtras* and in Nāgārjuna's works and those of his Mādhyamika School: "things do not possess an own being (=*substantiality), things do not arise, do not cease ... they are calm from the beginning and completely nirvāṇized by nature*".

-*Text 4 (Pañcaviṃśatisāhasrikāprajñāpāramitāsūtra*). The exhortation to the delighted cultivation of the Six Pāramitās (or moral Perfections) aiming at the obtention of the Supreme Perfect Enlightenment (*anuttara-saṃyakṣambodhi*).

---

[2] It is not possible to settle with certainty the epoch in which each one of these new doctrines appeared.

The Pāramitās (whose number differs) constitute the moral values that the Mahāyānist must realize in order to arrive at the moral and intellectual perfection which will allow him to attain the supreme goal of Buddhism: the condition or nature of a Buddha with the sublime attributes that mark it out.

-*Text 5 of the article in Cahiers* (not included in the enumeration of the first section) (*Mahāprajñāpāramitopadeśa, Ta chih tu lun*, *Taishō* 1509, p. 145 a, lines 12-25). The exaltation of the extreme generosity that leads to heroic sacrifices, as the donation of one of his eyes to a beggar by Śāriputra: The Mahāyāna extolled this kind of sacrifices.

Moreover this passage of the *Mahāprajñāpāramitopadeśa* contains the Theravāda opinion that not everybody can be saved, contrarily to what the Mahāyāna maintains in the sense that all men and women will attain Buddhahood.

-*Text 6 of the article in Cahiers* (not included in the enumeration of the first section) (*Biography of Hsüan tsang*, *Taishō* 2087, p. 226 c, lines 22-25). The 'erroneous opinions' (without indication of which they are) of the *Yogācārabhūmi*, the treatise of the great Mahāyānist thinker Asaṅga.

This treatise in 17 volumes contains a large exposition of important doctrines of the Mahāyāna. Asaṅga's *Yogācārabhūmi* belongs to the IVth century A.D., i.e., it is located after the *Lotus Sūtra*.

-*Text 7 (Biography of Hsüan tsang)*. The doctrine exposed in the *Prajñāpāramitā Sūtras* and by Nāgārjuna and his Mādhyamika School is contemptuously referred to with the expression "the heretics of the sky-flower".

These *Sūtras*, Nāgārjuna and his school maintained that the empirical reality has the ontological status of a flower that grows up in the space. See *supra* in this same section the text 1.

This same text affirms (*in fine*) in a general way without any specification that "*the fundamental principles (of Buddhism) are damaged or spoiled by the Mahāyāna*".

-*Text 10 of the article in Cahiers* (not included in the enumeration of the first section) (*Ta t'ang hsi yü chi, Records of the Western Countries, Taishō* 2087, p. 891 c, lines 1-12). The non ascetic existence of the Bodhisattva Maitreya in the Tushitā Heaven according to the Mahāyāna – existence that strictly speaking corresponds to any Bodhisattva who is reborn in this heaven. This existence does not agree with the austere life proper to the Śrāvakayānist monks.

-*Text of p. 251 of the article in Cahiers* (included in the enumeration of the first section) (*Nikāya-saṅgraha*, p. 11). The Mahāyānist doctrines in general, whose comparison with the Śrāvakayānist writings gives as a result that they are false.

-*Lotus Sūtra, Chapter XIX* (p. 378, line 11 Kern-Nanjio edn.) (not included in the enumeration of the first section; included in our article in *Hokke Bunka Kenkyū*). The *Discipline of the Bodhisattvas* (*bodhisattvacaryā*) and the *Supreme Perfect Enlightenment* (*anuttarasaṃyaksambodhi*) as conceived by the Mahāyāna and to which the Bodhisattva Sadāparibhūta has referred to previously. The Śrāvakayānist monks to which Sadāparibhūta has addressed consider that both are *inexistent* and thereby *not desired by them* (*asattam anākāṅkṣitam*).

- Other Mahāyānist doctrines not accepted by the Śrāvakayānists are mentioned in Bhavya's *Tarkajvālā* to which we shall refer below in detail.

Other arguments against the authenticity of the Mahāyāna *mentioned in the* Madhyamakahṛdaya *and in the* Tarkajvālā *of Bhavya*

In connection with the subject we are dealing with a special place deserves the treatises of Bhavya called *Madhyamakahṛdaya* (in verse) and its commentary *Madhyamakahṛdayavṛttitarkajvālā*. In Chapter IV of these works Bhavya points out a long series of arguments adduced by the Śrāvakayānists against the authenticity of the Mahāyāna, and refutes them. *The majority of these arguments are constituted by (Mahāyānist) doctrines that not only are not found among the Śrāvakayānist doctrines, but even are also in an evident contradiction with them.* The *Madhyamakahṛdaya* as well as its commentary the *Tarkajvālā* are important sources for the study of the conflict of change in Buddhism; now we shall only mention the principal arguments pointed out by Bhavya that the Śrāvakayānists adduced in order to demonstrate that the Mahāyāna had not been preached by the Buddha, following the text (Tibetan version) of the *Tarkajvālā*:

- *Kārikā* IV, 7 *a, c* and *d*: *The Mahāyāna is not the Word of the Buddha – as the Vedānta (is not either), because it is not included in the Sūtrāntas (= Sūtras), etc.*: mdo sde sogs su ma bsdus daṅ / ... / theg chen saṅs rgyas gsuṅ ma yin / rig byed mtha' yi lta ba bźin //. The commentary specifies that the text is referring to the *Tripiṭaka, i.e., the Canon of the Nikāyas* (= Śrāvakayānist sects), *constituted by the three* (tri) *'baskets'* (piṭaka) *or sections: section of the doctrinaire texts* (mdo sde, sūtra), *section of the texts concerning the monastic discipline* ('dul ba, vinaya), *and section of doctrinal systematization* (mṅon pa, abhidharma).

- *Kārikā* IV, 7 *b, c* and *d*: *The Mahāyāna is not the Word of the Buddha – as the Vedānta (is not either) - because it teaches another salvific path*: ... / lam gźan ñe bar ston phyir daṅ / theg chen saṅs rgyas gsuṅ ma yin / rig byed mtha 'yi lta ba bźin //. The commentary points out some practices that the Mahāyāna would prescribe, as bathing in sacred rivers, to drink water from those rivers, to recite *mantras* and to fast, all this in order to purify oneself from the committed faults and to attain Liberation, which are proper to Brahmanism and contrary to the spirit of Buddhism in its first steps.[3]

Kārikā IV, 8, *a-b*: *(The Mahāyāna is not the Word of the Buddha), because it negates the cause and the effect, as* nāstikas *(atheists) do*: chad par lta ba de bźin du / rgyu daṅ 'bras bu skur 'debs pas / ...

- *Kārikā* IV, 8, *c-d*: *(The Mahāyāna is not the Word of the Buddha), because it is undoubtedly not included in any of the*

---

[3] *Kārikā* IV, 7 reads in Sanskrit: na buddhoktir mahāyānaṃ sutrāntādāvasaṃgrahāt / mārgāntaropadeśād vā yathā vedāntadarśanam //.

Eighteen Sects[4] : sde pa bco brgyad khoṅs su yaṅ / gtogs pa med pas ma yin ṅes //.[5]

- *Kārikā* IV, 9, *a-d*: *Since mind has as its object (or support) form-color, etc. and is self knowable, the ajātivāda (= doctrine of the inexistence of arising and thus the non- existence of things and beings maintained by those Mahāyānists as the Mādhyamikas, which implies the non-existence of objects of knowledge) is opposed to (the traditional theory of) perception,* pratyakṣa *(which requires the existence of mind and the object of knowledge for the production of cognition)*: gzugs la sogs la dmigs pa'i blo / raṅ rig ñid du yod pas kyaṅ / mṅon sum gnod pa gaṅ yin des / skye med smras ba de la gnod//.[6] The commentary introducing this *kārikā* makes clear that this *darśana* of the Mahāyāna is a teaching contradictory not only to (the traditional conception of) *pratyakṣa* but also to the other means of valid knowledge: theg pa chen po'i lta ba 'di mṅon sum la sogs pa daṅ śin tu 'gal bar ston pa /.

Moreover in *Tarkajvālā*, folio 155 b, line 7-156 b, line 1, Bhavya expounds a series of arguments constituted by *Mahāyānist doctrines not accepted by the Śrāvakas of the Eighteen Sects*, which they adduced against the authenticity of the Sūtras of the Mahāyāna:

- *Because of having taught that the Tathāgata is eternal, (the Mahāyāna) is in contradiction with (the Buddha's teaching that says that) 'all the conditioned things are impermanent'*: de bźin gśegs pa rtag pa ñid du ston par byed pas 'ḥdus byas thams cad mi rtag pa' źes bya ba daṅ ḥgal baḥi yaṅ phyir ro /.

- *Because of having taught that everything is pervaded by the* tathāgatagarbha *(= literally 'the embryo of the Tathāgata'*,

---

[4] Cf. *Tarkajvālā*, folio 155 b, line 7.

[5] *Kārikā* IV, 8 *a-d* reads in Sanskrit: phalahetvapavādād vā yathā nāstikadarśanam / aṣṭādaśanikāyāntar bhāvābhāvān na niścitam //.

[6] *Kārikā* IV, 9 *a-d* reads in Sanskrit: rūpādyālambanā buddhiḥ svasaṃvedyāpi vidyate / yathāḥ pratyakṣabādhāpi jāyate 'jātivādinaḥ //

the essence of the Tathāgata) and the ādānavijñāna *(=* ālayavijñāna, *i.e., receptacle-consciousness), (the Mahāyāna) has not abandoned the belief in the* ātman *(substantiality, soul)*: de bźin gśegs paḥi sñiṅ pos khyab pa ñid daṅ / len paḥi rnam par śes pa ston par byed pas bdag tu ḥdsin pa ma spaṅs paḥi yaṅ phyir ro /.

- *Because of having taught that Lord Buddha has not entered the* Parinirvāṇa, *(and) with the teaching (derived) from there that (for Him) there is no extinction, (the Mahāyāna) is in contradiction with the three* lakṣaṇas *(or* mudrās, *as essential characteristics or 'seals') of things* (dharmas) *(i.e., unsubstantiality, impermanence, suffering:* nairātmyam, anityam, duḥkham*)*: saṅs rgyas mya ṅan yoṅs mi ḥdaḥ źes ston par byed pas de la źi ba ñid med par bstan pas chos kyi phyag rgya gsum daṅ ḥgal baḥi phyir daṅ /.

- *(The Mahāyāna) predicts to the Great Disciples (their future Enlightenment), and criticizes in excess the* Arhants, *and teaches that the householders are to be venerated, and extols the* Bodhisattvas *more that the* Tathāgata: ñan thos chen po rnams luṅ bstan pa daṅ / dgra bcom pa rnams la śin tu smod pa daṅ / khyim pa la phyag bya ba ston pa daṅ / de bźin gśegs pa las khyad par du byaṅ chub sems dpa' la bsṅags par byed pa'i phyir daṅ /.

- *The vows of the Bodhisattvas as Gaganagañja, etc. are only words*: nam mkha' mdsod la sogs pa'i byaṅ chub sems dpa'i smon lam rnams kyaṅ tshig tsam yin pa'i phyir daṅ /.

- *Because of saying that Śākyamuni is a supernatural creation, also all his teachings are false*: śā kya thub pa sprul pa yin par smra bas bstan pa thams cad kyaṅ log pa yin pa'i phyir daṅ /.

- *It is not logical (what the Mahāyāna affirms) that He (= the* Buddha*) remains always absorbed in meditation*: rtag tu mñam par gźag pa yin źes bya bar yaṅ mi rigs pa'i phyir daṅ /.

- *(The Mahāyāna) in numerous Sūtras extols the inexistence of the effect*: mdo sde maṅ po las 'bras bu med pa'i bsṅags pa ston pa'i phyir te /.

- *On affirming that even a very great fault can be completely eradicated, (the Mahāyāna) teaches that the action is without effect*: śin tu sṅig pa chen po yaṅ rtsa ba nas 'byin par smra bas las la 'bras bu med par ston pa'i phyir /.

- *Because the dream of (the fabulous King of India) Krīkī did not teach either the (future) division (of Buddhism into Eighteen Sects wherein the Mahāyāna was not included), the Mahāyāna is not the Word of the Buddha*: krī kī'i rmi lam gyi dbye ba yaṅ ma bstan pas de'i phyir theg pa chen po 'di saṅs rgyas kyis gsuṅs pa ma yin te /.

- *The teaching concerning* pratyakṣa *and the other means of correct knowledge maintained by the Mahāyāna are in contradiction with the traditional conception of perception*, as already referred to on quoting *kārikā* IV, 9.

Bhavya's apologetic method

As it had to be, the Śrāvakayānist negative theses about Mahāyānist Sūtras were refuted by Mahāyānist authors. We present in this article two instances of this refutation, one offered by Bhavya, another by the Lotus Sūtra.

Bhavya refutes one by one the doctrinaire arguments adduced by the Śrāvakayānists against the Mahāyāna. Two forms of Bhavya's apologetic method interest us in the context of this article:

The first form consists in demonstrating by arguments that the Mahāyānist doctrines rejected by the Śrāvakayānists, when correctly understood, agree with the fundamental principles taught by the Buddha, to which the Śrāvakayānists adhere.

The second form consists in showing that these Mahāyānist doctrines have a support in the Theravāda scriptures, they were expressed in them.

The first form of Bhavya's apologetic method

As an example of his first way of procedure we offer the Tibetan text and the English translation of a passage of *Tarkajvālā* (folio

169 a, lines 1-4), where Bhavya refutes the accusation of the Śrāvakayānists that the Mahāyāna with the *Tathāgatagarbha* and the *ādānavijñāna* theories is adhering to the heretic theory of a substantial, eternal *ātman* (*ātmavāda*) (*de bźin gśegs pa'i sñiṅ pos khyab pa ñid daṅ / len pa'i rnam par śes pa ston par byed pas bdag tu 'dsin pa ma spaṅs pa'i yaṅ phyir ro,* folio 156 a, line 2).

In fact Bhavya intends to demonstrate that there is not difference between the Śrāvakayānist and the Mahāyānist doctrinaire positions. It could be said that this first form of Bhavya's method is an application of the *upāyakauśalya* ('ability in the use of means') method of the *Lotus Sūtra.*

Text of the Tarkajvālā, *folio 169 a, lines 1-4, and translation*

[1] " *'The Tathāgata pervades everything' – so it has been said (in the Mahāyāna). It is so because (His) knowledge pervades all knowable objects, but He does not dwell in everything in the same way Viṣṇu does.*

[2] *'(All living beings always) possess the Tathāgatagarbha'– so it has also been said (in the Mahāyāna). It is so because It exists in the series of all living beings that are void, without characteristics, and aimless, but It is not like an individual acting inside (man), eternal, all-pervading. Why? Because of the (following) assertions and others: 'All the dharmas have the nature of voidness, characteristiclessness, aimlessness', (and) 'That which is voidness, characteristiclessness, and aimlessness, that is the Tathāgata.'*

[3] *(Concerning your objection against the doctrine of the ādānavijñāna that the Mahāyāna affirms, let us say that) The adānavijñāna is the cause of entering (pravṛtti) in the saṃsāra and getting rid (nivṛtti) of it. Since it flows as the great current of a river, it has moved onwards (praVṚT-), and it moves onwards with the nature of a continuous series of instants (kṣanikasaṃtānavarttin), but it is not like the ātman, and consequently it is not in contradiction with the seal of the Dharma, the anātman conception.*"

[1] de bźin gśegs pa ni khyab pa'o źes bya ba ni ye śes kyi śes bya ma lus pa la khyab pas yin gyi / khyab 'jug daṅ 'dra bar thams cad du gnas pa ñid ni ma yin no /

[2] de bźin gśegs pa'i sñiṅ po can źes bya ba yaṅ stoṅ pa ñid daṅ / mtshan ma med pa daṅ / smon pa med pa la sogs pa rnams sems can thams cad kyi rgyud la yod pa'i phyir yin gyi / naṅ gi byed pa'i skyes bu rtag pa thams cad du khyab pa lta bu ni ma yin te / ji skad du / chos thams cad ni stoṅ pa ñid daṅ / mtshan ma med pa daṅ / smon pa med pa'i ṅo bo / gaṅ stoṅ pa ñid daṅ / mtshan ma daṅ / smon pa med pa de ni de bźin gśegs pa'o źes bya ba la sogs pa 'byuṅ bas so /

[3] len pa'i rnam par śes pa yaṅ 'khor bar 'jug pa daṅ ldog pa'i rgyur gyur pa / chu bo chen po'i rgyun bźin du 'bab pas 'jug tu zin kyaṅ / skad cig ma ñid kyi rgyun gyis 'jug pa yin gyi / bdag daṅ 'dra bar ni ma yin pa'i phyir bdag med pa'i chos kyi phyag rgya daṅ mi 'gal lo.

We do some remarks on the preceding text.

The first [I] and the second [II] assertions are found in numerous Mahāyānist texts

The doctrines that "the *Tathāgatagarbha* pervades everything" (first assertion [I]) and that "all beings are possessed of the *Tathāgatagarbha*" (second assertion [II]) are expressed in numerous Mahāyānist texts. Let us mention some of them:

1. *Tathāgatagarbhasūtra, Taishō* 666, p. 457 b, line 28-c, line 1: "*With my Buddha's eye I see that all living beings, although inside the impurities of desire, hatred and error, possess the Tathāgata's knowledge, the Tathāgata's eye, the Tathāgata's body.*"

2. *Ibidem*, p. 457 c, lines 7-8: "*Either if Buddhas arise in the world or if they do not arise in the world, all living beings are endowed with the Tathāgatagarbha.* Cf. *Uttaratantra*, commentary *ad kārikā* I, 152, where the Sanskrit text of this *kārikā* is quoted: utpādād vā tathāgatānām anutpādād vā sadaivaite sattvās tathāgatagarbhā iti.

3. *Avataṃsakasūtra*, *Taishō* 278, p. 623 c lines 23-25: "*Moreover, O sons of the Buddha, there is no place where the Tathāgatajñāna does not reach. Why? There is no living being in the totality of living beings who is not fully possessed of the Tathāgatajñāna.*" Cf. *Uttaratantra*, commentary *ad kārikā* I, 25, where there is the Sanskrit text of this quotation: na sa kaścid sattvaḥ sattvanikāye saṃvidyate yatra tathāgatajñānaṃ na sakalam anupraviṣṭam.

4. *Uttaratantra*, commentary *ad kārikā* I, 16: "*... Since with their supramundane knowledge which reaches the extreme limit of all the knowable things they [= the Bodhisattvas] see the existence of the Tathāgatagarbha in all living beings, even in those reborn as animals...*": ... sarvajñeyavastuparyantagatayā lokottarayā prajñayā sarvasattveṣv antaśas tiryagyonigateṣu api tathāgatagarbhāstitvadarśanād... [The expression *tathāgatagarbhāstitva°*, "existence of the *Tathāgatagarbha*", in the commentary glosses the expression *sarvajñādharmatā°* of the *kārikā*].

5. *Ibidem*, *kārikās* 27-28: "*... All beings possess the Buddhagarbha*" (27), "*...because of the pervasion by the Body of the Perfectly Enlightened, all beings are always possessed of the Buddhagarbha*" (28): ...sarve dehino buddhagarbhāḥ (27), ...saṃbuddhakāyaspharaṇāt ... sadā sarve buddhagarbhāḥ śarīrinaḥ (28).

6. *Ibidem*, commentary *ad kārikā* I, 152: "*In every living being there exists the Tathāgatadhātu as an embryo, but the living beings do not know it*": tatra ca sattve sattve tathāgatadhātur utpanno garbhagataḥ saṃvidyate na ca te sattvā budhyante.

The quoted texts use as synonyms the expressions *tathāgatagarbha*, *buddhagarbha*, *tathāgatajñāna*, *tathāgatakāya*, *sambuddhakāya*, *tathāgatadhātu*, *sarvajñādharmatā*.[7]

---

[7] On the *Tathāgatagarbha* theory, see Jikido Takasaki, *A Study on the Ratnagotravibhāga (Uttaratantra), Being a Treatise on the Tathāgatagarbha Theory of Mahāyāna Buddhism*, Roma: IsMEO, 1966; D.S. Ruegg, *La Théorie du*

How does Bhavya understand the Tathāgatagarbha *doctrine*

Now let us see how Bhavya in his answer to the Śrāvakayānist accusation understands the *Tathāgatagarbha*'s doctrine. He, as a Mādhyamika, did not adhere to that doctrine, but, as a Mahāyānist thinker, he intended to clarify the real meaning of this doctrine in order also to defend the Mahāyāna from that erroneous Śrāvakayānist accusation.

In relation to the first assertion [I] (the pervasion of all by the *Tathāgata*) Bhavya answers identifying *Tathāgatagarbha* with *Tathāgatajñāna* (the Tathāgata's knowledge). The 'embryo' of Tathāgata is nothing else than the knowledge that the Buddha possesses, His Omniscience. This identification is expressed in many texts, as for instance in the texts quoted *supra* under the numbers 1., 3. and 4. And Bhavya argues that the assertion that *Tathāgatagarbha* [*Tathāgatajñāna*] pervades everything means that the knowledge of the *Tathāgata* encompasses everything and everybody, that it encounters no obstacle. In fact Bhavya is affirming Buddha's Omniscience, which was also accepted by the Śrāvakayānists.

As regards the second assertion [II] (the possession of the *Tathāgatagarbha* by all living beings) Bhavya admits that in (some schools of) the Mahāyāna the existence of the *Tathāgatagarbha* in all living beings is affirmed, but *he denies that it can be considered as an ātman*, soul, because it exists in the series of consciousnesses that constitute sentient beings who are "void, without characteristics, and aimless" by nature, and also because the *Tathāgata* is "void, without characteristics, and aimless", as all the *dharmas* are, but it does not exist with the essential characteristics of an *ātman.*

The expression "void, without characteristics, and aimless", *śūnyatā*, *animitta*, *apraṇihita* is found in *Saddharma-*

Tathāgatagarbha et du gotra, Paris: École Française d'Extrême-Orient, 1969, and *Le traité du Tathāgatagarbha de Bu ston rin chen grub*, Paris: École Française d'Extrême-Orient, 1973; B.E. Brown, *The Buddha Nature. A Study of the Tathāgatagarbha and Ālayavijñāna*, Delhi: Motilal Banarsidass, 1991.

puṇḍarīkasūtra IV, p. 101, line 1, Kern-Nanjio edn., where it is emphatically declared "all is void, without characteristics, aimless": *śūnyatānimittāpraṇihitaṃ sarvam.* In Candrakīrti, *Prasannapadā ad* XXII, 11, we also find the same idea: *śūnyāḥ' sarvadharmāḥ … nirnimittāḥ' sarvadharmā(ḥ)… apraṇihitā(ḥ) sarvadharmāḥ.* Cf. *Laṅkāvatārasūtra*, p. 78 Nanjio edition = p. 33 line 17 Vaidya edition (*śūnyatā…animittāpraṇihita°*).

The quoted texts express the Mādhyamika thesis accepted by the Mahāyāna "that *all* is void", in other words: "all is unsubstantial, submitted to causes and conditions". These texts authorize to apply the Voidness principle, i.e., unsubstantiality, to the *Tathāgatagarbha* also, as Bhavya does, since the word *sarvam* admits no exception and shows the absoluteness of the principle. And if the *Tathāgatagarbha* is void, unsubstantial, it is not an *ātman.* The universal unsubstantiality was a fundamental tenet of the Śrāvakayānists.

As a consequence of Bhavya's reasoning in relation to the first and second assertions there is no place for the Śrāvakayānist accusation that the *Tathāgatagarbha* is an *ātman*; there is no place for asserting that, with the *Tathāgatagarbha* theory, the Mahāyāna "has not abandoned the belief in the *ātman*".

Agreeing with Bhavya's position and confirming it, the so-called *Tathāgatagarbhasūtras*, the *Mahāparinirvāṇasūtra* and the *Laṅkāvatārasūtra* – to which we shall refer in the next section - affirm that the *Tathāgatagarbha*, whose existence they proclaim, is not an *ātman.* This doctrine has been preached by the Buddha.

The attribution of positive qualities to the Tathāgatagarbha *is only an* upāya

Moreover the *Tathāgatagarbhasūtras*, the *Mahāparinirvāṇasūtra* and the *Laṅkāvatārasūtra* add a most important idea. If sometimes the *Tathāgatagarbha* has been presented by the Buddha with attributes that bring it near the *ātmavāda* (doctrine of the existence of a soul), this has been only an *upāya*, an skillful means, on the part of the Buddha: He did not want to scare the brahmins/heretics with the thesis of the inexistence of an *ātman* in sentient beings; He wanted that, with the removal of the fear produced in them by the *anātmavāda* or *nairātmya*, they were able to approach the Buddhist Community, to receive the Buddhist Message, and consequently to be saved.

In what follows we quote some texts were the preceding ideas are developed.

1. The *Śrīmālāsiṃhanādasūtra*,[8] has a section consecrated to the *Tathāgatagarbha* [*Taishō* 353,? p. 221 b. line 8-p. 222 c, line 7; Tibetan text, p. 885, line 3-p. 899, line 5].

This Sūtra in its Chinese version clearly identifies the *Tathāgatagarbha* with the *Dharmakāya* [*Taishō*, p. 222 b, lines 22-23].[9] In that section the *Śrīmālāsiṃhanādasūtra* attributes *passim* to the *Tathāgatadharmakāya/Tathāgatagarbha* extolling characteristics (*Taishō*, p. 221 c, lines 8-10; Tibetan text, p. 888 line 7-p. 889, line 3). In *Taishō*, p. 222 a, lines 23-24; Tibetan text, p. 894, lines 3-4, the Sūtra attributes to the *Tathāgatadharmakāya* the four so-called *guṇapāramitās*: eternity (*nitya*), bliss (*sukha*), self (*ātman*) and purity (*śuddha*), what seems to lean, at least in the expression, towards an *ātmavāda* inspiration.

But the same Sūtra (*Taishō*, p. 222 b, lines 19-20; Tibetan text, p. 897, lines 5-6: *bdag ma lags, sems can ma lags, srog ma lags, gaṅ zag ma lags*...) categorically declares that the *Tathāgatagarbha* is neither an *ātman* nor a sentient being nor a soul (*jīva*) nor a person (*pudgala*), pointing out in an evident way that the *Tathāgatagarbha* must not be conceived as the *ātman* of the Brahmanical schools (heretics).

---

[8] Preserved in Chinese [*Taishō*?353 and 310 (48)] and in Tibetan [Lhasa edition (Dharamsala), *Dkon brtsegs*, Cha, p. 835, line 6-p. 907, line 4 = *Tōhoku* 92 = *Catalogue* 760 (48)].

[9] Cf. *Taishō*, p. 221 c, lines 10-11, and, with a different understanding of this last passage, the Tibetan text p. 889, lines 3-4, and the Sanskrit quotation in the *Uttaratantra* commentary *ad kārikā* I, 12: *ayam eva ca bhagavaṃs tathāgatakāyo 'vinirmuktakleśakośas tathāgatagarbhaḥ sūcyate*, which supports the two Chinese versions and their interpretation.

2. Another important text in relation with the *Tathāgatagarbha* theory is the *Mahāparinirvāṇasūtra* (*Taishō* 374). It contains, in page 525 a, line 14-b, line 1, the well-known dialogue between the Buddha and the group of five hundred brahmins. The brahmins were thinking that if Gautama had not taught the *ucchedavāda*, they would have entered His monastic order. Buddha, thanks to His power of knowing the thought of others, discovers what they were thinking and asks them why they attribute to Him the *ucchedavāda* (annihilation of the individual). They answer that He in many Sūtras has taught that the ātman does not exist, and consequently he is teaching the *ucchedavāda*. Buddha says that He has never taught that the *ātman* does not exist, and adds that He has always taught that in all sentient beings exists the Buddha Nature. He asks the brahmins whether the Buddha Nature is not an *ātman*. And He affirms that therefore He has not taught the *ucchedavāda*. Immediately the thought of the Supreme Perfect Enlightenment arises in all of them. Afterwards Buddha explains that in fact the Buddha Nature is not an *ātman* but that "for the benefit (*wei...ku*) of sentient beings" He declares it to be an *ātman*.[10]

3. Although the *Laṅkāvatārasūtra* cannot be considered a *Tathāgatagarbhasūtra* the *Tathāgatagarbha* doctrine has a very important place in this Sūtra. We find in it, pp. 77-79, Nanjio edition = p. 33, Vaidya edition, a very outstanding passage about the *Tathāgatagarbha* theory, its relation with the *ātmavāda*, and the real intention of its preaching by the Buddha. In this passage the Bodhisattva Mahāsattva Mahāmati asks the Buddha how is it that the *Tathāgatagarbhavāda*, which describes the *Tathāgatagarbha* as permanent (*nitya*), firm (*dhruva*), auspicious (*śiva*), eternal (*śāsvata*), etc., is not similar to the heretic *ātmavāda*, which posits an *ātman* conceived as permanent (*nitya*), creator (*kartṛ*) or permanent creator (*nityakartṛ*), without determinations (*nirguṇa*), all-pervading (*vibhu*), not liable to change

[10] Cf. the Tibetan translation of this passage in volume Kh, pp. 273, line 7-p. 275 line 6, Lhasa edition (*sems can gyi phyir*: "for the benefit of sentient beings"), and also Kh, pp. 441, line 3-442, line 4.

(*avyaya*). Buddha expresses that the *Tathāgatas* teach the doctrine of the *Tathāgatagarbha* only with the purpose of eliminating the fear that ignorant people feel in relation to the doctrine of unsubstantiality (*bālānāṃ nairātmyasaṃtrāsapadavivarjanārtham*), having recourse to their knowledge and to their skill in the use of methods (*prajñopāyakauśalyayogair*), and emphatically affirms that the *Tathāgatagarbha* is not the *ātman* of the heretics.

The third assertion

In relation to the third assertion (the doctrine of the *ādānavijñāna*) let us first indicate that as in the case of the *Tathāgatagarbha* doctrine Bhavya, being a Mādhyamika, does not adhere to this Mahāyānist doctrine, but nevertheless is going to refute the objection against it from the point of view of those Mahāyānists who maintain that doctrine.

Bhavya begins explaining in his answer, which is the function of the *ādānavijñāna*. Its important function is to give rise to the *saṃsāra* and to put an end to it (*len pa'i rnam par śes pa yaṅ 'khor bar 'jug pa daṅ ldog pa'i rgyur gyur pa*). This thesis agrees with the teaching of other texts, as for instance, Sthiramati *ad* Vasubandhu, *Triṃśikā* 19, p. 39, lines 1-2, Sylvain Lévi's edition: *evam ālayavijñāne* [11] *sati saṃsārapravṛttir nivṛttiś ca*, and Hsüan-tsang, *Siddhi, Taishō* 1585, p. 45 b, lines 28-29: "In the beginning, in the middle, and at the end the wheel of *saṃsāra* turns without depending on external conditions, since (it turns) due to the internal consciousness".

After dealing with the theme of the causal connection between the *ādānavijñāna* and the *saṃsāra* (function of the *ādānavijñāna*), Bhavya *rejects the Śrāvakayānist objection that equates ādānavijñāna* and *ātman*. Bhavya expresses that the *ādānavijñāna* moves onwards with the nature of a continuous series of instants (*skad cig ñid kyi rgyun gyis 'jug pa yin gyi* :

---

[11] *Ālayavijñāna* = *ādānavijñāna*.

kṣanikasaṃtānavarttin),[12] in other words the *ādānavijñāna* is a series formed by punctual instantaneous consciousnesses, each of which disappears as soon as it arises, and which are connected among them by the law of causality.[13] The notion of *ādānavijñāna* is completely different fromthe notion of *ātman*, which is a compact mass of consciousness (*vijñānaghana*, *Bṛhadāraṇyaka-Upaniṣad* IV, 5, 13), existent always *in se et per se*, existent as a whole, and being beyond time and causality.

This conception of the *ādānavijñāna* as a series, and consequently that it is not an *ātman*, is a fundamental thesis of the Yogācāra School. The *Saṃdhinirmocanasūtra* in a frequently quoted verse compares the *ādānavijñāna* to a current of water (*ogha*) (in the quotation of Sthiramati's commentary *ad Triṃśikā* 15, p. 34, lines 3-4 S. Lévi's edition, and in the Chinese translation: *Taishō* 676, p. 692 c, lines 22-23); the comparison is to a river (*chu bo'i kluṅ*) in the Tibetan translation (V, 7, p. 58 at the bottom, É. Lamotte's edition).[14] The *Laṅkāvatārasūtra* II, 100, refers to the flood of the *ālayavijñāna* (*ālayaugha*). The expression of the same idea is found in Hsüan-tsang, *Siddhi*, *Taishō* 1585, p. 12 b, line 28-c, line 15 (L. de la Vallée Poussin's translation, pp. 156-157), and in p. 14 b, lines 17-18 (L. de la Vallée Poussin's translation, p. 172).

Śrāvakayānist antecedents of the ādanavijñāna

Some Mahāyānist authors maintained that the *ādānavijñāna* had its antecedents in the Śrāvakayānist Scriptures. Asaṅga, *Mahāyānasaṃgraha* I, 11, É. Lamotte's edition, develops the thesis that the *ādānavijñāna* "was also taught in the Śrāvakayāna"

---

[12] Cf. *Yogācārabhūmi*, *Sde-dge* edition (*Tōhoku* 4038) Zi 4b line 5, where the same expression is used.

[13] Cf. L. Schmithausen, *Ālayavijñāna. On the Origin and the Early Development of a Central Concept of Yogācāra Philosophy*, Tokyo: The International Institute for Buddhist Studies, 1986, Part I, Chapter 3, pp. 41-47.

[14] Cf. Asaṅga, *Mahāyānasaṃgraha* I, p. 4, É. Lamotte's edition, where this verse is also quoted with minor variants.

(*ñan thos kyi theg par yaṅ bstan te*) although by other names (or under synonyms) (*rnam graṅs kyis*), and he refers to some sects of the Śrāvakayāna that accepted it: Theravādins, Mahāsaṃghikas, Mahīśāsakas. Cf. the commentaries of Vasubandhu (*Bhāṣya*), and of Asvabhāva (*Upanibandhana*) *ad locum.* Hsüan-tsang, *Siddhi*, *Taishō* 1585, p. 15 a, line 18-b, line 18 (L. de la Vallée Poussin's translation, pp. 178-182 with important notes), maintains the same thesis, adding other sects to the previously indicated: Vibhajyavādins, Sarvāstivādins. Vasubandhu, *Karmasiddhiprakaraṇa*, É. Lamotte's edition, p. 199 (Tibetan text), p. 250 (French translation), *Taishō* 1509, p. 785 a, lines 14-15, besides the Mahāsaṃghikas and the Mahīśāsakas mentions also the Tāmraparṇīyas among the Śrāvakayānist sects that admitted the existence of the *ādānavijñāna*. Cf. L. Schmithausen, *op. cit.*, Chapter 3.

In fact there are important points of contact between the Śrāvakayānist conception of *viññāṇa* / *vijñāna* and the Mahāyānist conception of *ādānavijñāna*. It is possible to consider the Mahāyāna conception as *a development* of the Śrāvakayāna conception.

1. The Mahāyānist *ādānavijñāna* is nothing else than 'a part', an aspect, a level of the *vijñāna* and not an element outside and different from the *vijñāna*. The Śrāvakayānists had analyzed the *viññāṇa* / *vijñāna* into six parts, the six acts of perception; the Mahāyānists deepening this study of consciousness analyzed it into eight parts, including thus the *ādānavijñāna*. What they both analyze was the same entity. Cf. L. Schmithausen, *op. cit.*, Part I, Chapter 5.

2. The conception of the *viññāṇa* / *vijñāna* as a series had already been conceived by several schools of the Śrāvakas. Cf. A.B. Keith, *Buddhist Philosophy*, Varanasi: Chowkhamba, 1963, pp. 169-176.

3. For the Mahāyānists the *saṃsāra* depends on the presence of the *ādānavijñāna* as expressed by Bhavya. For the Śrāvakayānists the *saṃsāra* depends on the existence of an individual (*nāma-rūpa*) and the individual has the *viññāṇa* /

vijñāna as its necessary condition. Cf. *Dīgha Nikāya* II, pp. 63-64 (XV *Mahānidānasuttanta*), PTS edition; *Saṃyutta Nikāya*, II, p. 13 (*Moḷiyaphaggunasutta*), and II, p. 91 (*Viññāṇasutta*); and P.Oltramare, *La Formule bouddhique des douze causes*, Genève: Librairie Georg & Cie, 1909, pp. 14-15; L. de la Vallée Poussin, *Théorie des douze causes*, Gand: Librairie Scientifique E. van Goethem, 1913, pp.12-18.

4. According to the Śrāvakayānists the *viññāṇa / vijñāna* 'carries' in itself or is composed by the *saṅkhāras / saṃskāras* or *bījas*, the karmic residues left by any corporal action, any vocal act, any mental (cognitive or emotive) operation (*kā ceyaṃ santatiḥ? hetuphalabhūtās traiyadhvikāḥ saṃskārāḥ*, Vasubandhu, *Abhidharmakośa ad* II, 36, Vol. I, p. 217, Swami Dwarikadas Shastri edition). The *ādānavijñāna* of the Mahāyāna fulfills the same function of being a 'carrier'. Cf. in the already quoted verse of the *Saṃdhinirmocanasūtra*, in Sthiramati *ad Triṃśikā* 15, Tibetan translation, p. 58 É. Lamotte's edition, the expressions: *sarvabījo* and *sa bon thams cad*.

The second form of Bhavya's apologetic method

In the case of the accusation regarding the *Tathāgatagarbha* and the *ādānavijñāna* Bhavya has had no recourse to Śrāvakayānist texts in order to prove that the Śrāvakas also maintained the doctrine they criticize as not being a doctrine taught by the Buddha, he does not mention the fact of the *ādānavijñāna* having antecedents in the Śrāvakayānist scriptures as we have said other Mahāyānist authors do. But in other cases he adduces Śrāvakayānist texts that prove that the Mahāyānist doctrine rejected by the Śrāvakas was also contained in their own texts.

One of the cases in which Bhavya adopts this procedure is in relation to the Theravāda accusation (contained in folio 156 a lines 3-4) that the Mahāyāna preaches that *gṛhapatis* must be honored (*khyim pa la phyag bya ba ston pa*). Under the name '*khyim pa*' (*gṛhapati*) we must understand "a layman who practises the *bodhisattvacāryā*" without having yet attained the condition of a Buddha - not any householder without qualifications. The prototype of a lay-Bodhisattva is Vimalakīrti to whom we shall refer afterwards.

Māhāyanist *texts that express that homage must be rendered to* gṛhapatis *and* Bodhisattvas *must be worshiped*

1. In fact we find in the *Lotus Sūtra* some instances of the Buddha enjoining people to honor the *kulaputras* or *kuladuhitas* (lay Buddhist devotees) who knew the *Lotus Sūtra*, taught it and venerated it (X, p. 226, line 1-p. 227, line 3, Kern-Nanjio edition), and the *dharmabhāṇakas* whether they be lay devotees or wandering monks (*ibidem*, p. 227, line 6: *gṛhasthānaṃ vā pravrajitānāṃ vā*). Cf. *ibidem,* verses 1-14.

2. In Candrakīrti's *Triśaraṇasaptati*, Per K. Sorensen edition, Wien: Universität Wien, 1986, verses 50-51, is prescribed that Arhants should honor Bodhisattvas, i.e., persons who have not yet become Buddhas.

3. It is interesting to mention Hsüan-tsang's *Ta t'ang hsi yü chi* (Records of the Western Lands), *Taishō* 2087, p. 891 c lines 1-12, where he narrates how Guṇaprabha, a 'Hīnayānist' monk was taken by the Arhant Devasena to the Tuṣita Heaven and how he respectfully saluted the Bodhisattva Maitreya but did not consider appropriate to worship him as Devasena would have liked, giving reasons for his behaviour. Cf. F. Tola and C. Dragonetti, "The Conflict of Change in Buddhism: The Hīnayāṇist Reaction", in *Cahiers d'Extrême Asie* 9, 1996-1997, pp. 242-243.

4. P. Skilling in his valuable article "Citations from the Scriptures of the 'Eighteen Schools' in the *Tarkajvālā* ", in *Bauddhavidyāsudhākaraḥ Studies in Honor of Heinz Bechert*, Swisttal-Odendorf: Indica et Tibetica, 1997, pp. 605-614, gives another instance of the "*practical ramification of the controversy*" - to use his own expression - taken from G. Roerich, *Biography*

of Dharmasvāmin, Patna: K.P. Jayaswal Research Institute 1959, p. 19.5, where a Śrāvaka criticizes Dharmasvāmin for having worshiped images of Avalokiteśvara: "You seem to be a good monk, by it is improper [for you as a monk] to worship a householder" (*khyod dge sloṅ legs pa źig 'dug pa la, khyim pa la phyag byed pa ma legs so zer*).

In the two last cases there was the idea – in the first case on the part of Devasena and in the second case on the part of Dharmasvāmin – that Maitreya and Avalokiteśvara had to be worshipped.

5. We could add another instance related to the present theme. Vimalakīrti to whom is dedicated the famous *Vimalakīrtinirdeśa*, is portrayed as a perfect *gṛhapati*, a wealthy man and a prominent citizen, and at the same time as a perfect lay believer, as a perfect lay Bodhisattva. Although it is not said in the *Vimalakīrtinirdeśa* that he must be worshipped, he inspires, due to his intellectual and spiritual superiority, a sentiment of fear and respect in the old Buddha's disciples as Shāriputra, Maudgalyāyana, Kāśyapa, etc.

Śrāvakayānist texts that express that homage must be rendered to Bodhisattvas

In folios 175 a, line 7-181 a, line 6 Bhavya rejects the accusation that the Mahāyāna, when it enjoins to worship Bodhisattvas, is acting against a Buddhist norm, since Bodhisattvas have not yet become Buddhas, the only ones - according to Śrāvakas – entitled to that honor. And Bhavya refutes this accusation of the Śrāvakas by quoting seventeen texts of the 'Eigtheen schools' where either it is enjoined that Bodhisattvas should be honored by monks, or antecedents are presented of Bodhisattvas being honored by monks. Peter Skilling, in his quoted article, has completed the quotations giving the folios of the Peking, Cone, and Derge editions where they are found.

We give two examples of texts from the 'Eigtheen schools' used by Bhavya in his defense of the Mahāyāna.

The first one is the passage concerning the *Vidyādharapiṭaka* of the Siddhārthikas, a sub-sect of the Mahāsaṃghika sect, included in folios 175 b, line 1-175 b, line 3 of Bhavya's treatise:

"...*'O monks, he who (thinking:) 'The Supreme Perfect Enlightenment (will be) mine through faith in Maitreya' pays homage to Maitreya, he is paying homage to me and is venerating me, the Supremely Perfectly Enlightened. By those of whom I am the teacher, for whom I am the Supreme Venerable, homage must be paid to the Bodhisattva Maitreya and also (by them) he must be venerated. By all the Four Assemblies, monks, nuns, male and female lay devotees, homage must also be paid to Prince successor Maitreya, (the future Buddha)'...*". On hearing these words from the Buddha, 1250 Arhants resolved to pay homage to all the Bodhisattvas.

...dge sloṅ dag ṅa'i bla na med pa yaṅ dag par rdzogs pa'i byaṅ chub ni byams pa 'di la dad pas gaṅ byams pa la mṅon par phyag byed pa de ni bla na med pa yaṅ dag par rdzogs pa'i saṅs rgyas ṅa la phyag byas pa daṅ mchod pa byas par gyur ro / ṅa gaṅ dag gi ston pa yin pa daṅ / gaṅ dag gi mchod gnas bla na med pa yin pa de dag gis ni byaṅ chub sems dpa' byams pa 'di la yaṅ phyag bya ba daṅ mchod pa bya ba yaṅ yin no / dge sloṅ daṅ / dge sloṅ ma daṅ / dge bsñen daṅ / dge bsñen ma daṅ / 'khor bźi po thams cad kyis kyaṅ rgyal tshab byams pa 'di la yaṅ phyag bya'o...

The second example is offered by the four verses of the *Jātakapiṭaka* of the Haimavatas, a sub-sect of the Mahāsaṃghika sect, included in folio 177 a, lines 3-4 of Bhavya's treatise where in a dialogue with the Buddha, Bhikṣu Ānanda, His well-known Disciple, praises the Bodhisattva Avalokiteśvara and venerates him:

"*O Bhagavan, I bow down to Avalokiteśvara,*
the Great Muni,
the Hero without fear
and endowed with compassionate nature."

bcom ldan 'das 'di dpa' bo ni /
mi 'jigs sñiṅ rje'i bdag ñid can /
spyan ras gzigs gyi dbaṅ phyug ni /
thub pa che la rab tu 'dud //

Position of the Lotus Sūtra *concerning the negation of the authenticity of the Sūtras*

Let us see now how the *Lotus Sūtra* faces the affirmation that the Buddha is not the author of the Mahāyānist Sūtras.

In the *Lotus Sūtra*, p. 22, lines 14-16, Kern-Nanjio edition, the Bodhisattva Mañjushrī expresses that Buddha Śākyamuni will preach soon the Exposition of the Doctrine called "The Lotus of the True Doctrine"; and in fact in Chapters II-XXVI Buddha appears doing diverse expositions on the Mahāyānist Doctrine and predicting to many of his followers their future Supreme Perfect Enlightenment.

The announcement of Mañjushrī and the presentation of the Buddha as preaching imply, on one hand, the rejection – in relation to the *Lotus Sūtra* - of the Śrāvaka's thesis that deny the authenticity of the Mahāyānist Sūtras, and, on the other hand, the affirmation that the Buddha has preached it, that He is its true author. It happens the same with the other Sūtras of the Mahāyāna: the Buddha is *directly* presented as preaching them, as being their author.

This is a *de facto* rejection of the Śrāvakayānist ideas regarding the authenticity of the Mahāyāna Scriptures.

The method of the Lotus Sūtra *in face of the Śrāvaka's criticisms. The* Lotus Sūtra *as an apologetic work: Its argument*

The *Lotus Sūtra* does not construct *individual* arguments in order to refute one by one the accusations of the Śrāvakas; the *Lotus Sūtra* presents *only one* argument destined to discard not only the Śrāvakayānist arguments pointed out by Bhavya, but any argument that could be elaborated against the authenticity of the Mahāyāna Sūtras, based on the idea that they teach doctrines different to those taught by the canonical Śrāvakayānist texts.

The argument of the *Lotus Sūtra* is centered around the notion of *upāyakauśalya* or "ability in (the use of) methods", and obviously it represents a Mahāyānist perspective.

Among the powers (*bala*) acquired by the Buddha in his spiritual perfection there was the faculty of knowing the different capacities, tendencies, proclivities, levels of understanding, and specially receptivity (*adhimukti*) of beings.

The Buddha, by knowing the psychological, intellectual and spiritual characteristics of beings, and their particular religious needs and expectations, adequates His preaching to the audience He has in front of Him, transmits to the disciple that part of His doctrine that the disciple is prepared to receive and assimilate in that moment, graduates His teaching for the hearer, passing from the stage which is within his reach to other stage that will demand him effort and work, He gradually leads him to the acceptance of an instruction, which shocks the received convictions, transmits him the knowledge that the disciple needs most as a help and support for overcoming the conflicts, the anxieties, the discouragement, the fears that in that moment are in possession of him. The Buddha is the Great Physician that provides each sick person the appropriate medicine, the Great Master that adjusts His teaching to the personal situation of the pupil, the Great Guide that leads His companions to the goal through the paths more in accordance with their training. With this form of acting the Buddha succeeds in not scaring, not scandalizing the beings that have recourse to Him, and in this way He does not separate them away from Him, and He makes possible that, remaining at His side, they gradually come to possess in its whole integrity and authentic sense the Doctrine that will be for their good, for their happiness, for their Salvation.

To His Śrāvakas, to whom the Buddha preached in the first years of His life as a Master, He gave of His Doctrine only what, according to their psychological and spiritual circumstances at that moment, they were capable of receiving, what they could grasp and assimilate at that moment, what they most required at that moment, as Liberation from suffering and Nirvāṇa. The teaching so transmitted to Śrāvakas was, necessarily, *provisional*, i.e., it was to be completed; and to many of its formulations a richer meaning, more profound, more complex, with greater novelty, was to be attributed afterwards – a meaning different from that meaning they seemed to express *prima facie*, and that was the only meaning the Śrāvakas were in that moment able to grasp.

With the Mahāyānist disciples, to whom the Buddha preached after He had preached to the Śrāvakayānist ones, it was different. They were intellectually, psychologically and spiritually prepared for receiving the *definitive* teaching of the Buddha, as Omniscience and Supreme Perfect Enlightenment, and this was transmitted to them provided with all its elements, freely, without secrets, clearly and directly expressing its proper and authentic meaning.

The teaching transmitted to the first disciples (Śrāvakas) and the teaching transmitted to those who followed them (Mahāyānists) constitutes a sole and unique teaching, a unique salvific 'Vehicle' (*Ekayāna*). What was transmitted to Śrāvakas is *Doctrine of the Buddha*, even not being the totality of it, and the Śrāvakas, adhering to the Mahāyāna, can easily complete it integrating it with the elements that were missing. And, at its turn, the *prima facie* meaning with which the Śrāvakas had taken the teachings of the Master, becomes larger, richer, more precise, when the Disciples have become able to place themselves in the perspective of the Mahāyāna and from this perspective interpret, grasp, and understand such teachings.

The doctrine of *upāyakauśalya* or 'ability in the use of the methods', provides with the argument for the refutation of any accusation presented by the Śrāvakayāna against the Mahāyāna consisting in it that the Mahāyāna is not the Word of the Buddha because it contradicts the teachings of the Śrāvakas: the Śrāvakayāna cannot be taken as the criterion of what is "the Word of the Buddha", because the teaching the Theravāda presents as teaching of the Buddha is only a part of this teaching and because the meaning with which the Theravāda took the formulations of the Buddha, is not the definitive and last meaning with which they have to be taken. The Mahāyāna is the correct criterion of authenticity because the Mahāyāna is the totality of the teaching of the Buddha and because the Mahāyāna took the formulations of the Buddha in the meaning in which the Buddha wanted them to be finally taken.

The argument based in the *upāyakauśalya* exempts from the necessity of having recourse to other arguments in order to refute the accusations that the Śrāvakas could adduce against the authenticity of the Mahāyāna Sūtras, founded in the existence of contradictions among the Śrāvakayānist and Mahāyānist doctrines.

Will of harmony in Bhavya and in the Lotus Sūtra

The attitude revealed by Bhavya and the *Lotus Sūtra* in their defense of the Mahāyāna does not imply the intention to present the Mahāyāna doctrines as the *only true* Doctrine of the Buddha, and consequently the exclusion of the Śrāvakayānist doctrines out of the Teaching of the Buddha.

The only thing that Bhavya basically tries to do is to demonstrate through arguments that the Mahāyāna doctrines either agree with the Śrāvakayānist doctrines or have in these ones their antecedents. Bhavya's apologetic attitude safeguards the coherence and unity of Buddhism in his historical evolution. In Bhavya there is a clear *will of harmonization.*

We find this same *will of harmonization* in the *Lotus Sūtra.* Although the *Lotus Sūtra* has sometimes very harsh expressions regarding the first Disciples of the Buddha, anyhow for the *Lotus Sūtra* the Śrāvakayāna and the Mahāyāna are *the same*

Doctrine presented by the Buddha *in two different forms* according to the special circumstances of the audience, and in His desire to save all living beings. This difference does not hinder that those who adhere to one or the other form of Buddhism can attain the same salvific goal, Buddhahood. Nobody is excluded from this achievement. The *Lotus Sūtra* in the numerous *vyākaraṇas* it contains has many examples that point out to the universality of its message. If Bhavya puts emphasis on the agreement of the doctrinaire point of view of Śrāvakayānists and Mahāyānists, the *Lotus Sūtra* put it in the identity of the religious aim of Salvation.

The Mahāyāna Sūtras are the Word of the Buddha

Bhavya, an important Mahāyānist Buddhist author, maintains in his *Tarkajvālā* that the Mahāyāna doctrine, correctly understood, is the same as the Śrāvakayāna doctrine. The *Lotus Sūtra*, a most important Mahāyānist Buddhist text, considers that the Śrāvakayāna doctrine and the Mahāyāna doctrine are one and the same although they are presented for didactic reasons in different forms and gradually, for the sake of the beings that hear it.

Neither Bhavya nor the *Lotus Sūtra* take into account an idea to which we are remarkably accustomed: the idea of evolution. Many doctrinaire elements are common to both, the Śrāvakayāna and the Mahāyāna; in relation to others there are more or less profound divergences, but neither Bhavya nor the author(s) of the *Lotus Sūtra* thought that they were non-Buddhists, that they constituted a new, non-Buddhist religious movement. They considered themselves true and faithful disciples of the Buddha. This was their feeling. Thus they did not accept the idea that the Mahāyāna Sūtras were not the Word of the Buddha. Similarly in our days a Mahāyānist Buddhist scholar and devotee could not deny the fact that the Mahāyāna Sūtras originated several centuries after Buddha's life, but nevertheless he deposits his faith in these Sūtras as expressing

Buddha's Teaching.

We think that Bhavya, the author(s) of the *Lotus Sūtra*, the modern Buddhist scholar are all of them right. In its long and dynamic existence Buddhism has evoluted. In some aspects Śrāvakayāna and Mahāyāna are the same; in some aspects Mahāyāna Buddhism in nothing else than the normal natural legitimate evolution of the Śrāvakayāna Buddhism. It could be said that all that the Mahāyāna teaches and may seem different from the Śrāvakayāna teachings was already in the Buddha's Preaching of the Śrāvakayāna epoch as a *garbha*, as a *bīja*, as a *śakti*, as an effect that is really existing in the cause. In due moment, thanks to the action of time, it blossoms as a Mahāyāna doctrine.

This is not a process exclusive of Buddhism; all religion has experienced it. The Buddha preached a rich lofty message, and as such in the course of its unavoidable evolution this message had to present itself under novel forms developing its inexhaustible potentialities.

IV

Śūnyatā in the *Lotus Sūtra*

Diverse points of view for the study of the Lotus Sūtra

The *Lotus Sūtra* can be considered from several points of view. The *Lotus Sūtra* is a foremost religious book. Its central teaching is the possibility for all living beings to achieve Supreme Perfect Enlightenment, i.e., to become a Buddha. Even Devadatta who attempted against the Buddha's life can reach that state. The Sūtra shows also the way to attain the supreme goal of Buddhahood, the discipline to which one has to submit: the severe *bodhisattvacaryā*. Linked with its central thesis other notions are dealt with in the *Lotus Sūtra*: the *upāyakauśalya* or ability, on the part of the Master, in the use of teaching methods, which allows him to adequate the message he will impart to the peculiar psychological and intellectual condition of the person who receives it; the *adhimukti* or open-mindedness, which permits the reception of a new beneficial message, even if it is contrary to deeply-rooted convictions; the *saṃdhābhāṣya* or that special form of discourse which, without deflecting from truth and as a result of the appliance by the Master of the ability in the teaching methods, presents the message in such a way that it can be grasped by the person, to which it is intended, with a certain (*provisional*) meaning that he accepts, and to which, later on, in the convenient moment, the Master will give its true, richer, more complete, *definitive* meaning; the *ekayāna* which affirms that the Buddha has taught only a single Vehicle although it can be wrongly imagined that He taught several Vehicles in the course of His life, incurring by doing so into changes or even falsities; in fact this wrong impression is due to His having recourse to the *upāyakauśalya* which makes Him grant the *one* and *same* Teaching to His followers under *diverse* forms. Many other religious aspects of Buddhism are dealt with in the Sūtra.

The *Lotus Sūtra* can be considered also as a source of historical information. For instance it informs us about the reactions of the Hīnayānists in face of the Mahāyānists' new message. In Part II of this book have included an article concerning this matter, "The conflict of change in the *Lotus Sūtra*: the Hīnayānist reaction".

References to the society of its time are also found in the *Lotus Sūtra*. The Sūtra describes the way of life, behaviour, reactions, feelings of monks and nuns, lay male devotees, lay female devotees, of the father that saves his sons from fire (Chapter III), of the rich householder and his son of low dispositions (Chapter IV), of the physician who, with herbs found in the Himalaya and a special treatment, restores the sight to a blind-born man (Chapter V), of the guide that safely leads the caravan through the dangerous forest (Chapter VII), of the two intimate friends (Chapter VIII), of the Preachers of the Dharma (*dharmabhāṇaka*), etc.

The *Lotus Sūtra* partakes of the conception of reality maintained by Buddhism. Cf. F. Tola and C. Dragonetti, "Buddhist Conception of Reality", *Journal of Indian Council of Philosophical Research*, Vol. XIV, Delhi (1996), pp. 35-64. The *Lotus Sūtra* refers to the inexistence of temporal beginning, the infinitude of space, the limitless number of worlds and beings, the dynamic form of existence, the laws that govern the empirical reality, the universal causality, etc.

In the present article we want to study the theory of *Śūnyatā* as manifested in the *Lotus Sūtra*. Of course, given the predominantly religious character of the Sūtra, we cannot expect to get on this matter a great amount of information. Nevertheless references to this important philosophical theory are found in several chapters.

Meanings of the word dharma

The word *dharma*, so much connected with *Śūnyatā*, in singular or plural has a wide range of meanings. Cf. Magdalene and Wilhelm Geiger, *Pāli Dhamma vornehmlich in der Kanonischen Literatur*, in *Kleine Schriften*, Wiesbaden: Franz Steiner Verlag, 1973, pp. 101-228, and the articles by Rupert Gethin, "He Who Sees Dhamma Sees Dhammas: Dhamma in Early Buddhism", in *Journal of Indian Philosophy* Volume 32, Nos. 5-6 December 2004, pp. 513-542, and by Collett Cox, "From Category to Ontology: The Changing Role of *Dharma* in Sarvāstivāda Abhidharma", in *Journal of Indian Philosophy* Volume 32, Nos. 5-6 December 2004. pp. 543-597.

Of all the meanings of the word *dharma* two are of special interest from the philosophical point of view: a. *laws* as the rules, norms, principles that govern the behaviour, the processes, the evolution of beings and things, and b. *elements of existence* as the components or factors of the all that exists. The second meaning is specially related to the theory of *Śūnyatā*.

Passages referring to dharmas *and* Śūnyatā

Śūnyatā and *dharmas* in relation to it are referred to in many passages of the *Lotus Sūtra* (we quote according to Kern-Nanjio edition, Osnabrück: Biblio Verlag, 1970), as for instance in:

1. Chapter II, p. 48, verse 68 a-b:
   evaṃ ca bhāṣāmy ahu nityanirvṛtā ādipraśāntā imi sarvadharmāḥ /
   "And so I declare that all these *dharmas*
   are eternally extinguished and calm from the beginning."

2. Chapter III. p. 62, verse 12 b:
   ... *śūnyāṃś ca dharmān ahu sparśayitvā /...*
   "... I, having attained (the knowledge of) the void *dharmas* ..."

3. Chapter IV, p. 101, line 1:
   ... *śūnyatānimittāpraṇihitaṃ sarvam āviṣkurmo.*

"... We manifest that all is Voidness, (the state) devoid of causes, (the state) devoid of purpose."

4. Chapter IV, p. 117, verse 45 a-b:
nirvāṇaparyanti samucchraye 'smin paribhāvitā śūnyata dīrgharātram /
"In this body, whose end is the *Nirvāṇa*,
having long been thoroughly imbued
with (the idea of) Voidness."

5. Chapter V, p. 124, line 10 – p. 125, line 1:
so 'haṃ ... °dharmaṃ viditvā ... ākāśagatikam ...
"I, knowing the *Dharma* ... leading to Voidness."

6. Chapter V, p. 131, verse 41:
ya ṛddhimantaś catudhyānadhyāyino ye śūnyatāṃ śrutva janenti prītim /
raśmīsahasrāṇi pramuñcamānās te caiva vuccanti mahādrumā iha //
"Those who possess the supernatural powers,
who meditate the four meditations,
who hearing about Voidness
feel delight,
and who emit thousands of rays,
they are called 'Great Trees'."

7. Chapter V, p. 133, line 1:
sarvadharmasamatāvabodhād dhi kāśyapa nirvāṇam.
"Since from the knowledge of the sameness of all the *dharmas* [comes forth], O Kāśyapa, the Nirvāṇa."

8. Chapter V, p. 136, lines 9-10:
tatra yathā ta ṛṣayaḥ pañcābhijñā viśuddhacakṣuṣa evaṃ bodhisattvā bodhicittāny utpādyānutpattikīṃ dharma-kṣāntiṃ pratilabhyānuttarāṃ samyaksaṃbodhim abhisaṃbudhyante.
"As the *ṛṣis* there (= in the parable) possess the five supernatural powers and a clear vision, so the Bodhisattvas,

producing the Mind of Enlightenment and acquiring the *kṣānti* (patience, acquiescence) in regard to (the theory of) the *dharmas* having no origination, obtain the Perfect Supreme Enlightenment."

9. Chapter V, p. 136, line 13 – p. 137, line 2:
yathā catasra oṣadhayas tathā śūnyatānimittāpraṇihitanirvā ṇadvāraṃ ca draṣṭavyam / ... evaṃ śūnyatānimittāpraṇihitāni vimokṣamukhāni bhāvayitvā sattvā avidyāṃ nirodhayanti.
"The four herbs are to be considered (to represent) Voidness, (the state) devoid of causes, (the state) devoid of purpose, the door of Nirvāṇa ... thus producing in themselves Voidness, (the state) devoid of causes, (the state) devoid of purpose - the doors of Liberation, beings suppress ignorance."

10. Chapter V, p. 137, lines 10-13:
so 'vabudhya traidhātukaṃ daśasu dikṣu śūnyaṃ nirmitopamaṃ māyopamaṃ svapnamarīcipratiśrutkopamaṃ lokaṃ paśyati / sa sarvadharmān anutpannān aniruddhān abaddhān amuktān na tamo 'ndhakārān na prakāśān paśyati / ya evaṃ gambhīrān dharmān paśyati sa paśyaty apaśyanayā sarvatraidhātukaṃ paripūrṇam anyonyasattvāśayādhimuktam.
"He, having obtained the knowledge, perceives that the Triple World in all directions is void, similar to a magic creation, similar to an illusion, similar to a dream, a mirage, an echo. He perceives that all the *dharmas* are not produced, do not cease, are not bound, are not released, that they are not darkness, gloom, nor light. Whoever perceives that the *dharmas* are profound in such a way, perceives, by not seeing, the whole Triple World with the various dispositions and propensities of beings."

11. Chapter V, p. 138, verse 51:
yas tu śūnyān vijānāti dharmān ātmavivarjitān /
saṃbuddhānāṃ bhagavatāṃ bodhiṃ jānāti tattvataḥ //

"But he who perceives
that the *dharmas* are void, devoid of substantiality,
knows according to Truth
the Enlightenment of the perfectly enlightened Bhagavants."

12. Chapter V, p. 138, verse 52 c-d:
śūnyajñānavihīnatvāc chrāvaka' saṃprabhāṣyate //
"Because of being deprived of the knowledge of the Void, he is called 'śrāvaka'."

13. Chapter V, p. 139, verse 53 a-b:
sarvadharmāvabodhāt tu samyaksaṃbuddha ucyate /
"Because of (possessing) the (true) knowledge
(of the true nature) of the *dharmas*,
he is called 'a perfectly enlightened'."

14. Chapter V, p. 140, verse 64 c-d:
sarvadharmāvabodhātu nirvāṇaṃ prāpyate 'mṛtam //
"By means of the (true) knowledge
(of the true nature) of all the *dharmas*
immortal Nirvāṇa is obtained."

15. Chapter V, p. 142, verses 75-76-77:
upāya eṣa buddhānāṃ vadanti yad imaṃ nayam /
sarvajñatvam ṛte nāsti nirvāṇaṃ tat samārabha //75//

tryadhvajñānam anantaṃ ca ṣaṭ ca pāramitāḥ śubhāḥ /
śūnyatām animittaṃ ca praṇidhānavivarjitam //76//

bodhicittaṃ ca ye cānye dharmā nirvāṇagāminaḥ /
sāsravā nāsravāḥ śāntāḥ sarve gaganasaṃnibhāḥ //77//
"This is the method of the Buddhas
that they declare this principle:
Without omniscience there is not Nirvāṇa
– try to get it (75),

and the limitless knowledge
of the three times and the six pure Perfections
and the Voidness devoid of causes, devoid of desire (76),

and the Mind of Enlightenment
and the other *dharmas* leading to Nirvāṇa
with impurities, without impurities, calm,
all similar to the sky (77)."

16. Chapter V, pp. 142-143, verses 79-80-81-82-83:
yaś ca dharmān vijānāti māyāsvapnasvabhāvakān /
kadalīskandhaniḥ sārān pratiśrutkāsamānakān //79//

tatsvabhāvaṃ ca jānāti traidhātukam aśeṣataḥ /
abaddham avimuktaṃ ca sa vijānāti nirvṛtim //80//

sarvadharmān samāñ śūnyān nirnānākaraṇātmakān /
na caitān (var.) *prekṣate nāpi kiṃcid dharmaṃ vipaśyati* //81//

sa paśyati mahāprajño dharmakāyam aśeṣataḥ /
nāsti yānatrayaṃ kiṃcid ekayānam ihāsti tu //82//

sarvadharmāḥ samāḥ sarve samāḥ samasamāḥ sadā /
evaṃ jñātvā vijānāti nirvāṇam amṛtaṃ śivam //83//

"He who knows
that the *dharmas* have the nature of illusion and dreams,
that they are without substance
like the trunk of the *kadalī*,
similar to an echo (79),

and knows
that the Triple World has throughout that (same) nature
and that it is neither bound nor released,
he knows extinction (80).

All the *dharmas* that are alike,
void,
whose essence is devoid of difference
– he does not see them;
he does not perceive even a single *dharma* (81).
He, a man of great wisdom,
sees the mass of the *dharmas* entirely.
There is not any Triple Vehicle;
but there is only One Vehicle in this world (82).

All *dharmas* are alike,
all are alike,
always exactly alike
– knowing that they are thus,
he knows the immortal, auspicious Nirvāṇa (83)."

17. Chapter VII, p. 186, lines 8-10:
yasmin bhikṣavaḥ samaye tathāgataḥ parinirvāṇakāla-samayam ātmanaḥ samanupaśyati pariśuddhāṃ ca parṣadaṃ paśyaty adhimuktisārāṃ śūnyadharma-gatiṃgatāṃ dhyānavatīṃ mahādhyānavatīm.
"When, O monks, the Tathāgata perceives (that) the moment, the occasion of His *Parinirvāṇa* (has arrived), and sees (that) the Assembly is completely pure, full of faith, expert in (the knowledge of) *dharmas* being void, devoted to meditation, devoted to great meditation (He enters *Nirvāṇa*)."

18. Chapter VIII, p. 200, lines 9-10:
tadyathāpi nāma mamaitarhi sarvatra cāgryo dharmakathikānām abhūt sarvatra ca śūnyatāgatiṃgato 'bhūt.
"As it is now with me, so he always was the best of the preachers of the Doctrine, he always was expert in (the knowledge of) Voidness."

19. Chapter X, p. 234, line 10:
sarvadharmaśūnyatāpraveśaḥ khalu punar bhaiṣajyarāja tathāgatasya dharmāsanam.
"Entering (ascertaining) the Voidness of all *dharmas* is, Bhaiṣajyarāja, the seat for (preaching) the *Dharma* proper of the Tathāgata."

20. Chapter X, p. 236, verse 24 c – d:
śūnyatā cāsanaṃ mahyam atra sthitvā hi deśayet //
"Voidness is my seat and standing in it he should preach."

21. Chapter XI, p. 262, line 2:
sarve ca te sarvadharmāñ śūnyān iti saṃjānanti sma mahāyānaguṇāṃś ca.
"They all knew that all the *dharmas* are void and even the virtues of Mahāyāna."

22. Chapter XI, p. 266, line 1:
trayāṇāṃ prāṇisahasrāṇām anutpattikadharmakṣāntipratilābho 'bhūt.
"Three thousand beings acquired the *kṣānti* (patience, acquiescence) in regard to (the theory that) the *dharmas* have no origination."

23. Chapter XIII, p. 275, lines 9-11:
yathābhūtaṃ ca dharmāṇāṃ svalakṣaṇaṃ vyavalokayati / yā khalv eṣu dharmeṣv avicāraṇāvikalpanā ayam ucyate mañjuśrīr bodhisattvasya mahāsattvasyācāra'.
"He sees the nature of the *dharmas* according to Truth. The absence of doubt and of false discrimination in relation to the *dharmas*, O Mañjuśrī, is called 'the good behaviour of the *Bodhisattva Mahāsattva*'."

24. Chapter XIII, p. 277, line 11 – p. 278 line 5:
punar aparaṃ mañjuśrīr bodhisattvo mahāsattvaḥ sarvadhamāñ śūnyān vyavalokayati yathāvatpra tiṣṭhitān dharmān aviparītasthāyino yathābhūtasthitān acalān akampyān avivartyān aparivartān samādāya yathābhūtasthitān ākāśasvabhāvān niruktivyavahāravivarjitān ajātān abhūtān na saṃskṛtān nāsaṃskṛtān na sato nāsato 'nabhilāpapravyāhṛtān asaṃgasthān asthitān saṃjñāviparyāsaprādurbhūtān.
"Moreover, O Mañjusrī, the *Bodhisattva Mahāsattva* looks upon all the *dharmas* as void, assuming the *dharmas* as they are, not being otherwise, being as they are, immovable, not to be shaken, not liable to turn back, not changing – being as they are, having the nature of space, devoid of explanation and of designation, unborn, not becoming, not

conditioned, not not-conditioned, not being, not not-being, inexpressible by words, without contact with anything, not existing, coming forth from false notions and error."

25. Chapter XIII, p. 281, verse 17 (c-d):
sarvadharma ajātatvā gaveṣanto na paśyati //
"Owing to their being unborn,
even looking (for them), he does not perceive any *dharma*."

26. Chapter XIII, p. 281, verse 19:
asantakā dharma ime prakāśitā aprādurbhūtāś ca ajātakāś ca /
śūnyā nirīhā sthita nityakālaṃ ayaṃ gocaro ucyati paṇḍitānām //
"*Dharmas* have been taught to be non existing,
not manifested, not born,
void, without activity, eternally standing
- this is called 'the field of sages'."

27. Chapter XIII, p. 281, verse 21:
ekāgracitto hi samāhitaḥ sadā sumerukūṭo yatha susthitaś ca /
evaṃ sthitaś cāpi hi tān nirīkṣed ākāśabhūtān ima sarvadharmān //
"With mind fixed in one entity, permanently concentrated,
firm like the peak of Sumeru, and, standing thus,
let him look upon all *dharmas* as being like the space."

28. Chapter XIII, p. 282, verse 22:
sadā pi ākāśasamā na sārakā aniñjitā manyanavarjitāś ca /
sthitā hi dharmā imi nityakālaṃ ayu gocaro ucyati paṇḍitānām //
"Always similar to space,
inconsistent, without movement, beyond vain imagining,
for the *dharmas* are eternally standing
- this is called 'the field of sages'."

29. Chapter XV, p. 318, lines 8-10:
dṛṣṭaṃ hi tathāgatena traidhātukaṃ yathābhūtaṃ na jāyate na mriyate na cyavate nāpapadyate na saṃsarati na parinirvāti na bhūtaṃ nābhūtaṃ na sattaṃ nāsattaṃ na tathā nānyathā na vitathā nāvitathā nānyathā na tathā / traidhātukaṃ tathāgatena dṛṣṭaṃ yathā bālapṛthagjanā na paśyanti.

"The Triple World has been seen by the *Tathāgata* as it really is: it is not born, it does not die, it does not fall dawn, it does not run away, it does not transmigrate, it does not become extinct, it is not real nor non-real, it is not existing nor non-existing, it is not such nor otherwise, it is not false nor non-false, it is not otherwise nor such. The ignorant do not see the Triple World as it has been seen by the *Tathāgata*."

30. Chapter XVI, p. 327, line 4:
bodhisattvakoṭīnayutaśatasahasrāṇāṃ anutpattikadharma-kṣāntir utpannā.
"In hundreds of thousands of millions of millions of Bodhisattvas the *kṣānti* (patience, acceptance), in regard to (the theory of) the *dharmas* not being produced, was born."

31. Chapter XVII, p. 351, verse 5 (c):
sarve bhavāḥ phenamarīcikalpā.
"All beings are like foam and mirage."

32. Chapter XXI, p. 403, lines 7-8:
aṣṭāṣaṣṭīnāṃ prāṇisahasrāṇām anutpattikadharma-kṣāntipratilābho 'bhūt.
"Sixty thousand beings acquired the *kṣānti* (patience, acceptance) in regard to (the theory of) the *dharmas* not being produced."

33. Chapter XXII, p. 419, lines 6-7:
anutpattikadharmakṣāntiṃ ca pratilapsyate.
"And he will obtain the *kṣānti* (patience, acceptance) in regard to (the theory of) the *dharmas* not being produced."

34. Chapter XXIII, p. 437, line 1:
dvācatvāriṃśatāṃ bodhisattvasahasrāṇām anutpatti-kadharmakṣāntipratilambho 'bhūt.
"Forty two thousand *Bodhisattvas* acquired the *kṣānti* (patience, acceptance) in regard to (the theory of) the *dharmas* not being produced."

Something that calls the attention is the fact that the references to the *dharmas* and *Śūnyatā* theory in the quoted passages 1-28 from Chapters I-XIII of the Sūtra are more numerous and richer in contents than those in passages 29-34 from Chapters XIV-XXIII of the Sūtra, which limit themselves to point out the acquisition of *anutpattikadharmakṣānti*. As it is known, the first thirteen chapters, which correspond to Chapters I-XIV of Kumārajīva's Chinese translation, refer to Śākyamuni as the historical Buddha, while Chapters XIV-XXVII, corresponding to Kumārajīva's XV-XXVIII, refer to the eternal Buddha.

Tenets of the Śūnyatā theory *in the above passages*

First of all let us see which are the characteristics attributed to the *dharmas* and to *Śūnyatā* in the quoted texts.

a. *Dharmas* (numbers refer to the quoted passages):

nityanirvṛta, ādipraśānta: 1;
śūnya: 2, 11, 16 (81), 17, 19, 24, 26;
anutpattika: 8, 22, 30, 32, 33, 34;
anutpanna, aniruddha, abaddha, amukta, na tamo'ndhakāra, na prakāśa, gambhīra: 10;
ātmavivarjita: 11;
nirvāṇāgamin, sāsrava nāsrava, śānta, gagaṇasaṃnibha: 15 (77);
māyāsvapnasvabhāvaka, kadalīskandhaniḥsāra, pratiśrutkāsamānaka: 16 (79);
tatsvabhāvam ... traidhātukam: 16 (80);
samatā, nirnānākaraṇātmaka: 7, 16 (81, 83);
na caitān (= dharmān) prekṣate nāpi kiṃcid dharmaṃ vipaśyati: 16 (81);
yathāvatpratiṣṭhita, aviparītasthāyin, yathābhūtasthita, acala, akampya, avivartya, aparivarta, ākāśasvabhāva, niruktivyavahāravivarjita, ajāta, abhūta, na saṃskṛta, nāsaṃskṛta, na sat nāsat, anabhilāpapravyāhṛta, asaṃgastha, asthita, saṃjñāviparyāsaprādurbhūta: 24;

sarvadharma ajātatvā ... na paśyati: 25;
asantaka, aprādurbhūta, ajātaka, nirīha, sthita nityakālam: 26;
ākāśabhūta: 27;
ākāśasama, na sāraka, aniñjita, manyanavarjita, sthita nityakālam: 28;
na jāyate na mriyate na cyavate nāpapadyate na saṃsarati na parinirvāti na bhūtaṃ nābhūtaṃ na sattaṃ nāsattaṃ na tathā nānyathā na vitathā nāvitathā nānyathā na tathā: 29;
sarve bhavāḥ phenamarīcikalpā: 31.

b. *Śūnyatā*

śūnyatānimittāpranihitaṃ sarvam : 3;
śūnyatām animittaṃ ca praṇidhānavivarjitam : 15 (76);
sarvadharmaśūnyatā ° : 19.

The preceding analysis shows that the characteristics attributed to the *dharmas* and *Śūnyatā* in the *Lotus Sūtra* are the same as those attributed to them in the *Prajñāpāramitā Sūtras* and in the treatises of Nāgārjuna and Nāgārjuna's disciples. It can be said that the Sūtra adheres to the classical Mahāyānist conception of the *dharmas* and *Śūnyatā*.

Now let us examine which is the importance attributed to the *Śūnyatā* and *dharmas* theory in the *Lotus Sūtra*. We shall approach this question from two points of view: a. Number of references to that theory in relation to number of references to other important notions that appear in the Sūtra, and b. Context where these references are made.

a. *Number of references*

The number of references to the *dharmas* and *Śūnyatā* theory is 34. The number of references in the *Lotus Sūtra* to other notions, that have in it an important function, is as follows:

adhimukti: 33, to which should be added the quotations of °*bala* (2), °*virahita* (1), °*saṃpanna* (1), °*sāra* (4), which increase its number to a total of 41;

upāyakauśalya: 74, to which should be added the quotations of *°jñāna* (5), *°jñānadarśana* (2), *°jñānadarśanadeśanā* (1), *°jñānanidarśana* (1), *°jñānābhinirhāra* (1), *°deśanābhinirhāranirmitta* (1), *°pāramitā* (1), *°viṣaya* (1), *°śata* (3), *°śatasahasra* (1), *°sahasrakoṭi* (3), *°suśikṣita* (1), which increase its number to a total of 95;

ekayāna : 6;

nirvāṇa : 55, to which should be added the quotations of *°kāla* (1), *°gāmin* (1), *°dvāra* (1), *°dhātu* (3), *°nagara* (1), *°paryanta* (1), *°paryavasāna* (5), *°prāpta* (8), *°bhūmi* (5), *°bhūmisthita* (1), *°mātra* (2), *°marga*, (1), *°śabda* (1), *°saṃjñin* (2), *°samavasaraṇa* (1); *parinirvāṇa* (23), *°kālasamaya* (5), *°vaineya* (1), *°saṃjñin* (1), which increase its number to a total of 119.

buddhakṣetra : 75, to which should be added the quotations of *°koṭinayutaśatasahasra* (7), *°guṇavyūha* (3), *°pariśuddhi* (1), *°vyūha* (1), *°sahasra* (3), *°upapatti* (1), which increase its number to a total of 91;

bodhi : 186, to which should be added the quotations of *°kāraṇa* (2), *°caryā* (1), *°citta* (5), *°cittāvinivartin* (1), *°pakṣika* (1), *°prasthita* (1), *°maṇḍa* (31), *°maṇḍavarāgragata* (10), *°maṇḍasaṃprasthita* (1), *°margopadeśa* (1), *°vṛkṣa* (14), *°vṛkṣamūla* (10), *°hetu* (1), *°aṅga* (2), which increase its number to a total of 267, without taking into account *bodhisattva* (a great number of references) and its compounds, which would increase its number to a remarkable amount.

samyaksaṃbodhi : 127.

The number of references to the *dharmas* and *Śūnyatā* theory is inferior to that of the other notions, with the exception of *ekayāna*. It is possible to explain this fact taking into account that the principal themes of the *Lotus Sūtra* are those indicated at the beginning of this article. Thus, it is normal that the notions that are in a direct relation to those themes have more presence in the Sūtra. Nevertheless, the study of the question from the second point of view will reveal us that, notwithstanding the relatively low number of references to the *dharmas* and *Śūnyatā* theory, to this theory is attributed in the Sūtra a foremost importance.

b. *Context where references are made*

Passage 5 (V, p. 124, line 10 – p. 125, line 1):

The *Dharma* leads to Voidness.

Passage 6 (V, p. 131, verse 41):

Possession of the supernatural powers (*ṛddhi*), meditation of the four meditations and feeling delight on hearing about *Śūnyatā* are the requisites for being called 'Great Tree' as a mark of distinction.

Passage 7 (V, p. 133, line 1):

By the knowledge of the sameness of the *dharmas* Nirvāṇa is obtained.

Passage 8 (V, p. 136, lines 9 - 10):

Bodhisattvas, who produce in themselves the Enlightenment-Mind (*bodhicitta*) and obtain the *kṣānti* in regard to the theory of the *dharmas* being unborn, are compared to the seers (*ṛṣi*) who possess the five supernatural knowledges (*pañcābhijñā*) and a pure vision, and they obtain the Supreme Perfect Enlightenment.

Passage 9 (V, p. 136, line 13 – p. 137, line 2):

Śūnyatā, the state devoid of causes, the state devoid of purpose and the door of Nirvāṇa are compared to the four beneficial herbs that restored the vision to the blind man.

Śūnyatā, the state devoid of causes and the state devoid of purpose are considered the doors of Liberation, and beings, meditating on them suppress ignorance.

Passage 10 (V, p. 137, lines 10 - 13):

He who possesses the knowledge of *Śūnyatā* and of the true nature of the *dharmas*, perceives (= knows the essence of) the whole reality with its diverse beings.

Passage 11 (V, p. 138, verse 51):

He who knows that the *dharmas* are void and without substantiality, truly reaches the Enlightenment of the Buddhas.

Passage 12 (V, p. 138, verse 52 c - d):

Śrāvakas are so called because they do not possess the knowledge of *Śūnyatā.*

Passage 13 (V, p. 139, verse 53 a - b):

On the contrary, he who knows the true nature of the *dharmas* is called 'a perfectly enlightened'.

Passage 14 (V, p. 140, verse 64 c – d):

Nirvāṇa is obtained through the knowledge of the true nature of the *dharmas*, i. e. Voidness.

Passage 15 (V, p. 142, verses 75 – 77):

Voidness among other *dharmas* leads to *Nirvāṇa.*

Passage 16 (V, pp. 142-143, verses 79 - 83):

He who knows the illusory nature of the *dharmas* and that the three worlds have that nature, knows extinction = *Nirvāṇa.*

Knowing that all the *dharmas* are always equal (*sama*) among themselves, one knows *Nirvāṇa* without death and auspicious.

Passage 17 (VII, p. 186, lines 8 - 10):

Buddha Śākyamuni will enter *Nirvāṇa* only when his disciples have become pure, full of faith, fully conscious of *dharmas* being void, and devoted to meditation.

Passage 18 (VIII, p. 200, lines 9 - 10):

The Buddha praises Pūrṇa, because he was the best of preachers and possessed the understanding of *Śūnyatā.*

Passage 19 (X, p. 234, line 10):

Knowing that *dharmas* are void is the seat where the *Tathāgata* preaches the *Dharma.*

Passage 20 (X, p. 236, verse 24 c - d):

Śūnyatā is the seat of Buddha, and sitting in it the *Bodhisattva* should preach the *Dharma.*

Passage 22 (XI, p. 266, line 1):

The *anutpattikadharmakṣāntipratilābha* by many persons was the great auspicious effect of the conversion of the daughter of the Nāga king into a Buddha.

Passage 23 (XIII, p. 275, lines 9 - 11):

The good behaviour of a *Bodhisattva* is to know the true nature of the *dharmas.*

Passage 24 (XIII, p. 277, line 11 - p. 278, line 5):

The second 'field of action' (*gocara*) of the *Bodhisattva* is to know that the *dharmas* are void and possess the corresponding characteristics.

Passage 26 (XIII, p. 281, verse 19):

The field (*gocara*) of the *pandits* are the *dharmas* taught as not being (*asantaka*), etc.

Passage 27 (XIII, p. 281, verse 21):

What the *Bodhisattva* perceives, when concentrated in meditation, is that the *dharmas* are like the space, i.e., void.

Passage 28 (XIII, p. 282, verse 22):

This passage repeats what passage 26 expresses: the field (*gocara*) of the *pandits* is the knowledge of the *dharmas* being similar to space, etc.

Passage 29 (XV, p. 318, lines 8-10):

What distinguishes the *Tathāgata* is that He knows the true nature of the world, i.e., Voidness, while the ignorant do not.

Passage 30 (XVI, p. 327, line 4):

The first effect of the teaching of the Chapter on the "Extension of the life of the *Tathāgata*", to which a great importance is attributed, is that a very great number of *Bodhisattvas* acquired the *kṣānti* in regard to the theory of the *dharmas* being un-born.

Passage 32 (XXI, p. 403, lines 7 - 8):

The effect of the teaching of the Chapter on the *Dhāraṇis* is that a great number of beings acquired the *anutpattikakṣānti.*

Passage 33 (XXII, p. 419, lines 6 - 7):

The woman who keeps in her memory the Chapter on a previous existence of *Tathāgata* Bhaiṣajyarāja and makes it known, will be reborn as a *Bodhisattva,* who immediately after her birth will get the supernatural knowledges (*abhijñā*) and the *kṣānti* in regard to the theory of the *dharmas* being unborn.

Passage 34 (XXIII, p. 437, line 1):

The effect of the teaching of the Chapter on Gadgadasvara was that a great number of beings acquired the *anutpattikadharmakṣānti.*

Conclusion

The remarks that precede allow us to conclude that the *Śūnyatā* and *dharmas* theory as established by the *Prajñāpāramitā Sūtras* and in the Mādhyamika treatises is present in the *Lotus Sūtra* and that, although the number of references to it is inferior to the number of references to many other main doctrines in the Sūtra, anyhow the important contexts in which it appears leave no doubt that it has in the *Lotus Sūtra* also a foremost position.

V

On Translating into Spanish the *Sadharmapuṇḍarīkasūtra*

A. The Language of the Lotus Sūtra*

In this paper we shall present some of the reflections that the translation of the *Sadharmapuṇḍarīkasūtra* (from its original text into Spanish) has provoked in us regarding some linguistic, semantic and communication problems.*

1. After translating some few pages of Kern's edition, we asked ourselves: which is the nature of the *Sadharmapuṇḍarīka's* language? We found many points of contact with Sanskrit, but it was not at all the Sanskrit of the *Kāvya* or of the philosophical or literary prose with which we were acquainted; we found also numerous points of contact with Pāli, in such a way that many times it was more useful for us to have recourse to the Pāli Dictionaries and Grammars than to the Sanskrit ones, but nevertheless it was not Pāli. We thought that to have a clear idea about the language of the *Sūtra* is a necessary requisite for a correct approach to the *Sūtra*, specially if one intends to translate it, since the nature of the language will determine the limits within which one has to move and the devices one can apply in the solution of semantic problems.

2. All languages, as any of the elements that constitute society, constantly evolute in a more or less swift way. Of course this does not happen with artificial languages, as for instance the artificial Sanskrit of the literary circles, which is forcibly submitted to Pāṇini's rules and thereby kept away from the so-called "danger" of the transformations, which are characteristic of any language that is

---

* This paper is based upon a lecture given by us in *The International Institute for Buddhist Studies*, Tokyo, 1989.

immersed in the ever-changing current of social life. Latin has also been preserved as an artificial language, without changes, by some European literary or academic circles: always there have been and there are still now poets and prose writers who compose their poems, treatises and speeches in the Latin employed twenty centuries ago by Cicero, Horatius and Virgilius. But what has happened with Sanskrit and Latin is not exclusive of these two languages. Any colloquial, or what is the same, living and popular language, which is used as literary language and is consequently fixed as such, tends to become in a more or less degree an artificial language; and in the same degree in which it becomes an artificial fixed language, it becomes also more and more different from the colloquial language from which it originated and which, precisely because of its being a colloquial language, continues its evolution or transformation.

The language brought to India by the Indo-europeans, the Old Indian, evoluted. Products of that evolution were the language of the *Vedas*, the Sanskrit, and the Middle Indian. Probably already in that epoch the Old Indian presented two aspects or variants: on one side the colloquial language and on the other side the literary-religious language. Probably also the Middle Indian derived from the colloquial aspect or variant of the Old Indian, and the language of the *Vedas* and the Sanskrit derived from the literary-religious aspects of the Old Indian

But perhaps to say that the language of the *Vedas*, the Sanskrit and the Middle Indian are 'products' of the Old Indian or that they 'derive' from it, is not very precise and creates misrepresentations. It would be better to say that the language of the *Vedas*, the Sanskrit and the Middle Indian are forms adopted by the Old Indian, in its literary and colloquial aspects, in the course of its evolution and that these forms are fixed in the texts that use them, but this fixation does not mean that the Old Indian stops its evolution; on the contrary, it continues its evolution adopting new forms that are at their turn fixed in other texts - as for instance in those of the New Indian languages.

Now if we call 'Vedic' instead of Old Indian the language used by the Indo-europeans when they came to India and established themselves in the North-western regions, we can say that the language of the *Vedas*, Sanskrit and Middle Indian are forms adopted by the Vedic in its evolution, as it is also said by some scholars.[1]

Very probably the differences between the colloquial or popular aspects of the Old Indian and its literary aspects, and likewise the differences between their respective lines of evolution were at a certain moment minimal and they increased with the progress of their evolution until at a certain moment there was an opposition between the Middle Indian as the language for colloquial use of the great number of people in India, and the Sanskrit as the literary language, which notwithstanding remained the spoken language of small groups.

3. The Mahāyāna *Sūtras* were written in Middle Indian [2] or better to say: in one of the dialects under whose forms the Middle Indian manifested itself in the different regions of India in which it was used, since it is beyond doubt that Middle Indian was divided in dialects.[3] It is not possible to determine the geographical area to which the Middle Indian dialect of the *Sūtras* belonged,[4] although there is some probability that it belonged to the region around Mathurā.[5] Pāli also has its origin in one of these Middle Indian dialects, which probably was very near to that in which the

---

[1] For the Sanskrit, Renou 1956, pp. 83-84; for the Middle Indian, von Hinüber 1986, p. 24.

[2] Edgerton 1953-1954, p. 3, and 1956, p. 134, Renou 1953, p. 283; von Hinüber 1986, pp. 19, 39. The principal reasons that oblige to admit that the so called Mixed, Hybrid or Buddhist Sanskrit is a Middle Indian Language are the following ones: 1. great part of the vocabulary of the Sūtras is Middle Indian, *i.e.*, is constituted by words with meanings not found in Sanskrit (Edgerton 1936, Dictionary 1953; Yuyama 1972), 2. in many verses in order to comply with the meter it is necessary to replace Sanskrit or Sanskritized words by their corresponding Middle Indian words (Edgerton 1935, 1946), 3. the older manuscripts even of the same texts present less Sanskrit or Sanskritized forms than the newer manuscripts (Edgerton, Grammar, 1953, pp.6-9).

[3] Bechert 1980, p. 14.

[4] Edgerton 1953-1954, p. 3; Von Hinüber 1986, p. 39 and 41. Cf. Roth; Lamotte 1958, p. 645.

[5] Lamotte 1958, p. 645; Damsteegt 1978, p. 263; von Hinüber 1986, p. 41; Roth 1980, p. 85.

Mahāyāna *Sūtras* were composed, taking into account their similarities.[6]

4. But either because the Middle Indian employed by the Mahāyāna *Sūtras* was still very near to Sanskrit, which had developped parallel to it, or because already at an early stage of its evolution, even before the composition of the *Sūtras*, it was submitted to Sankritization,[7] or because it was Sanskritized by the composers of the *Sūtras* or by their reciters and copyists which transmitted them, under the influence of the ever increasing prestige of Sanskrit - the fact is that the language of the *Sūtras* as we have them now presents itself as a *mixed language* in which Middle Indian forms coexist with Sanskrit forms.

But the language of the *Sūtras* is a mixed language not only because it presents together Middle Indian forms and Sanskrit forms, but also because all the Middle Indian forms do not derive from a single Middle Indian dialect but from several ones.[8]

This *Sūtra* language, besides being called 'Buddhist Sanskrit', also is called 'Hybrid Sanskrit' or 'Mixed Sanskrit', but taking into account that in reality it is a Middle Indian language that has been Sanskritized, it could also be called 'Mixed Middle Indian' or 'Hybrid Middle Indian'.[9]

This feature of the language of the *Sūtras* of being a mixed language reminds us the dialect of the Homeric pomes, the *Iliad* and the *Odyssey*. This dialect is in the main a Ionic (*yavana*) dialect but besides the Ionic element we find in it forms that belong to other Greek dialects: Attic forms, Aeolic forms, Cyprian and Arcadian forms, and besides that some very old Greek forms that were not understood in later times, and even forms that come from pre-Greek language. This is a feature common to traditional literature.

5. The *Sūtra* language, as we have it, i.e., in an advanced stage of evolution, in an advanced stage of Sanskritization, is a literary

---

[6] Von Hinüber 1986, p. 39.

[7] Von Hinüber 1982, p. 138.

[8] Edgerton, Grammar, 1953, p. 1; Lamotte 1958, p. 645.

[9] Edgerton 1956, p. 134.

language, that is to say: it was used for written or literary composition, not for colloquial, common, daily use; [10] it was not learned in infancy; it contains morphological forms created in order to comply with the requirements of the meter, [11] archaic poetic or hieratic words and even artificial forms invented by purely grammatical theoretical thinking.[12] But this literary nature does not mean that it could not be understood by the persons for whom the *Sūtras* were composed. Ourselves, after reading and translating some pages of the *Saddharmapuṇḍarīka*, we felt at home with it, not finding strange or problematic or odd the language it presents. This is undoubtedly what happened to the Buddhist believers in India some centuries ago, when they attended a recitation of the *Sūtra*, taking into account that their own daily language presented many similarities with the *Sūtra*'s language (as being one the popular aspect and the other the literary aspect of the same language, the Middle Indian), that they were immersed in the spiritual life that had produced the *Sūtra*, and that many of the phonetic and morphological variants presented by the written text of the *Sūtras* may disappear or become imperceptible when the *Sūtra* is orally delivered.

The literary nature constitutes another remarkable similarity between the language of the *Sūtras* and the language of the Homeric poems. The language of Homer's poems was also a literary language, not a colloquial one and (what is more striking) it was also in great part a product of the epic style and of the hexameter, the characteristic meter of the epic compositions.

6. The use of the Mixed Sanskrit, Hybrid Sanskrit or Buddhist Sanskrit was not restricted to the composition of Buddhist works (*Sūtras* or narrative texts). Mixed Sanskrit is not a strictly Buddhist phenomenon but a stage in the general evolution of the Indian

---

[10] Edgerton 1953-1954, p. 2.

[11] Smith 1952.

[12] Von Hinüber 1982, p. 140. We do not think that the fact of being a 'mixed language' can be considered as a characteristic of 'literary language'.

language,[13] as it is shown by its use in non-Buddhist inscriptions,[14] and even in some technical works,[15] as for instance in the medical treatise contained in the Bower Manuscript, specially in Parts IV-VII on divination and incantation,[16] in the mathematical treatise found in Bakhshālī[17] and in the astronomical treatise and the *Kośa* contained in the Weber manuscript found "near Kugiar, a place just across the border of Chinese Yarkhand".[18]

7. Another question that was provoked in us on reading the *Saddharmapuṇḍarīka* was: is the language of the *Sūtras* 'bad', 'barbaric' Sanskrit as sometimes it has been qualified? Were the authors of the *Sūtras* uneducated persons, who had no access to brahmnic education and to the learning of Sanskrit?

Notwithstanding the names it has received of 'Mixed' or 'Hybrid' 'Sanskrit' (which can provoke misunderstanding), it is accepted that the language of the *Sūtras* is not Sanskrit, that it is a Middle Indian language which was submitted to a more or less intense Sanskritization. As it is unfit to judge the language of a particular text by applying to it the grammatical rules of another, it is not possible to condemn the language or the *Sūtras* as 'bad' or 'barbaric' simply because it does not comply with the rigids norms of Pāṇini that are valid for Sanskrit.

The following consideration confirmed us in this idea. Every colloquial language evolutes in the course of time in an unceasing transformation, while the literary language has more resistence to change. But during all its evolution it is always the *same* language that remains, having adopted new forms of presentation. When the differences between that language on a certain moment of its development and that same language several centuries before have become very numerous and deep, it is usual to give to that language

[13] Lamotte 1958, p. 638.

[14] Damsteegt 1978; Lamotte 1958, pp. 639-642.

[15] Renou 1957, p. 20 and notes 286 and 498.

[16] Ed. Hoernle 1893-1912, Chapter VII.

[17] Ed. Kaye 1927, p. 11 and pp. 78-79.

[18] Bühler 1893.

a new name that conceals their basic identity but at the same time 'legitimates' those differences. So new names were given to Latin in Europe, as for instance in Spain, around the 10th century when the form it got in its evolution was very much different from the form it had several centuries before. It is how Latin has come to be known as 'Spanish', although 'Spanish' is nothing else than transformed Latin, since there has been no interruption of its identity.

Now if we analize Spanish in reference to classical Latin, we find in it many forms completely in disagreement with the grammar of classical Latin. For instance, we find in Spanish, when referred to Latin, confusion of gender, use of one case ending for another, formation of participles from the theme of present and not from the theme of supine, adding of perfect endings to the theme of present, etc. From the point of view of Latin grammar, twenty centuries ago in Rome, all that is 'bad' or 'barbaric', but from the point of view of Spanish and its own grammar, now twenty centuries after in Spain or in South America, all that is correct.

As for the second question we agree with Renou when he says[19] that the language of the *Sūtras*, the so-called 'Hybrid Sanskrit', was not the language of persons bad cultivated or lacking ability,[20] as the language of some *Purāṇa* of early date or of some *Śilpa* treatises is, since it has served to note down some of the most beautiful texts of Buddhism, and stanzas which are the richest in spiritual sensibility.

---

[19] Renou 1953, p.284.

[20] This appreciation is supported by the rich vocabulary employed by the authors of the Sūtras and by many passages of really literary value.

B. Problems of Translation And Communication*

The linguistic point of view we have dealt with in the previous article is not the only point of view from which we have to approach the *Lotus Sūtra.*

The *Saddharmapuṇḍarīka* is the work of a religious Buddhist author, it carries a religious Buddhist message, and it is directed to religious Buddhist hearers or readers. Our decision to translate it into Spanish introduces three new elements in this scheme: 1. the translators, 2. the Spanish-speaking readers, and 3. the translation itself.

1. Happily in our case we have been in contact with Buddhist texts since more or less 30 years, we have translated several Buddhist texts, we feel respect and appreciation for Buddhism, and Buddhism is for us in reality the religion with which we have more affinities. These circumstances, we think, facilitate our work in order to give a translation as faithful as possible, i.e., a translation that transmits, as much as possible, the contents and spirit of the translated work. We know that it is impossible to convey in a translation all what the original text says or inspires; great part of this is lost; the translator must do his best in order that the loss be reduced to its minimal proportion.

2. The readers, to whom our translation is directed, offer more serious difficulties. They are not acquainted at all or, in very few cases, only superficially, with Buddhism, they have not been educated in a Buddhist tradition, they do not belong to a Buddhist culture. Even more: they belong to a tradition and to a culture not only different from, but in many cases even contrary to Buddhism: Catholicism. So it is necessary to capacitate them to grasp, to understand and to appreciate the *Lotus Sutra*'s message as far as that is possible in the given circumstances.

For that purpose we have had recourse to some *upāya* (we could say):

---

* This work is the second part of the lecture given by us in *The International Institute for Buddhist Studies*, Tokyo, 1989.

The Introduction of our translation will help the Spanish-speaking reader to grasp the spiritual world of Buddhism in general and specially that of the *Saddharmapuṇḍarīka*, its doctrines, its importance in Buddhist culture, its spread, its transmission and so many other interesting aspects.

The sub-titles we are giving to the different parts into which the text can be divided and the notes that will accompany the translation will also help the reader to grasp the message of the *Sūtra* as it unfolds itself in the different chapters.

We have generously resorted to the use of capital letters as the first letter of many words. In Spanish capital letter at the beginning of a word enhances the status of the being or thing designated by the word. And we want this to be done in relation to many Buddhist concepts, specially those that pertain to the Buddha and his Doctrines, in order that the Spanish-speaking reader unconsciously perceive that he is dealing with concepts that are above the common and ordinary level of daily life.

3. The last element we must take into account is the translation itself. As any text, the *Lotus Sūtra* is to be considered in its external, formal aspect, and in its internal aspect or contents.

As for the formal aspect we have decided to translate the verse portions of the *Saddharmapuṇḍarīka* in what we call 'free verses', that is to say in series or sequences of a few words, which are not subject either to a metrical scheme or to rhythm, with other series or sequences that follow or precede them, but which nevertheless have in themselves a smooth flowing that harmonizes with the smooth flowing of the preceding and following series or sequences.

Happily we have some experience in verse translation, because we have already published verse translation of several *kāvyas*, which have been well received by literary critics. The free verse has (we can say) a neutral intensifying power, it gives more expressive force to what is said and predisposes the reader to an easier acceptance of what is transmitted to him. We have made the experiment with some very famous Spanish verses: when they are deprived of their verse-form and are converted into prose, although maintaining all their words and transmitting the same idea, these verses lose great part of their expressive force and the impression they cause in the reader is reduced.

As for the internal aspect or contents of the text, i.e. the message of the *Lotus Sūtra*, we have adopted several norms in order to convey it as faithfully as possible, and to misrepresent it as less as we can. These norms fundamentally refer to the semantic value of a series of words, but they have also to do with the problems of communication that all translation presents.

(a) When we fix the meaning of a word we must fix it in the context of the Mixed or Hybrid Sanskrit. Many words that appear in the *Sūtras* (such as *vyākaraṇa*, *ātmabhāva*, *ādikarmika* and many others, in spite of their correct Sanskrit form, have meanings that are not found in Sanskrit but are proper of the Middle Indian languages, specially Pāli. It is obvious that we must be careful not to give to these words the meaning they have in Sanskrit. That could originate an erroneous understanding of the text.

(b) Equally important is to determine the value of many words in the light of the Buddhist doctrines to which the *Lotus Sūtra* is related. A translation without reference to these doctrines runs the risk not to grasp the real meaning of the text. This has happened, we think, in two passages of Burnouf and Kern translations that can serve as examples.

In III, 12 we have:

vimucya tā dṛṣṭikṛtāṇi sarvaśaḥ, śūnyāṃś ca dharmān ahu sparśayitvā /
tato vijñānāmy ahu nirvṛto 'smi na cāpi nirvāṇam idaṃ prabudhyate /

In this verse what interest us is the second *pāda*. It has been translated by Burnouf:

"Après m'être complétement dégagé des opinions des fausses doctrines, et avoir touché aux lois du vide..."

and by Kern:

"After having completely freed myself from all (heretical) views, and reached the laws of void..."

We think that, if these authors had had in mind the *śūnyatāvāda*, they would have grasped better the meaning of that verse or at least would have transmitted more clearly that meaning to the readers.

Other translators have given more faithful translations of that verse, as for instance Kumārajīva; his Chinese version is rendered by Murano (p. 48):

"And (I) attained the truth that nothing is substantial."

and by Hurvitz (p. 51):

"I...directly witnessed the empty dharmas."

Likewise Matsunami, Nagao and Tanji (p. 80); Sakamoto and Iwamoto (p. 141) in their Japanese translations from the Sanskrit text. All these translators have naturally related that verse to the *śūnyatā* doctrine.

Another instance is given in II, 67 (68):

evaṃ ca bhāṣāmy ahu nityanirvṛtā ādipraśāntā imi sarvadharmāḥ
caryāṃ ca yo pūrayi buddhaputro anāgate 'dhvāni jino bhaviṣyati /

Here we refer to *pādas a* and *b.* They are translated by Burnouf (p. 31):

"C'est ainsi que j'expose toutes les lois qui sont perpétuellement affranchies, qui sont dès le principe parfaitement pures..."

and by Kern (p. 48):

"And so I reveal all those laws that are ever holy and correct from the very beginning".

Here also reference to the *śūnyatāvāda* could have allowed a better translation as it is shown by the translation by Kumārajīva; his Chinese translation is rendered by Murano (p. 35):

"All things are from the outset
In the state of tranquil extinction."

and by Hurvitz (p. 37):

"The Dharmas from the very origin
Are themselves eternally characterized by the marks of quiet extinction."

Likewise Matsunami, Nagao and Tanji (p. 63); Sakamoto and Iwamoto (p. 111) in their Japanese translation from the Sanskrit text.

(c) We must have great care not to distort the meaning of many important words of the *Sūtra* translating them by words that in a strong way evoke Christian notions, giving in this way a Christian flavour to the *Sūtra*.

It is well known that when the Jesuits came to Japan they translated into Japanese several of their religious books. They used Buddhist Japanese words for Spanish words expressing more or less similar Christian notions. The Christian religion was thus presented under a Buddhist appearance. Perhaps this was done with the deliberate purpose of facilitating the conversion of people from Buddhism to Christian creed, since the distance between both was made to appear as insignificant. A ludicrous and unexpected result of this method of translation was that in an old Japanese encyclopaedia it was stated that Christianity was only a Buddhist sect.

A similar misunderstanding happened with the well known book entitled "The Story of Barlaam and Josaphat". This book tells the story of two Christian saints: Barlaam and Josaphat. This book was very popular in Christian countries in its Greek and Latin recensions. Its popularity and spread in the West as well as in the East is shown by its translations into Syriac, Arabic, Hebrew, Persian, Armenian, Georgian, German, Italian, Slavonic, Servian, Czech, French, Spanish, Portuguese, Swedish, Danish, Icelandic, English, Irish, etc.

"Both Barlaam and Josaphat have a formal place on the roll of Christian saints, and special days in the calendar are set apart to their memory. In the Menology of the Greek Church, August 26 is the commemoration of St. Josaphat; and, in the sister Church of Rome, November 27 is dedicated to the joint service of the two saints".[1] But what is strikingly remarkable is that it has been established in an indubitable way [2] that the story of Barlaam and Josaphat is nothing else than the story of the Buddha's life as it is

---

[1] Geden *ERE* VII, p. 568 b.

[2] Wallis Budge 1923, pp. XXXIX-LVII.

told in the *Lalitavistara* for instance; and 'Josaphat' is a corrupted form of '*Bodhisattva* ' and 'Barlaam', of '*Bhagavant* '.[3]

So we must take utmost care to avoid that some Spanish-speaking reader, on reading our translation, may think he is perusing an exposition of Christian teachings made in India.[4]

This danger threatens any Western translator. Kern (p. 55) for instance in II, 119 and 120 translates the words '*sādhum*' and '*sādhu*' used by the Buddhas to signify their approval of the Buddha's decision to teach the *Dharma*, by '*Amen*'. '*Amen* ' is a Hebrew word, which means '*Be it so*'. It is much used in Catholic liturgy and is learnt by every Christian child since the first years of life. The same Kern (pp. 57, 207, 209) translates '*tāyin*' by '*saint*', a word connected with Catholicism as tightly as '*bodhisattva*' or '*arhant*' with Buddhism or '*sadhu*' with Hinduism. Kern also translates (for instance pp. 5, 20, 21) '*asura*' by '*demon*', a word that conveys a very peculiar religious significance for Western readers.

Another example is: the words '*loi*' and '*law*' employed by Burnouf and Kern respectively to translate the Sanskrit '*dharma*'. '*Saddharmapuṇḍarīka*' is translated by the first author as "Le Lotus de la Bonne Loi" and by the latter as "The Lotus of the true Law" and, of course, in many places of their translations we find the words 'loi' and 'law' in singular or plural, rendering the word '*dharma*'. For instance in II, 13:

ekībhavitvāna vicinteyur mamāgrādharmāna pradeśamātram /
kalpāna koṭīnayutān anantān na tasya bhūtaṃ parijāni artham /

Burnouf (p. 21) has for *pāda c*:

"...de mes lois suprêmes..."

and Kern (p. 33) has for *pāda c* :

"...of my superior laws..."

[3] On the change from *Bodhisattva* to *Iōásaf* and of *Bhagavant* to *Barláam*, see Wallis Budge 1923, pp. LXXXVIII-XC.

[4] An example of a Christianized translation of a Buddhist text is the translation by Timothy Richard of the *Śraddhotpāda*.

Now it happens that the terms '*lois*' and '*law*' have in Western countries, since many centuries ago, a very strong relation with Christian religion. This relation is very easily called to mind especially when these words are employed in religious context. '*Law*' according to *The Oxford English Dictionary*, among its various meanings, has the following ones: "*The body of commandments which express the will of God with regard to the conduct of His intelligent creatures*", and which has been "*communicated by express revelation, especially in the Bible*". It also means a '*dispensation*', *i.e.*, '*religious order or system*' and as such the expressions '*The old law*' and '*The new law*' designate respectively the Old Testament (or first part of the Bible) and the Gospel.[5]

So it is possible that for many readers the words 'loi' or 'law' carry with themselves implicit connotations alien to the text.

This possibility is very dangerous when the words 'loi' and 'law' are used in sentences like those already quoted that are put in the Buddha's mouth: 'mes lois suprêmes', 'my superior laws'. The Christian God is a legislator; he, thanks to his power, creates the laws that govern the physical reality, the logical processes, and the moral life. Owing to the biblical resonances, that the words 'loi' and 'law' have in themselves and which they transmit to the sentences in which they appear, it is not impossible that many readers unwittingly attribute to the Buddha the same function of a law-giver, ignoring that the Buddha already in the most ancient texts had declared that these laws, which rule reality, exist independently of the appearance and existence in the world of *Tathāgatas*, who thanks to their intellectual power and effort, discover and reveal them to the others.

Another conflictful word is '*bodhi*', which has so important place in Buddhism. It is translated by Kern usually by '*enlightenment*', to which corresponds the Spanish word '*iluminación*'. Both words belong to the terminology of Christian mystics. They mean the act of receiving spiritual light from God and generally this light is represented as coming from the heights, from the sky, where heaven

[5] *The Oxford English Dictionary* sub '*law*', p. 114, Par. 9 and p. 115, Par. 11.

and Christian God were traditionally located. We think this image does not correspond to the original notion indicated by *bodhi.* This word derives from the root *BUDH-*, whose primary meaning is '*erwachen*', '*wachen*', '*to awake*', '*to wake*'. So '*enlightenment*' or '*iluminación*' are not even a correct translation of the word '*bodhi*'. But, apart from its etymological derivation and its correct meaning, the word *bodhi* refers to a fundamental conception, when it is metaphorically employed in Buddhist context. *Bodhi* is a trascendental state of being produced not by any external factor, alien to oneself, but by an internal transformation of oneself as a result of the intellectual and moral Buddhist discipline to which one has submitted oneself. If we want to employ the metaphor of light, we could say that in Christian *enlightenment* light comes from outside, in *bodhi* from inside.

Happily the word 'enlightenment' (or 'iluminación') belongs to Christian mysticism. And, although the diverse mysticisms are related to diverse systems of thought, many times opposed among themselves, the experience that constitutes their aim, the practices they adopt to reach that aim, and the terminology they employ to describe that experience and those practices have much in common. And so '*enlightenment*', '*iluminación*', and '*bodhi*' have also something that they partake: they refer to a super-natural state in which one comes into contact with, touches, knows, realizes, the Absolute.

So, taking into account the previous fact, we have decided to translate '*bodhi*' by '*iluminación*', but informing the reader in a note that in the case of Christian enlightenment the 'light' has an external origin, and in the case of Buddhist enlightenment it has an internal source.

(d) There is also the danger of a Westernized translation of some words. For instance Kern usually translates '*rākṣasa*' by '*Titans*' (with initial capital letter). The Titans were a race of Gods expelled from the Olympus by Zeus, the supreme God. It is a term belonging to ancient Greek religion. '*Asantagrāha*' in III, 103, is rendered by 'chimera', which originally designated a monster created by Greek mythology. And Kern translates '*kalpa*' by 'eon', which is also a

Greek word equivalent to a long period of time. And he translates '*yakṣas*' by '*goblins*'. The goblins were mischievous and ugly demons who herassed people in European Middle Ages.

(e) The next remark concerns the numerous words that cannot be translated from one language to another. Each culture creates peculiar things and notions, for which it also creates new words and for which there is no correspondent in other languages.

For instance in II, 90, 91, 92, we have the enumeration of a series of Indian musical instruments: *bherī, śāṅkā, paṭaha, sughoṣaka, dundubhi, vīṇā, tāla, paṇava, mṛdaṅga, vaṃśa, jhallarī, jalamaṇḍaka, maṇḍaka.* Regarding these terms, we have left in our translation the Sanskrit words, when we do not know the form or the nature of the instrument; and, in case we know, we translate the Sanskrit word by a Spanish word that designates a more or less similar instrument. The misrepresentation that this way of behaving can produce in the reader is not grave at all.

Regarding other words of more intellectual or abstract nature, it is not convenient at all to translate them, and it is much better to maintain the original Sanskrit words, although we know their meaning. We refer to terms like *bodhisattva, arhant, buddha, nirvāṇa, tathāgata* etc. We remember that when we were translating the *Yogasūtras* of Patañjali, first into Spanish, and then into English, we found that it was impossible to translate, for instance, the word '*samāpatti*', because there is not in Spanish or English a word that can express the rich and complex psychological process to which the word *samāpatti* refers. The same happens with the words we have just mentioned like *bodhisattva* etc.: there are not Spanish (or English) words able to express the rich and complex notion to which these words refer. So, following the example of Chinese and Japanese translators, who have preserved the Sanskrit word *bodhisattva* under the forms of '*pu ti sa to*' or '*pu sa*' and *bosatsu*, we have preferred to maintain *bodhisattva* in its original Sanskrit form in our translation. The reader will have to learn from the Introductions of from the notes, which are the rich and complex notions that these words convey and to integrate these notions to his knowledge, enriching it thereby.

(f) Another norm we fixed for our translation has to do with the words that have in Sanskrit several meanings as for instance *dharma* and *adhimukti*. In first place let us examine the word '*dharma*'. This word, most important in Buddhism, has numerous values, as for instance: 1. *law*, 2. *teaching*, *doctrine*, specially *Buddhism*, 3. *nature*, *characteristic*, *attribute*, and 4. *factor* or *element of existence*.[6]

If somebody is explaining or commenting in a class or a seminar the *Saddharmapuṇḍarīka*, whenever the word '*dharma*' appears, very probably he will indicate which of these numerous meanings is the most apropriate in each case, in order to transmit to his hearers the true significance of the passage of the text he is dealing with. The translator must behave in a similar way. If he has not at his disposal in his own language a word that possesses all the meaning of the word '*dharma*', he must translate it, whenever it appears, by that word that in the translator's language has that special meaning with which the word '*dharma*' in this case is used, in order to provide the reader with a correct understanding of the text.

But it can happen that in the translator's language there is a word that has *all* the meanings of the word '*dharma*'. For instance Japanese, Chinese and Tibetan translators have at their disposal words that traditionally are used to translate '*dharma*': the Japanese '*Hō*', the Chinese '*Fa*', and the Tibetan '*Chos*'. These words have all the meanings of the word '*dharma*', although their principal meaning is respectively '*law*' for the two first and '*religious doctrine*', '*the doctrine of Buddha*' for the third one. In this case, when the translators do not indicate in some way which is he meaning to be given to '*Hō*' or '*Fa*' or '*Chos*' each time these words appear, they are leaving to the reader (who may have not the special training for that purpose) the task of making each time the election, and very probably the reader will understand '*Hō*', '*Fa*', and '*Chos*' the most of the cases with their first and principal (but not unique) meaning, not grasping the true import of the text.

---

[6] Geiger 1973; Burnouf 1876, pp. 36-37, 1927, pp. 840-841; Kern 1901, I, p. 293; Tola and Dragonetti 1977.

Hurvitz, who translates the *Lotus Sūtra* from the Chinese, has replaced the '*Fa*' character of Kumārajīva by the Sanskrit word '*dharma*' explaining in his Glossary that "*Of the many possible meanings of this word in Buddhist Sanskrit, two seem to stand out in the Lotus: (1) A constituent of existence, even a 'thing'; (2) A truth, a true idea, or even the Buddha's Truth in its totality; a doctrine. In the sense of the Buddha's Truth or Doctrine, the word is always capitalized*" in his translation.

Burnouf and Kern have translated '*dharma*' by '*loi*' and '*law*' respectively. Of the numerous meanings that the word '*dharma*' has according to them, they have chosen one, giving in this way a great uniformity to their translation, but discarding also the true idea of many passages of the original text, as for instance in II, 68 and III, 12, to which we have already referred.

As for our translation, we have translated '*dharma*' in each case with the Spanish word most apropriate to the context.

In relation to '*adhimukti*', several meanings are attributed to this word: 1. 'understanding, assuring or convincing oneself through penetration, comprehending expectantly'[7]; 'intelligence, pénétration'[8]; 2. 'trust, confidence'[9]; 3. 'faith'[10]; 4. 'open-mindedness'[11]; 5. 'the being inclined to, inclination'.[12]

It is not possible to think that the word '*adhimukti*' designates *one* complex mental state constituted by several elements, that as such it corresponds to *one* rich notion, and that consequently it should be translated by a single word (if it were possible to find a word adequate to that state and notion). In Chapter III, p. 73, line 15 Kern's edition, it is said that the father who tries to save his children from the burning house knows their inclinations (*āśaya*)

[7] Kurumiya 1982.

[8] Burnouf 1925, pp. 337-339.

[9] Mochizuki K. and Tsukamoto K., quoted by Kurumiya 1982, p. 337.

[10] Fujita K., quoted by Kurumiya; also in Tibetan: Sarat Chandra Das, *A Tibetan-English Dictionary*. Jäschke: *mos pa*.

[11] Kubo 1987, pp. 45-50, and English Summary, pp. 7-8.

[12] Burnouf (see note 8) and Sarat Chandra Das: *mos pa*.

and their '*adhimukti*': *kumārakāṇām āśayajño bhaved adhimuktiṃ ca vijānīyāt.* Here we cannot attribute to the children any complex mental state and according to the context the sentence means simply that the father knows the childish inclinations and likings of his sons. So it is better to consider that the word '*adhimukti*' refers to several psychological states of mind related among themselves and, as in the case of '*dharma*', we must translate '*adhimukti*' each time it appears by the word most appropriate for the context.

Among the various meanings of the word '*adhimukti*' the one that we consider the most interesting is precisely that of 'open-mindedness'.

When we began our study of Buddhism, one of the values exalted by the Buddhist texts that seemed to us of prevalent interest was that of 'alertness and vigilance' (*appamāda, sati, sampajañña*) in regard to one's own emotional reactions and to the outward world, which surrounds us and constantly invades our subjectivity and intimacy modifying the flow of our lives and our personal attitudes and states of mind. Thanks to this value, awareness increases, one becomes more master of his own acts and less a toy of the external world and of the internal unconscious reactions. This value of 'alertness and vigilance' is not taken into consideration by Western traditional ethics and is almost unknown to it.

'Open-mindedness' is another value not taken into account by Western traditional ethics. We consider '*adhimukti*', '*open-mindedness*', '*receptivity*' as a most important attitude in relation to religious life, as it predisposes man to receive a new message, to change his erroneous convictions, to increase his aspirations. But it is also a value that concerns human personality as a whole. It must be considered as the basis of a true humanism, which intends to develop all the possibilities of man, to broaden his personality, to unfold all his latent faculties. And this is possible only when man opens himself to new fruitful ideas, to new sound emotions, to new noble experiences, which on one side enrich him with new intellectual, aesthetic, spiritual acquisitions and, on the other side, awake in him his dormant possibilities.

(g) The last remark concerns some words in regard to which there is not complete agreement between tradition and philology. One of these words is '*tāyin*'. It can be said that most scholars consider that '*tāyin*' corresponds to Pāli '*tādin*', Sanskrit '*tādṛś*'[13], and that consequently it means '*such*', '*ein solcher*', '*tal*' in Spanish. This interpretation from the scholarly, philological point of view must be accepted.

But there is a different interpretation that we can call 'the traditional interpretation'. The word '*tāyin*' has been understood also with the meaning of '*protector*'. In the *Dhātupāṭha*[14] (appendix to Pāṇini's grammar) 1518 the root '*TĀYṚ*' appears with the menaing of '*to protect*' (*tāyṛ saṃtānapālanayoḥ*), in *Mahāvyutpatti* (first quarter of 9th century)[15]: *trāyī* (*tāyī*) No. 15 and *tāyī* (*-in*) No. 1746, are translated in Tibetan by '*skyob pa*', which means '*to protect*' and by '*skyo ba*', which means '*to guard*', '*to defend*', '*to preserve*', and in Chinese by several Chinese characters, which mean '*to save*', '*to deliver*', '*to protect*'; Surendrabodhi and Sna-nam Ye-śes sde (end 8th - beginning 9th centuries)[16] in their version into Tibetan of the *Saddharmapuṇḍarīka* translate '*tāyin*' by '*skyob pa*', '*skyob mdsad*', '*skyoṅ ba*', which mean '*to protect*';[17] Sarvajñadeva and Dpal-brtsegs (end 8th - beginning 9th centuries)[18] in their translation into Tibetan of the *Bodhicaryāvatāra* (III, 2; V, 9) render in the same way the word '*tāyin*'; some Jain commentators of canonical works[19] understand '*tāyin*' with the meaning of '*to protect*'; and finally Kumārajīva (350-410 A.D.) in his Chinese translation of *Saddharmapuṇḍarīka*, in 7. 47 interprets '*tāyin*' as '*protector*' or '*saviour of the world*'.

---

[13] Yuyama 1965-1966.

[14] On the *Dhātupāṭha*, Scharfe 1977, pp. 101-102.

[15] Vogel 1979, pp. 381, considers the *Dhātupāṭha* as authentic and 'as a whole' old, but admits that many single roots may have been introduced in it in a late epoch.

[16] Naudou 1968, pp. 88-89.

[17] Ejima 1988 *sub* '*tāyin*'.

[18] Naudou 1968, p. 86.

[19] Bapat 1940, pp. 256-257.

Shall we, on translating '*tāyin*', follow the philological interpretation (*tāyin*: *such*) or the traditional one (*tāyin*: *protector*)?

'*Tāyin*', '*tādin*', '*tādṛś*', '*such*', '*ein solcher*', '*tal*' are in themselves neutral words, void words;[20] they do not indicate anything by themselves. A meaning is assigned to them, when one specifies to whom or to what is similar the person or the thing they designate. So very early was felt the need to give a content to that word. In Pāli[21] the word '*tādin*', from '*such*', '*such like*' came to mean '*of such (good) qualities*', '*as the Buddha*', '*as a religious man ought to be*', '*holy*', '*following the path of true religion*'. And even Edgerton who interprets '*tāyin*' as '*tādṛś*' provides it with a concrete meaning: '*holy*'.[22] And many translators have given to '*tāyin*' a mening elected by themselves, preferentially '*sage*', '*mighty*', '*holy*'.[23]

Now, if a concrete meaning is to be arbitrarily assigned to this empty word, why not to give it the meaning of '*protector*', which has in its favour Indian, Tibetan and Chinese sponsors? For the moment we have decided to follow the traditional interpretation, but informing the reader in a note about the existence of the philological one.[24]

These are the modest remarks that the translation into Spanish of the *Lotus Sūtra* has provoked in us. We feel this translation as a rewarding task: we are dealing with a text, which is rich in literary beauties and in deep ideas and feelings, and which presents to us interesting and manifold thought provoking problems.

---

[20] Other words of the same nature are many times: '*tathā*' (as in *tathāgata*) '*evaṃrūpa*', '*īdṛś*', '*idṛśa*'.

[21] *PTS Dictionary*, Childers 1976 (reprint), *sub voce*.

[22] *Dictionary sub voce.*

[23] In English '*such*' "*acquires an emphatic force: so great, so eminent and the like*", and can also be used "*as an absolute intensive, the implied clause of comparison being indeterminate and quite lost sight of*". (Cf. *The Oxford English Dictionary sub voce*, p. 86, Par. 14). A similar thing happens in Spanish.

[24] The word '*tāyin*' of *Bodhicaryāvatāra* III, 2 and V, 9 has been translated by several authors by '*protector*' or '*saviour*' as for instance L. de la Vallée Poussin, Finot (only V, 9), Schmidt (only III, 2), Steinkellner, Matics (only V, 9). They have filled the 'empty' '*tāyin*' with one of the traditional 'contents' ascribed to it.

REFERENCES

Bailey, H.W., "Buddhist Sanskrit", in *Journal of the Royal Asiatic Society of Great Britain and Ireland*, 1955, pp. 13-36.

Bechert, H., *Die Sprache der ältesten buddhistischen Überlieferung. The Language of the Earliest Buddhist Tradition* (Symposien zur Buddhismusforschung, II), Göttingen, Vandenhoeck & Ruprecht, 1980.

Berger, H., *Review* of H. Lüders, *Beobachtungen über die Sprache des buddhistischen Urkanons* in *Göttingische Gelehrte Anzeigen*, 210. Jahrgang, Nr. 1/2, 1956, pp. 96-111.

Bloch, J., *Indo-Aryan from the Vedas to Modern Times*, Paris, A. Maisonneuve, 1965.

Brough, J., "The Language of the Buddhist Sanskrit Texts", in *Bulletin of the School of Oriental and African Studies*, University of London, XVI, 1954, pp. 351-375.

Bühler, G., "New Manuscripts from Kashgar", in *Wiener Zeitschrift für die Kunde des Morgenlandes*, VII, 1893, pp. 260-273.

Budge, Sir E.A. Wallis, *Baralâm and Yewâsef: being the Ethiopic version of a Christianized Recension of the Buddhist Legend of the Buddha and the Bodhisattva*, an English Translation and Introduction, etc., Cambridge: at the University Press, 1923.

Burnouf, E., *Le Lotus de la Bonne Foi*, Paris, Librairie Orientale et Américaine, Maisonneuve F., 1925.

—, *Introduction à l'Histoire du Bouddhisme Indien*, Paris, Maisonneuve, 1876.

Childers, R.C., *A Dictionary of the Pali Language*, Kyoto, Rinsen Book Company, 1976.

—, R.C., *A Dictionary of the Pali Language*, Kyoto, Rinsen Book Company, 1976.

Damsteegt, Th., *Epigraphical Hybrid Sanskrit*, Leiden, E.J. Brill, 1978.

Das, Sarat Chandra, *A Tibetan-English Dictionary*, Calcutta, the Bengal Secretariat Book Depôt, 1902.

De la Vallée Poussin, L., *Bodhicaryāvatāra, Introduction à la Pratique des futurs Bouddhas*, Paris, Bloud et Cie., 1907.

Dictionnaire Tibétain-Latin-Français par les Missionaires Catholiques du Tibet, Hong Kong, Imprimerie de la Société des Missions Etrangères, 1899.

Edgerton, F., "The Meter of the Saddharmapuṇḍarīka", in *Studies in Indology: Mahāmahopādhyāya Kūppuswāmī Sastri Commemoration Volume*, Madras, G.S. Press, 1935, pp. 39-45.

—, "The Prakrit underlying Buddhist Hybrid Sanskrit", in *Bulletin of the School of Oriental Studies*, VIII, 2/3, 1936, pp. 501-516.

—, "Meter, Phonology, and Orthography in Buddhist Hybrid Sanskrit", in *Journal of the American Oriental Society*, 66, 1946, pp. 197-206.

—, *Buddhist Hybrid Sanskrit I Grammar, II Dictionary*, New Haven, Yale University, 1953.

—, "The Nature of Buddhist Hybrid Sanskrit", in *Journal of the Ganganatha Jha Research Institute*, XI-XII, 1953-54, pp. 1-10.

—, *Buddhist Hybrid Sanskrit. Language and Literature*, Banaras, Banaras Hindu University, 1954.

—, "Semantic Notes on Buddhist Hybrid Sanskrit", in *Festschrift Albert Debrunner*, Bern, A. Franke Verlag, 1954, pp. 129-134.

—, "The Buddha and Language", in *The Indian Historical Quarterly*, XXXII, 1, 1956, pp. 129-135.

—, "On editing Buddhist Hybrid Sanskrit", in *Journal of the American Oriental Society*, 77, 1957, pp. 184-192.

Ejima, Y., *Index to the Saddharmapundarīkasūtra*, Tokyo, The Reiyukai, 1985.

Filliozat, J., *Review* of F. Edgerton, *Buddhist Hybrid Sanskrit*, in *T'oung Pao*, XLIII, 1955, pp. 147-171.

Finot, L., *La Marche à la Lumière*, Paris, Editions Bossard, 1920.

Geden, A.S., "Josaphat, Barlaam and", in Hastings, *Encyclopaedia of Religion and Ethics*, Edinburg, T. and T. Clark, 1964.

Geiger, W. and M., *Pāli Dhamma*, in *Kleine Schriften*, Wiesbaden, F. Steiner, 1973, pp. 101-228.

Hoernle, A.F.R., *The Bower Manuscript*, Calcutta, Superintendent Government Printing, India, 1893-1912 (Reprint: New Delhi, International Academy of Indian Culture, 1983).

Kaye, G.R., *The Bakhshālī Manuscript*, Calcutta, Government of India, Archaeological Survey of India, New Imperial Series, 1927.

Kern, H., *Histoire du Bouddhisme dans l'Inde*, Paris, E. Leroux, 1901.

Kubo, Tsugunari, *Hokekyō Bosatsu Shisō no Kiso* (The Fundamental Philosophy of the Lotus Sūtra with respect to the Practices of the Bodhisattva), Tokyo, Shunjū-shu, 1987 (with a resumé in English, pp. 1-45).

Kurumiya, Yenshu, "Adhimukti in the Saddharma puṇḍarīkasūtra", in *Indological and Buddhist Studies in Honour of Professor J. W. de Jong*, edited by L.A. Hercus and others, Canberra, Faculty of Asian Studies, 1982, pp. 337-351.

Lüders, H., *Beobachtungen über die Sprache des buddhistischen Urkanons*, Berlin, Akademie Verlag, 1954.

Lamotte, É., *Histoire du Bouddhisme Indien*, Louvain, Université de Louvain, 1958.

Lin Li-Kouang, *Introduction au Compendium de la Loi, (Dharma-samuccaya), L'Aide-Mémoire de la Vraie Loi*, Paris, Maisonneuve, 1949.

Mansion, J., *Esquisse d'une Histoire de la Langue Sanscrite*, Paris, P. Geuthner, 1931.

Mahāvyutpatti, Tokyo, Suzuki Research Foundation, 1962.

Matics, M.L., *Entering the Path of Enlightenment*, London, Allen & Unwin, 1970.

Matsunami, S., Nagao, G., and Tanji, A., Japanese translation of the *Saddharmapuṇḍarīkasūtra*, Tokyo, Daij Butten, 1988.

Newman, J., "Buddhist Hybrid in the Kālacakra Tantra", in *The Journal of the International Association of Buddhist Studies*, 11, 1, 1988, pp. 123-140.

Naudou, J., *Les Bouddhistes Kaśmīriens au Moyen Age*, Paris, P.U.F., 1958.

Nobel, J., *Suvarṇaprabhāsottamasūtra*, Leiden, E.J. Brill, 1950.

Rhys Davids, T.W. and Stede, W., *The Pali Text Society's Pali-English Dictionary*, London, The Pali Text Society, 1921.

Raghavan, V., "Buddhist Hybrid Sanskrit", in *Suniti Kumar Chatterji Jubilee Volume*. *Indian Linguistics*, XVI, Nov. 1955, Madras, Linguistic Society of India, 1955, pp. 313-322.

Regamey, C., "Lexicological Gleanings from the Kāraṇḍavyūhasūtra", in *Suniti Kumar Chatterji Jubilee Volume*, *Indian Linguistics*, XVI, 1955, pp. 1-10.

Renou, L., *Review* of F. Edgerton, *Buddhist Hybrid Sanskrit*, in *Journal Asiatique*, CCXLI, 1953, pp. 283-287.

—, *Histoire de la Langue Sanskrite*, Lyon, IAC, 1956.

—, "Introduction générale" of J. Wackernagel, *Altindische Grammatik*, Göttingen, Vandenhoeck and Ruprecht, 1957.

Rhys Davids, T.W. and W. Stede, *The Pali Text Society's Pali-English Dictionary*, London, The Pali Text Society, 1921.

Roth, G., "Particular Features of the Language of the Ārya-Mahāsāṃghika-Lokottaravādins and their Importance for Early Budhist Tradition", in Bechert 1980.

Richard, T., *The Awakening of the Faith* (Shangai, 1907), London, Charles Skilton Ltd., 1961.

Sen, S., *An outline Syntax of Buddhistic Sanskrit*, Calcutta, Calcutta University Press, 1928.

Smith, H., "Le futur moyen indien et ses rythmes", in *Journal Asiatique*, CCXL, 1952, pp. 169-183.

Sakamoto, Y. and Y. Iwamoto, Japanese translation of the *Saddharmapuṇḍarīkasūtra*, Tokyo, Iwanami Bunko, 1988.

Śāntideva, *Bodhicaryāvatāra*, ed. L. de la Vallée Poussin, Calcutta, Bibliotheca Indica, 1901-14 (Sanskrit text-imcomplete); and in *Tibetan Tripiṭaka*, Tokyo, Sekai Seiten Kanko Kyokai, 1978 (Tibetan translation - *Tōhoku* 3831).

Scharfe, H., *Grammatical Literature*, Wiesbaden, O. Harrassowitz, 1977.

Schmidt, R., *Der Eintritt in den Wandel in Erleuchtung*, Padeborn, F. Schöningh, 1923.

Senart, É., *Le Mahāvastu*, Tokyo, Meicho-Fukyū-kai, 1977 (Reprint).

Steinkellner, E., *Śāntideva, Eintritt in das Leben zur Erleuchtung*, Düsseldorf-Köln, E. Diedrichs Verlag, 1981.

The Oxford English Dictionary, Oxford, Clarendon Press, 1970.

Tola, F. and C. Dragonetti, "La teoría de los *dharmas* en el Budismo", in *Boletín de la Asociación Española de Orientalistas*, XIII, 1977, pp. 105-132.

von Hinüber, O., "Pāli as an artificial language", in *Indologica Taurinensia*, X, 1982, pp. 133-140.

—, "Die Bedeutung des Handschriftenfundes bei Gilgit", in *Zeitschrift der Deutschen Morgenländischen Gesellschaft, Supplement V, XXI. Deutscher Orientalistentag*, 1983, pp. 47-66.

von Hinüber, O., *Das ältere Mittelindisch im Überblick*, Wien, Verlag der österreichischen Akademie der Wissenschaften, 1986.

Vogel, C., *Indian Lexicography*, Wiesbaden, O. Harrassowitz, 1979.

Yuyama, A., "Supplementary Remarks", in *Indo-Iranian Journal*, Volume IX, 1965-66, pp. 85-112.

Yuyama, A., *A Bibliography of the Sanskrit Texts of the Saddharmapuṇḍarīkasūtra*, Canberra, Australian National University Press, 1970.

—, "Some Glossarial Notes on the Prajñā-pāramitā-ratna-guṇa-saṃcaya-gāthā", in *Proceedings and Papers of the XIV*th *Congress of the Australasian Universities Language and Literature Association*, 1972, edited by K.I.D. Maslen, Dunedin, 1972, pp. 30-37.

—, "Remarks on the Metre of the Prajñā-pāramitā-ratna-guṇa-saṃcaya-gāthā", in *Studies in Indo Asian Art and Culture, Commemoration Volume of the 70*th *Birthday of Acharya Raghu Vira*, New Delhi, International Academy of Indian Culture, 1973, Volume 2, pp. 243-253.

—, *A Grammar of the Prajñā-pāramitā-ratna-guṇa-saṃcaya-gāthā*, Canberra, Australian National University Press, 1973.

—, *Prajñā-pāramitā-ratna-guṇa-saṃcaya-gāthā*, Cambridge, Cambridge University Press, 1976.]

—, *A Bibliography of the Sanskrit Texts of the Saddharmapuṇḍarīkasūtra*, Canberra, Australian National University Press, 1970.

VI

Ekaṃ Samayam

Much has been written on the usual opening formula of the Pāli *suttas* or Sanskrit *sūtras*: *evaṃ me sutam ekaṃ samayaṃ bhagavā* (place name) *viharati / evaṃ mayā śrutam ekasmin samaye bhagavān* (place name) *viharati sma.* Is the temporal expression *ekaṃ samayam* ('once, at one time, on a certain occasion') to be connected to the preceding or the following words? Both possibilities have their adherents and it seems that until now no agreement has been reached at.

The uncertainty about this matter is well shown in the article on the *Nagaropamasūtra* by Gregory Bongard-Levin, Daniel Boucher, Takamichi Fukita and Klaus Wille. In this article, in the translation done by Boucher with suggestions of Fukita and Wille, the *apo koinou* or 'double-jointed' construction has been adopted [1] following P. Harrison's suggestion as expressed in *The Samādhi of Direct Encounter with the Buddhas of the Present*, p. 5, note 3.[2] Consequently no punctuation has been placed in the problematic sentence. T. Vetter, "*Compounds in the Prologue of the Pañcaviṃśatisāhasrikā*", p. 65 note 48, also follows Harrison's solution.[3] But it seems that the *apo koinou* construction complicates the problem since instead of two possibilities, there are three now. Moreover, it is to be noticed that Kamalaśīla in his commentary of the *Vajracchedikā* (*Tōhoku* 3817, Peking 5217) refers to the possibility of several

---

[1] In: *Sanskrit-Texte aus dem buddhistischen Kanon: Neuentdeckungen und Neueditionen* III, Bearbeitet von Gregory Bongard-Levin, Daniel Boucher, Fumio Enomoto, Takamichi Fukita, Hisushi Matsumura, Claus Vogel, Klaus Wille, Göttingen, Vandenhoeck and Ruprecht, 1996.

[2] P. Harrison, *The Samādhi of Direct Encounter with the Buddhas of the Present*, Tokyo, The International Institute for Buddhist Studies, 1990.

[3] In: *Wiener Zeitschrift für die Kunde Südasiens*, Band XXXVII, 1993, pp. 45-92.

interpretations of the opening formula, but does not favour the *apo koinou* construction.

After the *Nagaropamasūtra*'s edition, Mark Allon, in *Style and Function*, pp. 195, 246-247, and 287, points out the metrical and sound similarities of *evaṃ me sutam* and *ekaṃ samayam*, and punctuates after *sutam*, accepting the three-word preamble.[4]

We want to make a suggestion strengthening the point of view of Galloway, "Thus Have I Heard at one Time ..." (*Indo-Iranian Journal*, 34, 1991, pp. 87-104)[5], and of Allon regarding this problem. Why not to apply to it what can be called the "criterion of usefulness": Which connection gives a better function to the expression *ekaṃ samayam*? Which construction renders it more useful? With which construction is the whole meaning of the opening formula better served? This "criterion of usefulness" guides the interpretation and translation of texts. When a word with different meanings is used by an author, the interpreter or translator must choose the word that gives a better meaning to the context, cf. K. Kunjunni Raja, *Indian Theories of Meaning*, pp. 52-53, on *artha* and *prakaraṇa* as criteria given by Bhartṛhari for determining the correct meaning of a word in case of ambiguous and equivocal expressions.[6] The same procedure must be applied when a series of words offers the problem of how they are to be divided. Let us examine the two possible alternatives with this in view:

1. *evaṃ me sutam ekaṃ samayam / evaṃ mayā śrutam ekaṃ samayam*: "Thus have I heard once or at one time or on a certain occasion". What does the temporal expression add to *evaṃ me sutam / evaṃ mayā śrutam*? Nothing that is important, because even if that expression were not there, anyone would understand

---

[4] Mark Allon, *Style and Function, A study of the dominant stylistic features of the prose portions of Pāli canonical sutta texts and their mnemonic function*, Tokyo, The International Institute for Buddhist Studies, 1997.

[5] In *Indo-Iranian Journal*, 34, 1991, pp. 87-104. See also *ibid*, 40, 1997, pp. 367-371.

[6] Cf. K. Kunjunni Raja, *Indian Theories of Meaning*, Adyar, The Adyar Library and Research Centre, 1963.

that "what has been heard" has been heard once, at one time, on a certain occasion. The situation would be different and the use of the temporal expression would be meaningful, either if what the narrator heard was something particular, something different from what he normally has heard, something that he wanted to mark out (for instance: "*Once* I heard the Lord saying a rude word to one of his monks") or if his having heard it was for him a new experience (for instance: "I had never heard such a thing, but *once* I heard the Lord saying a rude word to one of his monks"). But in the present case the narrator did not hear anything extraordinary; he heard about an episode of Buddha's life and about episodes of Buddha's life he had heard hundreds of times before and he wanted to record them in the books of the Hīnayāna and of the Mahāyāna.

Moreover, the absurdity of the useless *ekaṃ samayam* added to *evaṃ me suttam / evaṃ mayā śrutam* becomes more evident if we take into account that this expression appears for instance 80 times in the *Udāna*: "Thus have I heard at one time...", "thus have I heard at one time", etc., and also many times in the other collections of the *Tipiṭaka / Tripiṭaka*. A useless expression repeated so many times!

Finally we must think that in fact the aim of the expression "Thus have I heard" is not to point out that the narrator has *heard* about the episode, but to serve as a "seal of authenticity".

2. *ekaṃ samayaṃ bhagavā* (place name) *viharati / ekasmin samaye bhagavān* (place name) *viharati sma.*

If we add the temporal expression to the following words it becomes fully meaningful. It is natural that, if we are to hear about an episode of Buddha's life, we would like to know the time and the place where the episode occurred. It is why in the commentary of the *Jātakas* its author informs the reader about the time and place of the tale of the anterior life of Gautama Buddha. There it was easy to indicate the time of the events because the tales belong to a mythic past: *Bārāṇasiyaṃ Brahmadatte rajjaṃ kārayamāne.* It was not so easy to do the same thing with the episodes of the present life of Buddha, because in that epoch there were no certain means to fix the time of events. It was safer to employ an undetermined expression: "Once, at one time, on a certain occasion".

But more important that the reason above is the fact that Buddha was a *wanderer*, that according to the rules of his Discipline he and his monks could not stay long in the same place. They went from one place to another. Thus the *Udāna* tells us that he stayed *once* in *Uruvelā* (I, 1), *once* in *Sāvatthi* (I, 5), *once* in *Rājagaha* (I, 6), *once* in *Pātali* (I, 7), *once* in *Gayā* (I, 9), etc. He complied with the rule of his own Discipline, he constantly wandered from one place to another and *ekaṃ samayam* reflects this fact.

This explanation is reinforced by the expression *tena kho pana samayena*: "at that time", "on that occasion", which many times appears in these texts. According to alternative 1, this expression (which introduces the episode to be narrated) would mean: "*when I heard*", but the episode told by the narrator *did not take place when the narrator* heard *about it*. According to alternative 2, this same expression would mean: "*when the Bhagavant was in such or such place*", and that was what really happened, and the formula is useful to locate the event.

VII

The Meaning of the Infinite Numbers in the *Lotus Sūtra*

In the *Saddharmapuṇḍarīkasūtra* are found several adjectives, nouns under the form of compounds, comparisons and expressions, etc, that denote great numbers and are employed in relation to beings and things of diverse kind.[1] These great numbers are of such a magnitude that in fact they are almost expressive of infinitude. The adjectives expressing great / infinite numbers are very numerous. Among them, we have for instance: *agaṇanīya*, *agaṇiya*, *asaṃkhya*, *asaṃkhyeya*, *aparimita*, *aprameya*, *apramāṇa*, *ananta*, *acintya*. We can indicate as the most representative ones among compounds, comparisons and expressions referring to great / infinite numbers the following ones:

Compound: *bahu ... koṭīnayutaśatasahasra*[2]: "many ... hundreds of thousands of ten millions of one hundred thousand millions of ...

Comparison with the sand of the Gaṅgā river: *aśitigaṅgānadīvālikāsama*: "equal to the sands of eighty Ganges rivers".

Comparison with atoms: *evāprameyā bahukalpakoṭyaḥ parinirvṛtasya sugatasya tasya / paramāṇu sarve na bhavanti lakṣyās tāvad bahu kṣīṇa bhavanti kalpāḥ* (VII, p. 158, v. 5): "And innumerable are the many ten millions of Cosmic Periods

---

[1] Cf. Shiro Yoshioka, *Index to the Saddharmapuṇḍarīkasūtra*, Informations num. 3, July 31, 1989. *Gleanings* 2: *Similes of the Innumerableness/Immeasurableness*, Tokyo, The Society for Studies of the Lotus Sūtra.

[2] The compound *koṭīnayutaśatasahasra* is equivalent to the following number: 10.000.000 (*koṭi*, ten millions) x 100.000.000 (*nayuta*, one hundred millions) x 100 (*śata*, one hundred) x 1.000 (*sahasra*, one thousand), that makes a total amount of number 1 followed by 20 zeros. This gives an idea of the enormity of the numbers one finds in the *Lotus Sūtra* and allows us to consider such great numbers as *infinite* numbers. When this compound is applied to *kalpas*, and is expressed in years, the number enormously increases, since each *kalpa* contains more than one billion years.

passed since that Sugata had entered into Nirvāṇa. The atoms in their totality cannot be counted and thus are the Cosmic Periods elapsed since that happened".

Expression: *kalpāna koṭīnayutā gaṇenta ekaika no cāntu labheya teṣām* (VII, p. 192, v. 77)[3]: "Counting them one by one you would not find the end of the ten millions of one hundred thousand millions of those Cosmic Periods.

We do not think that these great / infinite numbers are only examples of the exaggerations proper to an exuberant literary imagination, and that as such no importance is to be attached to them. On the contrary, we consider that these words, etc. contribute to the *Sūtra* important elements that enhance its richness of thought. All these words, etc., indicative of great / infinite numbers, possess a secondary or implicit meaning besides their numeral notions. Frequently the secondary or implicit meaning has more weight than the numeral notion in itself. In this article we shall deal with three of these secondary meanings:

1) In many cases these words, etc. serve to extol the persons, things, processes, etc. to which they are applied. We can consider them as rethorical or poetical devices of the *hyperbole* kind.

2) Sometimes these words, etc. reflect important Indian and / or Buddhist theories or teachings with which tight relations are established.

3) Other times the use of these words, etc. allows to clearly see some fundamental changes in the Buddhist Teaching or in some of its doctrinaire elements such as *Bodhi* or *Nirvāṇa*.

In this article we shall refer to some examples that illustrate all the mentioned three effects that derive from the words, etc. expressive of great / infinite numbers.

---

[3] Other examples can be easily found in the *Index of the Saddharmapuṇḍarīkasūtra*, mentioned in note 1, edited by Yasunori Ejima and others, Tokyo, The Reiyukai, 1985 ff., under the words *agaṇanīya*, *asaṃkhyeya*, etc., and specially *koṭi* and *nayuta*. Moreover almost in every page of the *Sūtra* it is possible to find references to great / infinite numbers. The *Index* also gives the Tibetan and Chinese equivalents of all the above quoted words.

Hyperbolic or extolling use of the words expressing great /infinite numbers

In the following paragraphs we indicate some examples of the hyperbolic or extolling use of the words, etc. that mean great / infinite numbers. In each case we point out one or two of the secondary or implicit meanings attached to these words, etc. Of course other secondary or implicit meanings could be found and taken into account.

1) Retinues of the Nāga kings, p. 4, lines 10-11, (*sārdhaṃ bahunāgakoṭīśatasahasraparivāraiḥ*: "together with many hundreds of thousands of ten millions of Nāgas"); of the Kinnara kings, p. 4, line 13 (similar expression); of the Garuḍa kings, p. 5 line 4 (similar expression); of the Asura kings, p. 5, line 2 (similar expression); of the Gandharva kings, p. 4, line 15 (similar expression without *ko61*: "ten millions"), present at Rājagṛha Assembly.

2) Beings that attended the Buddha's Assembly in Rājagṛha, p. 15, verse 48 (*ahaṃ vimāśca bahuprāṇakoṭya iha sthitāḥ*: "myself and these many ten millions of beings standing here").

The great / infinite number of these retinues and beings indicates the extraordinary magnitude of the Buddha's Assembly in Rājagṛha, therefore its importance and the great attraction had the Buddha's Teaching in all sorts of beings.

3) Maruts who together with other gods request the Buddha to teach his Doctrine, p. 55, verse 115 (*marudgaṇānāṃ ca sahasrakoṭyaḥ*: "a thousand of ten millions of troops of Maruts").

The great number indicates here the importance of the event and the interest of the gods in the Buddha's Preaching of his Doctrine.

4) Gods, Nāgas, Yakshas, Rākshasas, who aspire to obtain the Illumination, p. 35, verse 31 (*devāśca nāgāśca sayakṣarākṣasāḥ koṭīsahasrā yathā gaṅgavālikāḥ*: "Gods and Nāgas, together with Yakshas and Rākshasas – thousands of ten millions as numerous as the Ganges sands").

The great number indicates here the universality of the Buddha's Message and the great attraction the goal of the *Bodhi* has in all kinds of beings.

5) The Buddha's Disciples, p. 24, verse 68 (*tahi śrāvakāṇāṃ gaṇanā na vidyate te cāpramāṇāḥ sugatasya śrāvakāḥ* : "it is not possible to calculate the number of the Disciples; the Disciples of the *Sugata* are without measure; monks and nuns, p. āṭ, verse ḷṇ: *bhikṣū bahū tatha pi ca bhikṣuṇīyo ... analpakās te yatha gaṅgavālikā*: "Many monks and also nuns ... they were numerous like the sands of the Ganges"); and Bodhisattvas, p. 10, verse 13 (*bodhisattvā yatha gaṅgavālikāḥ* "Bodhisattvas as numerous as the sands of the Ganges"), p. 20, line 12 (*viṃśatibodhisattvakoṭyaḥ* : "Twenty times ten millions of Bodhisattvas"), p. 24, verse 70 (*bahubodhisattvā yatha gaṅgavālikāḥ*: "Bodhisattvas as numerous as the sands of the Ganges"). Cf. p. 4, lines 10-11; p. 4, lines 13; p. 4, line 15; p. 5, line 2; p. 5, line 4, and p. 15, verse 48.

All these followers of the Buddha's Teaching are a sign of the wide spreading of Buddhism in all its levels.

6) Beings saved by the Bodhisattvas, p. 2, line 10 and p. 3, lines 2-3 (*bodhisattvasahasrai. ... bahuprāṇikoṭīnayutaśatasahasḥ rasaṃtārakaiḥ.*: "With thousands of Bodhisattvas ... Saviours of many hundreds of thousands of ten millions of one hundred millions of beings").

The secondary meaning of the great numbers here is the great activity, the great compassion and the great efficiency of the Bodhisattvas.

7) Beings that received the Buddha's Teaching, p. 9, verse 7 (*buddhāṃśca paśyāmi ... praśāsamānān bahusattvakoṭīḥ* : "And I see Buddhas ... instructing many ten millions of beings").

8) Beings brought to their spiritual perfection by the Buddhas, p. 49, verse 73 (*ekasmi yāne paripācayanti acintiyā prāṇisahasrakoṭyaḥ* : "They bring to religious maturity in one single Vehicle unthinkable thousands of ten millions of beings").

These last two instances show the great and efficient activity of the Buddhas and the extraordinary diffusion of Buddhism in space.

9) Buddhas of the future, p. 52, verse 98 (*anāgatā pi bahu-buddhakoṭyo acintiyā yeṣu pramāṇu nāsti*: "many unthinkable ten millions of future Buddhas for whom there is no measure").

10) Tathagatas of the past, p. 49, verse 71 (*ye cāpyabhūvan purimās tathāgatāḥ parinirvṛtā buddhasahasraneke / atītam adhvānam asaṃkhyakalpe teṣāṃ pramāṇaṃ na kadāci vidyate*: "There is no measure at all for those who were the former Tathāgatas, the many thousands of Buddhas completely extinguished, in the numberless Cosmic Periods of the past times").

11) The Buddhas that have been seen and were respectfully served by the eight sons of Candrasūryapradīpa, p. 22, lines 1-2 (*taiś ca tataḥ paścād bahūni buddhakoṭīnayutaśatasahasrāṇi dṛṣṭāni satkṛtāni ca*: "And afterwards many hundreds of thousands of ten millions of one hundred millions of Buddhas were seen and respectfully served by them").

12) The Buddhas under whom the Tathāgatas have followed the Career of the Bodhisattva, p. 29, lines 4-5 (*bahubuddhakoṭīnayuta-śatasahasracīrṇacaritāvino*: "Many hundreds of thousands of ten millions of one hundred millions of the Buddhas under whom they followed the Course of conduct").

13) Beings to whom Buddhahood is predicted, p. 26, verse 82 (*āśvāsayitvā ... prāṇakoṭyo bahavo acintiyāmaḥ ... bhāviṣyatha buddha mamāntareṇa*: "Encouraging ... many inconceivable ten millions of beings ... you will become Buddhas after me"). Cf. p. 27, verse 93; p. 29, lines 4-5.

The last five instances prove that Ýhākyamuni is not the only Buddha, that there has been an unlimited number of them, that the possibility to obtain the condition of Buddha is very great, and that in fact many have attained it or will attain it.

14) *Stūpas* built by believers, p. 14, verso 44 (*stūpāna paśyāmi sahasrakoṭyo analpakā yathariva gaṅgavālikāḥ* : "I see not a few thousands of ten millions of *Stūpas* as the sands of the Ganges").

15) Flags and parasols adorning the *Stūpas*, p. 14, verso 45 (*chatradvajās teṣu sahasrakoṭyaḥ* : "And in them ten millions of thousands of flags and parasols").

16) *Stūpas* in honour of Candrasūryapradīpa's relics, p. 26, verse 84 (*stūpāna koṭīnayutā anantakā*: "Infinite one hundred millions of ten millions of *Stūpas*").

17) Offerings given in honour of the Buddhas, as garments, p. 13, verse 37 (*vastrāṇa koṭīśata te dadanti sahasrakoṭīśatamūlya*: "They give hundreds of ten millions of garments, of a value of hundreds of ten millions of thousands").

The four last instances show through the great numbers the magnificence of the *Stūpas*, the prestige of Candrasūryapradīpa, the great diffusion of Buddhist *Dharma* everywhere in the universe, and the profound faith and devotion of the donors.

18) Time dedicated to meditation by the Bodhisattvas, p. 13, verse 35 (*dhyāyanta varṣāṇa sahasrakoṭyā*: "Meditating during ten millions of thousands of years"). Cf. p. 159, lines 3-7.

The great numbers of years dedicated to meditation points out the importance of the meditative practices and the constancy of the Bodhisattvas in their efforts.

19) Time spent in teaching the Buddhist *Dharma* by Candrasūryapradīpa, p. 25, verse 76 (*prabhāṣate tajjina agradharmān paripūrṇa so antarakalpaṣaṣṭim*: "That Conqueror expounded the foremost *dharmas* during sixty complete Intermediate Cosmic Periods"), and by Varaprabha, p. 26, verse 86 (*aśīti so antarakalpapūrṇāṃ tahi śāsane bhāṣati agradharmān*: "During eighty Intermediate Cosmic Periods he preached the foremost *dharmas* according to this Discipline"). Cf. p. 21, lines 17-18, and line 1-2.

Both texts with the great period of time they assign to the Preaching of the *Dharma* make manifest the constancy and great compassion of the two Tathāgatas.

20) Time necessary for the appearance of a Buddha, p. 25, verse 80 (*sudurlabhā bhonti jinā maharṣayaḥ kalpāna koṭīnayutāna atyayāt*: "Very difficult to meet with are the Conquerors, the Great Rishis, even after one hundred millions of ten thousands millions of Cosmic Periods").

The great numbers serves here to emphasize that getting Buddhahood is not an easy task.

21) Duration of the Career of the Bodhisattva, p. 30, verse 4 (*tasyāṃ cīrṇāya caryāyāṃ kalpakoṭyo acintiyā*: "Having practised the

Career of the Bodhisattva during inconceivable ten millions of Cosmic Periods"). Cf. texts quoted under numbers 11, 12, and 18.

This passage hints at that the Career of the Bodhisattva requires a long space of time to be fulfilled.

22) Duration of the *Dharma* preached by the *Tathāgatas*, as for instance by Padmaprabha, p. 67, lines 7-8 (*padmaprabhasya tathāgatasya parinirvṛtasya dvātriṃśadantarakalpān saddharmaḥ sthāsyati*: "the True Doctrine of the Tathāgata Padmaprabha once extinguished will last thirty two Intermediate Cosmic Periods"); by Rashmiprabhāsa, p. 146, verse 9 (*saddharma viṃśāntarakalpa sthāsyati*: "his True Doctrine will last twenty Intermediate Cosmic Periods"); by Jāmbūnadaprabhāsa, p. 151, lines 11-12 (*viṃśatiṃ cāsyāntarakalpān saddharmaḥ sthāsyati*: "his True Doctrine will last twenty Intermediate Cosmic Periods"); by Tamāla-patracandanagandha, p. 154, line 2 (*catvāriṃśaccāntarakalpān saddharmaḥ sthāsyati*: "his True Doctrine will last forty Intermediate Cosmic Periods").

23) The false doctrine, adverse to the True Doctrine taught by Padmaprabha, Rashmiprabhāsa, Jāmbūnadaprabhāsa, Tamāla-patracandanagandha, has the same duration as the True Doctrine, p. 67, line 8; p. 146, verse 9; p. 151, line 12, and p. 154, lines 2-3 (where we find expressions similar to those recorded in the preceding paragraph).

The great / infinite duration of the preservation of the True *Dharma* shows its resistence, its capacity to survive thanks to its intrinsic value; the great / infinite duration of the false doctrine, opposite to the True *Dharma*, indicates how difficult is the appearance of the Buddhas who are the only ones that can teach the Truth and that can put an end to the erroneous comprehension and distortion of the *Dharma* preached by previous Buddhas.

24) Time during which beings were burnt by suffering before being saved by a Buddha, p. 91, verse 97 (*paridahyamānā bahukalpakoṭyas*: "being burnt during many ten thousand millions of Cosmic Periods").

This text alludes to the great magnitude of human suffering.

25) Examples and arguments, p. 9, verse 8 (*dṛṣṭāntahetūnayutāna koṭibhiḥ* : "by ten thousand millions of one hundred millions of arguments and examples"); p. 12, verse 27 (*dṛṣṭāntahetūnayutair anekaiḥ* : "by many one hundred millions of arguments and examples"); p. 14, verse 41 (*dṛṣṭāntahetūnayutair anekaiḥ* : "by many one hundred millions of arguments and examples").

The great infinite number of the arguments and examples employed by the Buddhas (p. 9) and the Bodhisattvas (p. 12 and p. 14) show their great intellectual and demonstrative strength.

26) Marvels revealed by the ray of light emitted by the Buddha, p. 10, verse 12 (*śṛṇomi paśyāmi ca ... iha sthito īdṛśakāni tatra / anye viśeṣena sahasrakoṭyaḥ* : "I hear and I see ... standing here such marvels there, and others - even more, by ten millions of thousands").

These infinite marvels reveal all the good things that are occurring in the universe due to the Preaching of the True Doctrine and by the extraordinary power of the Buddha.

Implicit references to other Indian / Buddhist theories. Limitless number of worlds

As we have already said the words, comparisons, expressions, etc. that denote great/infinite numbers impliedly establish connections with other well known Indian/Buddhist theories. For instance in Chapter VII of the *Sūtra* reference is made several times to the limitless quantity of worlds. In p. 163, lines 6-7, the number of worlds in each region of space is mentioned in a general way: *daśasu dikṣvekaikasyāṃ diśi pañcāśallokadhātukoṭīnayutaśatasahasrāṇi ṣaḍvikāraṃ prakampitānyabhūvan*: "In the ten regions of the space, in each region, the fifty hundreds of thousands of one hundred millions of ten millions of worlds trembled in six ways", and in the following pages (p. 167, lines 10-11; p. 171, lines 4-5; p. 174, lines 6-8) the same expression is employed to indicate in an individual way the number of worlds in each region of the space. In p. 157, lines 1-2, the infinitude of the worlds is also pointed out: *tat kiṃ manyadhve bhikṣavaḥ śakyaṃ teṣāṃ lokadhātūnām anto vā paryanto vā gaṇanayādhigantum/ta āhuḥ/no hīdaṃ bhagavan no hīdaṃ sugata*: "What do you think, O monks, is it possible to reach by calculation the end or the limit of the systems of worlds? They said: 'Certainly not, O Bhagavan, Certainly not, O Sugata'." Cf. p. 6, line 7; p. 8, line 6; p. 9, verse 4; p. 14, verse 44; p. 15, verse 49; p. 16, verses 53, 55, etc., where references to the infinite number of worlds and therefore to the limitlessness of space are found. It is obvious that the great / infinite numbers of worlds requires a limitless space in which these worlds can be located.

This cosmological conception of the *Saddharmapuṇḍarīka* of a limitless space, where an almost infinite number of worlds is situated, agrees with the general Hindu / Buddhist conception of space as a limitless entity.[4] The connection thus established between the passages of the *Sūtra* that refer to an infinite number of worlds and the general cosmological Indian theory and its implications, gives to these passages a profound background and enriches their contents.

The great / infinite number of kalpas

To the infinite number of worlds and the limitlessness of the space corresponds the infinite number of *kalpas*, Cosmic Periods that have existed in the past. We find in several passages of the *Sūtra* (p. 17, lines 8-9; p. 156, lines 1-2; p. 375, lines 9-10; p. 431, lines 6-7) the following expression referring to the infinitude of space (or expression similar to it): *atīte 'dhvanyasaṃkhyeyaiḥ kalpair asaṃkhyeyatarair vipulair aprameyair acintyair aparimitair apramāṇais tataḥ pareṇa parataraṃ yadāsīt tena kālena tena samayena ...*: "In a past time, innumerable Cosmic Periods ago, more than innumerable, numerous, countless, inconceivable, infinite, unmeasurable, when it was before, much more before than that, in

[4] Cf. W. Kirfel, *Die Kosmographie der Inder*, Darmstadt, Wissenschaftliche Buchgeselschaft, 1967, pp. 180-181. On the Buddhist cosmological conception in general see F. Tola and C. Dragonetti, "La Infinitud en el pensamiento de la India", in *Hitos* 3, Buenos Aires, 1979, pp. 37-39, and "Buddhist Conception of Reality", in *Journal of Indian Council of Philosophical Research*, Volume XIV, Number 1, September-December, 1996, pp. 35-64.

than time, in that occasion ..." In p. 484, lines 4-5, we have another expression of the great / infinite number of past *kalpas: asaṃkhyeyakalpakoṭīnayutaśatasahasrasamudānītamanuttarāṃ saṃyaksaṃbodhim ...*: "The Supreme Perfect Enlightenment attained by me after numberless hundreds of thousands of one hundred millions of ten millions of Cosmic Periods ..." Cf. p. 13, verse 35; p. 17, lines 8-9; p. 25, verses 57 and verse 76; p. 26, verse 86; p. 21, lines 1-2 and 17-18.

It is well known that beginninglessness, *anāditva*, is one of the fundamental principles of Indian thought, expressed in many theories and teachings.[5] The great / infinite number of past *kalpas* requires de existence of a similar great / limitless extent of time in the past. The *anāditva* principle makes possible the existence of the required extent of time during which so many *kalpas* have followed one another.

As in the previous case of the great / infinite number of worlds and the limitlessness of space, we have also in this case a connection between the idea of a great / infinite number of *kalpas* and another important Indian conception, that of the *anāditva*; and this connection gives to all the passages in which the infinite number of cosmic periods are referred to, a new light, a deeper significance.

References to the great / infinite number of past *kalpas* are very numerous in the *Sūtra.* The same does not happen with future *kalpas.* The references to these ones are not numerous, although we find some of this kind, as for instance, in p. 207, verse 22: *anantakalpasmi anāgate 'dhvani dṛṣṭvāna buddhān bahavo hyanantān ...*: "Seeing in the future time during an infinite Cosmic Period many, infinite Buddhas, ..." In p. 52, verse 98, reference is made to a great / infinite number of Buddhas of the future, whose existence seems to require a great / infinite number of *kalpas* where to appear: *anāgatā pi bahubuddhakoṭyo acintiyā yeṣu pramāṇu nāsti.*

[5] Cf. F. Tola and C. Dragonetti, "*Anāditva* or Beginninglessness in Indian Philosophy", in *Annals of the Bhandarkar Oriental Research Institute*, Poona, India, 1980, pp. 1-20.

Fundamental changes in Buddhist Doctrines.
Length of the life of the Tathāgata [6] *after obtaining the Bodhi*

The most interesting use of the great / infinite numbers in the *Sūtra* is the one related to the 'length of life' (*āyuṣpramāṇa*) of the Tathāgatas. In this case the use of the great / infinite numbers points out a most fundamental change in an equally fundamental Buddhist doctrine.

Early and Hīnayāna Buddhism

For Early and Hīnayāna Buddhism the Buddhist who has submitted himself to the intellectual and moral disciplines prescribed by Buddhism will obtain the *Bodhi,* and then, on the moment of his death, will reach *Nirvāṇa* without any remaining substratum. This was considered as the liberation from reincarnations or re-existences, and therefore from birth, old age, sickness, and death, and from the suffering inherent to human nature. This was what happened with Śākyamuni according to the first Buddhist texts. It can be said that in this stage of the history of Buddhism to attain *Nirvāṇa* as soon as possible was considered as the final goal of human effort.

Mahāyāna Buddhism

The position of Buddhist message, according to the definitive form it shows in the Sūtras of the Mahāyāna period, is quite different.

After a long and strenous Career of Bodhisattva which has lasted a great / infinite length of time and in which he has acquired the Supreme Knowledge and has accomplished numerous and heroic acts of Compassion, the Bodhisattva, becoming a *Tathāgata,* obtains the *Bodhi* (Enlightenment) and gets a *Buddhakṣetra,* a World of Buddha.[7] These Worlds of Buddha are described in terms of great

[6] Cf. Z. Ito, "A Study on the Meaning of Tathāgata's āyuṣ-pramāṇa in the *Saddharmapuṇḍarīkasūtra*", in *Hokke Bunka Kenkyū,* no. 11 and 12.

[7] Cf. *Saddharmapuṇḍarīkasūtra* I, verses 13-43, and Tsugunari Kubo, *Hokekyo Bosatsu Shisō Kiso,* Tokyo, Shunjū-sha, 1987, pp. 103-141.

beauty, are adorned with flowers and gems, brilliant with gold – true and magnificent Paradises.There the new Buddha lives and reigns (so to say), imparting the *Dharma* to a great number of disciples, guiding and inciting them towards the *Bodhi.* In this way he accomplishes a task of compassion and beneficence, which is the continuance of the task of compassion and beneficence he has accomplished during his Career of Bodhisattva. The life and (so to say) the reign of the *Tathāgata* in his *Buddhakṣetra* last a great / infinite length of time. During this infinite length of time he keeps his individual personality and consciousness, purified and enhanced by the Bodhisattva Career to which he has submitted himself. Only after the great / infinite number of *kalpas* spent in his compassionate activity, the *Tathāgata* enters the Supreme *Nirvāṇa,* the blissful extinction, which remains as the final aim of Buddhist effort. This destiny is generously open to anybody who decides to become a Bodhisattva, to live and act as such, and to make the *Bodhi* the supreme and unique goal of his existences.

In the *Lotus Sūtra* we have the history of several *Tathāgatas* and in each of these histories we find the same scheme, the same course of life that we have referred to in the foregoing lines, and the same great/infinite length of life.[8] Let us mention among these *Tathāgatas*, Padmaprabha, pp. 65-66 (p. 66 lines 11-12: *padmaprabhasya tathāgatasya dvādaśāntarakalpā āyuṣpramāṇaṃ bhaviṣyati sthāpayitvā kumārabhūtatvam*: "The length of life of the *Tathāgata* Padmaprabha will be of twelve Intermediate Cosmic Periods, without mentioning his youth"); Raśmiprabhāsa, pp. 144-145, (p. 144, línea 7: same *āyuṣpramāṇa*: 'length of life'); Śaśiketu, p. 148, (p. 148, línea 15: same *āyuṣpramāṇa*); Jāmbūnadaprabhāsa, pp. 150-151 (p.151, línea 11: same *āyuṣpramāṇa*); Tamālapatracandanagandha, pp. 152-154, (p. 154, línea 1: *caturviṃśatiṃ ... asyāntarkalpānāyuṣpramāṇam*:

[8] If we consider that an *antarakalpa* lasts for 336.000.000 years, the length of the life of the four first mentioned *Tathāgatas* has been of 4.032.000.000 years and that of *Tamālapatracandanagandha* of 8.064.000.000 years.

"And his legth of life will be of twenty four Intermediate Cosmic Periods ...").[9]

Position of Nirvāṇa in Mahāyāna Buddhism

Nirvāṇa, so difficult to grasp in its true meaning even by philosophically educated minds, the complete extinction (as that of a flame) with which it is likened, and which naturally produces a feeling of dread and uneasiness in the great majority of persons too much attached to themselves, to life and to the joys and pleasures it offers – *Nirvāṇa,* extinction, is postponed to a so far away future that it seems that it will never arrive, will never be produced. No other religious Master has discovered and offered to his adepts a destiny more magnificent and more in accordance with human aspirations than the one discovered and taught by Śākyamuni in the Mahāyāna Sūtras.

With the Mahāyāna Buddhism has been transformed from a religion that proclaims extinction as the final goal into a religion that presents as its goal a fully blossomed and blissful quasi-eternal existence under the signs of Knowledge and Compassion. Buddhism has become from a *Nirvāṇa-religion* a *Bodhi-religion.*

The quasi-eternity of the existence of the *Tathāgatas* after obtaining the *Bodhi* seems to indicate a fundamental change, a very profound transformation in Buddhist message. This quasi-eternity is one of the important elements that distinguish Hīnayāna from Mahāyāna Buddhism. Perhaps it is the change or transformation what allowed the quick acceptance of Buddhism by so diverse Asian peoples, and explains its formidable force of attraction.

The great / infinite numbers applied to the length of the existence of the *Tathāgatas* after obtaining the *Bodhi* are the clear indicative sign of this fundamental transformation.

---

[9] Cf. Jikido Takasaki, *An Introduction to Buddhism*, Tokyo, The Tōhō Gakkai, 1987, pp. 163-167.

Secondary or implicit effect of the great / infinite numbers taken as a whole

In the preceding paragraphs we have dealt with the secondary or implicit meaning of the great / infinite numbers and with their effect in relation to each of the cases in which they are employed. But these same numbers, taken as a whole, considered as a totality, have also a global effect. These numbers provide all facts narrated in the *Sūtra,* all the personages that appear in it, with a dimension of greatness. Nothing in the *Sūtra* is small, scanty, mediocre; on the contrary all is limitless, incommensurable, of cosmic proportions, magnificent, adequate in this way to the greatness of the Doctrines taught by the *Sūtra,* which are inspired in a spirit of generosity and which constitute *a message of universal character.*

VIII

Beginninglessness of the *Veda* and the *Dharma*

Beginninglessness (*anāditva*) is a fundamental theory in Indian thought, which distinguishes it from Western thought always eager to find a first principle, a first cause, a first moment to every thing. According to this theory, since a beginningless eternity, the series of reincarnations, the series of existences, the empirical reality (*saṃsāra*) as a whole has existed and has been in a constant process of change or transformation under manifold forms, especially as *evolution* and *involution*. The same thing can be said about all that exists in this empirical reality, about all that constitutes it: beings, things, existence, life, the words, etc. In an article published in *Annals of the Bhandarkar Oriental Research Institute* 1980, pp.1-20, we have given a number of texts which refer to this characteristic of reality in relation to many entities that exists in it or constitute it according to Indian Philosophy.

The *Veda*

One of the entities, which have had no beginning, is the *Veda*. Excepting some schools, as those of the materialists and Buddhists, who deny the supernatural origin and value and eternity of the Vedic texts, the philosophical and religious schools of India agree in the fact that those texts possess a supernatural character because of their origin, because of their unshakable validity as absolute norm of truth, and because of the eternity that in some way or other is attributed to them. The *Veda*'s eternity and, as a consequence of it, its absolute and inalterable identity through the infinite creations, its independence and autonomy are the guarantee of the absolute character of the moral laws that find their expression in the *Veda*: good has been always good in itself, bad has been always bad in itself and not as the product of the decision of some omniscient and omnipotent being: the moral law has in itself its fundament and justification.

The *Dharma*

Beginninglessness of the Empirical Reality

As Hinduism, Buddhism affirms also that the reincarnations cycle, the empirical reality (*saṃsāra*), has had no beginning. This principle is asserted in many texts: *Saṃyuttanikāya* II, pp. 178-182 (PTS ed.), III, pp. 149 and 151 (PTS ed.), V, pp. 226 and 441 (PTS ed.), cf. *Kathāvatthu*, p. 29 (PTS ed.); Divyāvadāna, p. 122, lines 18-20 (Vaidya ed. = p. 197 Cowell-Neil ed.); *Laṅkāvatārasūtra* II, verse 151; *Mahāvatsu* II, p. 264, verse 45; III, p. 34, verse 4; p. 396, verse 2, and p. 499, verse 3 (Basak ed. = II, p. 188, III, pp. 26, 300, 375 Senart ed.); Buddhaghosa, *Aṭṭhasālinī*, p. 10 (no. 25), p. 177 (no. 471), pp. 191 and 192 (nos. 515 and 519), p. 285 (no. 34) (Bapat / Vadekar ed. = pp. 10-11, 216, 235 and 236, 357 PTS ed.); Śāntideva, *Bodhicaryāvatāra* II, verse 28; Prajñākaramati, *Pañjikā ad* IX, verses 12 (*anādisaṃsāra*), 32 (*idem*), 33 (*anavarāgrasaṃsāra*), 84 (*idem*), 118 (*anavarāgrasya saṃsārasya pūrvakoṭir na prajñāyate*), 124 (*anavarāgro hi jātisaṃsāraḥ*); Śāntideva, *Śikṣāsamuccaya*, p. 94, lines 30 ff. (Vaidya ed. = p. 170, line 2, Bendall ed.); Vasubandhu, *Abhidharmakośa* III, verse 19; Nāgārjuna, *Madhyamakaśāstra* XI, verse 1 and *Candrakīrti*, *Prasannapadā*, *ad locum*, etc.

Laws that Govern the Empirical Reality

The empirical reality is not a chaotic universe. It is submitted to laws, principles, norms (*dharmas*), which regulate its existence and behaviour. There are in the universe laws which determine what necessarily must happen and *vice versa* what necessarily cannot happen in certain given circumstances, i.e., when definite causes and conditions occur or do not occur. Thanks to these laws the universe presents itself as an organized system, as a *cosmos*.

All that exists is in this manner under the sway of the law of causation, *pratītyasamutpāda*, which is expressed in the formula: *asmin satīdaṃ bhavati* (Vasubandhu, *Abhidharmakośa* III, verse 18). Nothing occurs in the realm of existence, due to chance or hazard, fortuitously. The *pratītyasamutpāda* is thus the first great *dharma* in the universe.

The strictest causality that controls the whole empirical reality implies the interdependence of all that exists, as everything is the effect of a multiplicity of causes and conditions, and at the same time everything gives rise to other effects; and all these (we may say) causal series are interconnected among themselves. This aspect of the *pratītyasamutpāda* can be considered as another great law of existence.

The law of causality manifests itself in the laws that regulate the physical order, the moral order and the salvific course of action.

Let us mention, as an example of a *physical law*, the law of the forcible destruction of anything that comes forth: *yaṃ kiñci samudayadhammaṃ sabban taṃ nirodhadhammam* (*Udāna* V, 3, p. 49, lines 15-16 PTS ed.), which affects human body and every kind of life in nature, being time the factor that allows the functioning of this law. An instance of a *moral law* is the law of *karman* or moral retribution of actions, associated with the cycle of rebirths, which connects an evil action with punishment and a good action with reward, accomplishing in this way a task of justice. Many laws regulate the *salvific* course of action. We can mention as examples of this type of laws the Four Noble Truths, according to which the human condition is necessarily submitted to suffering, suffering has attachment as its cause, suffering can be suppressed destroying its cause, and there is a specific method, which, when applied, gradually leads to the cessation of suffering through the cessation of its cause, attachment. This method is the Noble Eightfold Path.

Characteristics of these Laws

These laws have not been dictated by a Creator, since for Buddhism there is not a Creator of the world. These laws, as the empirical reality they regulate, exist since a beginningless eternity, existing by themselves, always the same, inalterable, acting with ineludible force. The Buddhas discover these laws that exist prior to the intellectual act that reveals to them their nature and their functioning.

The characteristics of these laws are clearly and forcibly described in the celebrate formula that appears, in its complete or shorter form, since the oldest Buddhist texts:

> *utpādād vā tathāgatānām anutpādād vā tathāgatānāṃ sthitaiveyaṃ dharmatā dharmasthititā dharmaniyāmatā tathatā avitathatā ananyatathatā bhūtatā satyatā tattvam aviparītatā aviparyastatā.*
> "Whether Tathāgatas arise or Tathāgatas do not arise, stable is the law, the stability of the law, the necessity of the law, its suchness, its invariable suchness, its inalterable suchness, its reality, its truth, its identity, its invariability, inalterability."

Yaśomitra, *Sphuṭārthā ad* III, verse 28 a-b (p. 452, Vaidya edn.). Cf. *Saṃyuttanikāya* II, p. 26 (PTS edn.); *Aṅguttaranikāya* I, p. 286 (PTS edn.); *Kathāvatthu* VI, 2 and commentary (PTS edn.); *Śālistambasūtra*, Tibetan translation in L. de la Vallée Poussin, p. 93, Sastri, p. 47, Schoening, pp. 498-500; *Laṅkāvatārasūtra*, pp. 143-144 and 218 (Nanjio edn. = p. 58, lines 18-19, Vaidya edn.); Vasubandhu, *Abhidharmakośa ad* III, 28 a-b; Candrakīrti, *Prasannapadā ad* I, verse 1, p. 40 (L. de la Vallée Poussin edn.); Prajñākaramati, *Pañjikā ad* IX, verse 150 a-b (p. 269, Vaidya edn.).

We find a resonance of this formula in *Lotus Sūtra* II, verse 103 a-b:

> *dharmasthitiṃ dharmaniyāmatāṃ ca*
> *nityasthitāṃ loke imām akampyām* ... // 103 //
> "the stability of the law and the necessity of the law,
> its eternal unshakeable stability in the world ..."

This formula was very well known by brahmanic authors, as for instance Kumārila, *Tantravārtika ad* I, 3, 11, p. 156 (Ānandāśrama edn., 1981); Vācaspati Miśra, *Bhāmatī ad* II, 2, 19, p. 526 (Nirnaya Sagar Press edn., 1938).

The characteristics of these laws are also referred to in texts such as, *Śālistambasūtra* (Tibetan translation in L. de la Vallée Poussin, pp. 92-93, Sastri, p. 46, Schoening, pp. 494-497, quoted in Prajñākaramati, *Pañjikā ad* IX, verses 15 and 142, pp. 186 and 269, Vaidya edn.):

> *ya imaṃ pratītyasamutpādaṃ satatasamitaṃ nirjīvaṃ yathāvad aviparītam ajātam abhutām asaṃskṛtam apratigham anālambanaṃ śivam abhayam ahāryam avyayam avyupaśamasvabhāvaṃ paśyati sa dharmaṃ paśyati.*
>
> "He who sees this Dependent Origination as eternal, without life, completely inalterable, not-born, not-become, not-composed, without obstacle, without support, calm, without fear, and ineradicable, having non-cessation as its own being – he sees the *Dharma.*"

This text was commented by Kamalaśīla in his *Ṭīkā ad Śālistambasūtra*, Tibetan translation in Schoening, pp. 688-721. Cf. *Aṣṭasāhasrikā*, pp. 560-562 (Wogihara edn. = p. 135 Vaidya edn.), Śāntideva, *Śikṣāsamuccaya* XIII, p. 127, XVIII, p. 171 (Vaidya edn. = pp. 236-237, 322-323, Bendall edn.), *Mahāvyutpatti* 1706-1723 (enumeration of synonyms of *paramārtha*).

Discovery and Exposition of these Laws by the Buddha

The Buddha has not created these laws; they had not been revealed to Him by any superior power; He has not invented them, they are not a construction of His mind. The laws are there, have always been there, and the Buddha, as already said, by an intense and painful intellectual effort was able to discover them. From the very moment He discovers these laws, they become His Teaching, the *Dharma.* His Teaching, His *Dharma* is thus the exposition, manifestation, explanation, elucidation, transmission, and revelation by Him of these laws. Cf. *Saṃyuttanikāya* II, pp. 25-26, PTS edn. We can say that at the beginning of the Buddhist doctrine there has been an intellectual act of cognition, laboriously conquered. From the first moment, the importance of knowledge and human effort have constituted distinguishing features of Buddhism.

Eternity of the Dharma *and of the* Dharmabhāṇakas

Till now we have referred to the eternity of the empirical reality (*saṃsāra*) and of the laws that rule in it; let us now consider the eternity of the *Dharma* on the basis of the *Saddharmapuṇḍarīka*.

The *Lotus Sūtra* II, verse 102 openly declares the lasting nature of the Path of the *Dharma*:

sthitikā hi eṣā sada dharmanetrī

and II, verse 134 expresses that the "Essence of the Doctrine" (*Dharmatā*) of the Buddhas of the past, of the Buddhas of the future and of Śākyamuni is *the same* and is not the product of vain imaginations:

yathaiva teṣāṃ purimāṇa tāyinām anāgatānāṃ ca jināna dharmatā /
mamāpi eṣaiva vikalpavarjitā tathaiva haṃ deśayi adya tubhyam // 134 //

Śākyamuni's Doctrine is described in the Pāli texts with the same terms as the Doctrine of Tathāgata Candrasūryapradīpa who lived in the past an infinite number of *kalpas* before (p. 17, Kern-Nanjio ed.). See the description in *Dīghanikāya* I, par. 40, p. 62 (PTS ed.), *Saṃyuttanikāya* I, p. 105, IV, pp. 121-122 (PTS ed.) (for other passages cf. *Pāli Tipiṭakaṃ Concordance* I, Part VI, p. 316 b *sub ādi-kalyāṇam*), and in *Lotus Sūtra*, p. 17, lines 11-13, and p. 18, lines 9-10 (Kern-Nanjio ed.). We give the text of the description as in the quoted passage of the *Lotus Sūtra*, p. 17:

sa dharmaṃ deśayati smādau kalyāṇaṃ madhye kalyāṇaṃ paryavasāne kalyāṇaṃ svarthaṃ suvyañjanaṃ kevalaṃ paripūrṇaṃ pariśuddhaṃ paryavadātaṃ brahmacaryaṃ saṃprakaśayati sma.

"He exposed the *Dharma*, beautiful at its beginning, beautiful in its middle, beautiful at its end, good in its meaning, good in its form; He proclaimed religious life, unique, perfect, completely pure, completely purified."

An infinite number of *Tathāgatas* in an infinite number of worlds, in the past, in the future and in the present have taught, will teach and teach one and the same Doctrine, that *Ekayāna* (*Lotus Sūtra*, pp. 40-44, Kern-Nanjio ed.).

It can also be said that the *Lotus Sūtra* exists since a beginningless eternity. The *Tathāgata* Candrasūryapradīpa existed

> *atīte dhvanyasaṃkhyeyai' kalpair asaṃkhyeyatarair vipulair aprameyair acintyair aparimitair apramāṇais tata' pareṇa paratarāṃ*
> "in the past, innumerable, more than innumerable, numerous, immeasurable, inconceivable, infinite countless *kalpas* ago – long and very long before that."

(p. 17, Kern-Nanjio edn.). And at that time, during sixty complete *antarakalpas*, Candrasūryapradīpa preached the same *Lotus Sūtra* that Śākyamuni is about to preach in the Great Assembly described in the beginning of the text – i.e., many Cosmic Periods afterwards, in the present. And before, much before than this Tathāgata Candrasūryapradīpa, there were twenty thousand other Tathāgatas Candrasūryapradīpa who preached the same *Lotus Sūtra* (p. 18, Kern-Nanjio edn.). This brings further back the *Lotus Sūtra* itself.

As a consequence of the beginningless *Lotus Sūtra* and of its Teaching, the existence of the *Dharmabhāṇakas* has also been without beginning.

Brahmanic Position towards the Eternity of the Dharma

This conception of an eternal *Dharma*, the Buddhist Doctrine, was harshly opposed by the Brahmanic thinkers, as for instance by Kumārila in his *Tantravārtika ad* I, 3, 11 and 12, especially because, if the Buddhist *Dharma* is as eternal as the *Veda*, the result would be that the *Veda* would not remain the sole and absolute authority.

Final Remarks

Thus we have two eternities side by side, each in its own context: the eternity of the *Veda* and the eternity of the *Dharma*. It would be possible to establish between these two eternities the differences that arise from the diverse contexts to which they belong. And it would be interesting to trace out the principles, valid in Indian thought, which have promoted the coming forth of these two theories, in two so close and different traditions, the Hindu and the Buddhist one. We leave the study of these two questions for another occasion.

REFERENCES

Ārya Śālistamba Sūtra, edn. N.A. Sastri, Adyar (India), Adyar Library, 1950.

Aṭṭhāsālinī, edn. P.V. Bapat and R.D. Vadekar, Poona, Bhandarkar Oriental Series, 1942.

L. de la Vallée Poussin, *Théorie des donze causes*, Gand, Librairie Scientifique E. Van Goethem, 1913.

Mahāvastu Avadāna, ed. R. Basak, Calcutta, Calcutta Sanskrit College Research Series, 1963-1968.

Pāli Tipiṭakaṃ, London and Boston, The Pali Text Society, 1952 ff.

The "Sālistamba-Sūtra" and its Indian Commentaries, by J.D. Schoenning, Ann Arbor MI (USA), UMI Dissertation Information Service, 1991 (Doctoral Dissertation).

Sāntideva, Bodhicaryāvatāra with Pañjikā commentary of Prajñākaramati, edited by P.L. Vaidya, Darbhanga, The Mithila Institute, 1960.

P.L. Vaidya, ed.: Buddhist Sanskrit Texts, The Mithila Institute, Darbhanga (India).

Vasubandhu, *Abhidharmakośa and Bhāṣya with sphutārthā commentary of ācārya Yaśomitra*, Varanasi, Bauddha Bharati Series, 1970-1973.

IX

On the Names of the *Bhikṣus* and the *Bodhisattvas* in the *Lotus Sūtra*

On translating from Sanskrit into Spanish the *Saddharmapuṇḍarīka*, we were struck by the names of the *Bodhisattvas* as mentioned in the initial description of the Great Assembly in Gṛdhrakūṭa, especially when we compared them with the names of the *Bhikṣus* also mentioned there.

I. THE *BHIKṢUS*

The description begins enumerating the *Bhikṣus*, Great Disciples (*mahāśrāvaka*) that attended the Assembly.

Inclusion of the names of the monks in the onomastic Indian tradition

The names of the *Bhikṣus* have, outside the *Lotus Sūtra* and before and after it, a constant presence in the onomastic Indian tradition and are applied to a great diversity of persons, as it will be seen by the observations that accompany the names of each *Bhikṣu* in the first part of the *Appendix* at the end of this article. We think it is necessary to remark that very probably the names of the *Bhikṣus* that designated *gotras* (as for instance Kauṇḍinya, Kāśyapa, Maudgalyāyana) were used, before the advent of Buddhism, only by the members of those *gotras*; but afterwards also by persons who did not belong to those *gotras* but who assumed them in honour of some ancient *Bhikṣu* who had that name as his own one.

Historical biographies of the Bhikṣus

The monks that bear these names have all of them rich biographies, plenty of events. It could also be said that the biographies of these *Bhikṣus* are *historical* biographies, narrating concrete, real events, connected with *real* persons and the actual social historical reality of India. All these biographies, although they present common elements, are different one from the other, making it clear that they belong to diverse individuals. They show the diverse circumstances of the life of each monk: place of birth, town, village, etc. where he lived, family name, name of the father, mother, brothers, sisters, cousins, etc., family relations, relationship with Śākyamuni, *gotra*, epithets, occupation before becoming a Buddhist monk, the locality where he was ordained, personal character, moral qualities and physical aspect, etc. For the biographies of these monks see Mochizuki, *Bukkyō Dai Jiten*, Malalasekera, *Dictionary of Pāli Proper Names*, and *Encyclopaedia of Buddhism*, under each name.

Realistic and individualistic iconography of the Bhikṣus

There are iconographic representations of the first disciples of Śākyamuni, *Bhikṣus* and *Arhants*, since very early in the history of Buddhism in all the Buddhist countries. Some of these representations are of the *Bhikṣus* mentioned in the First Chapter of the *Lotus Sūtra*. In general, all these artistic images have some predominant characteristics: realism, individualism, austerity and simplicity. They are portrait-like representations of individual personages, modelled with surprising truth and naturalness. The personages are represented with very human faces, attitudes and postures; they have quite different facial expressions; they offer a variety of psychological types. They have in common an almost absolute absence of extraordinary, supernatural, superhuman elements: they are human beings, monks.

Examples of iconography of the Bhikṣus

Let us mention as examples of this iconography:

- the Buddha preaching to the Congregation, in Ajanta, Cave XVII (wall-painting) (*The Way of the Buddha*, p. 98) ;

- the *Mahāparinirvāṇa*, from Gāndhāra in Victoria and Albert Museum (London) (Hallade, p. 134) ;

- Ānanda attending the Buddha's *Parinirvāṇa*, in Gal Vihāra, Sri Lanka (*The Way of the Buddha*, p. 112) ;

- *Bhikṣu,* in Ajanta Cave VI (wall-painting) (*The Way of the Buddha,* Chapter IV, colour plate III);

- Votive state representing, among others, Ānanda and Kāśyapa, from China, Northern Qi or Sui dynasty, in Victoria and Albert Museum (*Buddhism,* p. 200) ;

- *Lohan* (*Arhant*), from China, found at Yixian, Hebei province, Liao dynasty, British Museum (*Buddhism,* p. 205) ;

- the Buddha preaching, from China, Dunhuang, Gansu province, Tang dynasty (*Buddhism,* p. 214) ;

- *Lohan,* from China, in University Museum, Philadelphia (de Silva-Vigier, illustration No. 135) ;

- Head of a *Lohan,* from China, Ethnographic Museum, Leiden, Holland (de Silva-Vigier, illustration No. 136) ;

- *Lohan,* from China, by the painter Chang Shêng-wên, in Chinese National Palace Museum, Taichung, Taiwan (scroll) (Seckel, p. 249) ;

- Monk from Japan, Köln, Museum of Far-east Art (de Silva-Vigier, illustration No. 138);

- Five hundred *Rakan* (*Arhant*) from Japan, probably Mampukuji Temple, Uji near Kyoto, in British Museum (drawing) *(Buddhism,* illustration No. 407, p. 283);

- the *Arhants* depicted in paintings and sculptures included in *The Sacred Art of Tibet,* pp. 102-119;

- the *Bhikṣus* who accompany the Buddha in the illustrations in the work of Kurita Isao, *Gandhāran Art*, Parts III and IV;

- Statues of Śāriputra, Kātyāyana, Maudgalyāyana, Rāhula, Pūrṇa, Subhūti in Kōfukuji at Noborioji, Nara, Japan.

It is a pleasure to finish this enumeration with the wonderful "Five hundred" *Rakans* in the Gohyakurakanji Temple in Tokyo.

Let us refer to a personal remark which confirms the above mentioned characteristics of the *Bhikṣus* as represented in Rakanji Temple. When we were in Japan (1989), we met Venerable Senchu Murano, Chief Priest of the Myochoji Temple in Kamakura. When we told him about the strong impression the Rakanji Temple produced in us, he was very much pleased to explain to us that pleople used to go to that Temple to recognize in one or another of the faces of the *Rakans* there the faces of their beloved dead family members - to such an extent the faces of these *Arhants* are distinct, different and, in their realism, representative of the diverse human types of Japan.

On proper names

Most frequently it is imposible to translate proper names, because in general they have not meaning at all. Very probably they have had at some moment a meaning, but with the course of time they have lost it. Even when the proper name has a clear (etymological) meaning, there is a resistence to translate it. The translation of proper names can give rise to funny or odd effects or to misrepresentations. For instance it would be absurd to translate the Spanish proper names Dañino, Espantoso, Guerrero, Villa (family names), or the beautiful woman's name Dolores (personal name), whose literal meaning are respectively: 'noxious', 'horrid', 'warrior', 'town with peculiar privileges', and 'pains'!

The proper name has a meaning, which is not its literal or etymological meaning. It designates a certain person (or object) with his or her complex personality, with his or her peculiar attributes, with his or her untransferable individuality. When the proper name can be translated and is translated, it loses its significative force and ceases to signify that determinate person and comes to signify anything else that may or may not have a relation to that person. It happens with the proper names what happens with the names of the *yogarudha* category in the Indian theory of meaning, as for instance *paṅkaja* whose etymological (*yaugika*) meaning is 'what grows in the mud' and whose conventional (*rūḍha)* meaning is 'lotus'. Of these two meanings it is the conventional one that occurs to the mind in first place and imposes itself on it. Cf. Kunjunni Raja, pp. 61-62.

All this can be exemplified with the proper names of the *Mahābhārata.* Many of its heroes have transparent names, i.e., with a clear meaning, for instance Yuddhiṣṭhira ('firm in battle'), Duryodhana ('difficult to be conquered'), Dhṛtarāṣṭra ('whose empire is firm') etc.; nevertheless the use is to understand them in their *rūḍha* meaning, and consequently not to translate them, but to maintain them untranslated. When one translates these names, they do not fulfil any more their function. They are no more expressive and individualizing marks. 'Yuddhiṣṭhira' designates in a concrete, specific way, a certain individual with a past, a present, a future, with numerous personal attributes; but "firm in battle" designates only one attribute, in an abstract general way, and can be applied, as an epithet, to anybody possessing that attribute.

Phonetical transliteration by Kumārajīva of the names of the Bhikṣus

Let us see how Kumārajīva and the other translators have dealt with the names of the *Bhikṣus.* Kumārajīva has not translated the Sanskrit names of the *Bhikṣus* into Chinese, he has limited himself to *transliterate* them (i.e., to give by means of Chinese ideograms the approximate phonetic value of the syllables that compose the Sanskrit name), even when there was the possibility of a more or less correct translation. In other words, even in these cases Kumārajīva has preferred the conventional (*rūḍha*) meaning to the etymological (*yaugika*) meaning. He has left aside this last meaning.

The Japanese tradition, following Kumārajīva, adopted the same procedure as he did. Cf. the translations of the *Lotus Sūtra* either from Sanskrit or from Chinese into Japanese in the *Daijō Butten* and in *Iwanami* series, and into English by S. Murano, by Bunnō Katō and by Tsugunari Kubo and Akira Yuyama. The Western translators as Burnouf and Kern, who translate from Sanskrit, and Hurvitz, who translates from Chinese, do in the same way. In other words, they all have adopted the 'conventional meaning' of the names of the *Bhikṣus.*

Tibetan translation of the names of the Bhikṣus

The Tibetan translator has followed an ambiguous method: (a) sometimes he transliterates: Kauṇḍinya (1) (in the list included in the first part of the *Appendix* at the end of this article), Śari (10),

Maudgalyāyana (11), Kātyāyana (12), Kapphina (15), Pilinda (17), Bakkula (18), Bhāradvāja (20) (8 names in total); (b) he translates the epithets that accompany the names, which he transliterates: *ājñata* in (1), *putra* in (10), *mahā* in (11) and (12), *vatsa* in (17); (c) in all the other cases less one (18 names in total) he translates the name and the epithet when this one exists: Aśvajit (2), Bāspa (3), Mahānāmam (4), Bhadrika (5), Mahākāśyapa (6), Uruvilvakāśyapa (7), Nadīkāśyapa (8), Aniruddha (13), Revata (14), Gavāṃpati (16), Mahākauṣṭhila (19), (Mahā)nanda (20), Upananda (22), Sundarananda (23), Pūrṇa Maitrāyaṇīputra (24), Subhūti (25), Rāhula (26), Ānanda (27); and (d) in one case, Gayākāśyapa (18), he translates the name but transliterates the epithet (Gayā).

In his effort to translate anything that can be translated, the Tibetan translator assigns to some *Bhikṣus* very odd names: Horse tamer (2), Vapour or Steam (3), the name of a constellation: Revata (14), Great-stomach (19), Near-pleasure (22), Full (24), Great-Wealth (25), Eclipse of moon (26).

Why Kumārajīva keeps untranslated the names of the Bhikṣus *(*rūḍha *meaning)?*

In first place it cannot be said that Kumārajīva did not translate the names of the *Bhikṣus*, because it was impossible to translate them, as it generally happens with proper names, since among the names of the *Bhikṣus* there are several that could be easily translated, as for instance: Aniruddha (13), Gavāṃpati (16), Nanda or Mahānanda (21), Upananda (22), Sundarananda (23), Subhūti (25), Ānanda (27), and nevertheless he has not translated them. In fact, Kumārajīva adopts in face of the names of the *Bhikṣus* the same attitude that in modern times anybody instinctively and unconsciously adopts in face of proper names in any language: not to translate them, not to understand them in their etymological meaning, to take them in their conventional sense. And it was the same attitude adopted in Ancient India in face of the *yogarūḍha* words: the preference was given to the conventional meaning.

Kumārajīva did not translate the names of the *Bhikṣus*, because the only function of these names was to point out concrete individuals and nothing else. And this function could not be fulfilled if the names were distorted on being translated.

II. THE *BODHISATTVAS*

With the names of the *Bodhisattvas* that attended the Great Assembly the atmosphere has completely changed.

Scanty relation of the names of the Bodhisattvas *with the Indian onomastic tradition*

The first observation in regard to the names of the *Bodhisattvas* is that they do not really belong to the onomastic Indian tradition, since only few of them, as Mañjuśrī, Avalokiteśvara, Maitreya, Siṃha (which we mention in the third part of the *Appendix* at the end of this article), are applied to other persons in very few cases, and that occurs generally only several centuries after the constitution of Mahāyāna Buddhism and the development of the cult of the *Bodhisattvas.*

Names of the Bodhisattvas *as epithet-like names*

The names of the *Bodhisattvas* bring to our mind the epithets of several heroes (the so called *epitheta ornantia*) of the Homeric poems, the epithets of the *Mahābhārata*, and the (epithet-like) names of the personages (belonging to the Judeo-Christian tradition) that appear in Milton's *Paradise Lost.* In Homer we find epithets, which (almost) exclusively accompany the name of some particular hero, as *pódas ōkús*: 'of swift feet' (for Achilles), *klutótoxos*: 'of illustrious bow' (for Apollo), *polútlas*: 'who endures much' (for Ulysses). In the *Mahābhārata* we have similar epithets (with a difference consisting in it that these epithets are not proper to one hero; they can be applied to several), as *narapuṅgava* ('a bull among men'), *samitiñjaya* ('victorious in battle'), *kapidhvaja* ('whose ensign is the monkey') etc. In Milton's *Paradise Lost* are found names as: Ariel: 'Lion of God'; Arioch: 'Fierce Lion'; Gabriel: 'Man of God'; Lucifer: 'Light-bringer'; Michael: 'Who is like God?'; Ramiel: 'Exaltation of God'; Satan: 'The Enemy'.

Contrarily to what happens with the proper names, these epithets are usually translated; they indicate some characteristic - but only one - of the personality of the heroes, which they enrich.

From the formal point of view the names in the English poem and the names of the *Bodhisattvas* can be considered as epithet-like names that may or may not be translated. Notwithstanding, some of these epithet-like names, as Mañjuśrī (1), Maitreya (24), may have a tendency to become exclusively proper names possessing the characteristics indicated in the section of this article concerning the *Bhikṣus*. This tendency manifests itself in the fact that both names are not translated by Kumārajīva.

Supernatural biographies of the Bodhisattvas

It cannot be said that the *Bodhisattvas* have *historical* biographies as the *Bhikṣus*. Around several of them has been created a very rich supernatural, extraordinary, legendary, mythological biography, full of events that trascend all human dimension. These special characteristics also appear in full light when the texts tell us about the functions, transformations, names, attributes, worship, vehicles, dwelling-places (*buddhakṣetra)* etc. of these *Bodhisattvas*.

Let us mention, as examples,

- the case of Avalokiteśvara (cf. *Lotus Sūtra* XXIV; Mochizuki I, pp. 800-807, Haussig (ed.), pp. 322-326 with bibliography; L. de la Vallée Poussin, in *ERE*, 2, pp. 256-261), *Encyclopaedia of Buddhism* II, 3, pp. 407-415;
- the case of Mañjuśrī (cf. Mochizuki V, pp. 4875-4878, Lamotte, 'Mañjuśrī'; L. de la Vallée Poussin, in *ERE*, 8, pp. 405-406; Haussig (ed.), pp. 421-424);
- the case of Maitreya (cf. Mochizuki V, pp. 4815-4819, Lamotte, *Histoire*, pp. 775-788; Haussig (ed.), pp. 414-418);
- and the case of Bhaiṣajyarājan (cf. *Lotus Sūtra* XXII; Mochizuki V, pp. 4885-4886, Haussig (ed.), pp. 328-329).

While the *Bhikṣus* are immersed in the real life, the *Bodhisattvas* belong to a spiritual reality.

Relation of the Bodhisattvas *and of their names with Buddhist virtues*

It could be said that the *Bodhisattvas* are the personification of some particular moral Buddhist virtue, such as wisdom, compassion, etc. Each name transforms the *Bodhisattva* that bears it into an archetype. And consequently anything that has not directly to do with that particular virtue passes into a secondary plane - or completely disappears.

We have thus:

- Mañjuśrī (1) is the personification of knowledge and wisdom;

- Avalokiteśvara (2), of compassion;

- Mahāsthāmaprāpta (3), of *sthāma* (endurance, power, strength), a quality of which the *Bodhisattva* should be endowed (Tucci, p. 491);

- Sarvārthanāman (4), (perhaps) of the will of being helpful, of rendering service to others, of benefiting everybody (cf. Edgerton, Dictionary, p. 66, under the words *arthakriyā, arthacaryā, arthacara*; and *Bodhisattvabhūmi*, Wogihara ed., p. 4, lines 2-6, where it is stated that a mark that distinguishes the *Bodhisattva* from *Śrāvakas* and *Pratyekabuddhas* is that he cares for the welfare, well-being and benefit (*artha*) of all beings); this quality is, of course, tightly related with compassion;

- Nityodyukta (5), of a constant *udyoga*, concept related to *vīrya*, one of the Perfections. (Cf. *Dhammasaṅgaṇi*, p. 64, PTS edition, where a definition of *vīrya* is given by means of several synonyms);

- Anikṣiptadhura (6), of the virtue of 'not laying down the burden', i.e., of perseverance in the fulfilment of religious and ethical duties (cf. *Dhammasaṅgaṇi*, p. 64, PTS edition, where *anikkhittadhuratā* is reckoned among the synonyms of *vīrya*, Pāli *viriya*);

- Ratnapāṇi (7), (perhaps) of generosity, since the Chinese interprets this name as meaning: "The hand that gives alms and precious things" (Soothill, p. 477 a);

- Pradānaśūra (11), of generosity;

- Mahāpratibhāna (18), of eloquence, readiness in speech, brilliance especially as manifested in speech, by which a *Bodhisattva* brings creatures to religious maturity; *pratibhāna* is one of the *vaśitā* (power) and of the *pratisaṃvid* (special knowledge) (Edgerton, p. 366 *sub pratibhāna*; MacQueen, p. 310; Gonda, *The Vision of the Vedic Poets*, p. 318);

- Satatāsamitābhiyukta (19), of constant application to, of continuous zeal for the Buddhist Teaching and Discipline;

- Akṣayamati (21), of undecaying intelligence, which allows him to grasp, to preserve, to understand the Teaching; it is a mark of a *Bodhisattva*'s *gotra* (*Bodhisattvabhūmi*, Wogihara edn., p. 9, lines 12-13: *medhāvī ca dharmāṇāṃ grahaṇadhāraṇohanasamarthaḥ*); there are several *Bodhisattvas* which bear compound names with *mati*, cf. *Mahāvyutpatti*, 681, 682, 694, 695, 698, 706;

- Maitreya (24), of benevolence, love, kindliness, friendliness (*maitrī*).

-Mahāvikrāmin (15), Anantavikrāmin (16), Trailokya-vikrāmin (17) and Siṃha (25) could also be reckoned in this category as personifications of the highest degree of the *vīrya-pāramitā*: heroism at the service of pursuance of the *Bodhisattva*'s noble ideal.

Relation of the names of the Bodhisattvas *with the Buddha's attributes*

Some of the names of the *Bodhisattvas* or at least part of these names from the earliest times have been used in reference to the Buddha, as is the case with Mañjuśrī (1), Bhaiṣajyarāja (8), Bhaiṣajyasamudgata (9) and Siṃha (25).

- Mañjuśrī (1) is designated also with other names: Mañjughoṣa, Mañjunātha, Mañjubhāṇin, Mañjurava, Mañjuvajra, Mañjuvara (?), Mañjuśiri, Mañjuśirī, Mañjusvara, Vāgīśvara, Vādirāj (Edgerton, p. 414 b; Lamotte, 'Mañjuśrī', p. 1). Many of these names point to Mañjuśrī's 'sweet' voice or eloquence. The term *mañju* in Pāli is an adjective with the meaning of 'sweet, charming, pleasant, lovely'; it appears also in compounds as *mañjubhāṇin, mañjubhāṇaka, mañjubhāṇikā,* with similar significance: 'sweet-voiced, speaking sweetly'. *Mañju* is applied to the voice of the Buddha, cf. *Majjhima-Nikāya* II, p. 140, lines 5-8 (PTS ed.); *Jātaka* I, p. 95, two last lines - p. 96, line 3 (PTS ed.), and for *brahmassara* see *Dīgha-Nikāya* II, p. 211, paragraph 19 = p. 277, paragraph 18 (PTS ed.).

- Bhaiṣajyarāja (8) ('King of medicines') and Bhaiṣajyasamudgata (9) ('Excellent in medicines'): from early times, in many texts, the Buddha is considered as the Great, Insuperable Physician (*mahāvaidya, mahābhiṣaṭka, anuttara bhisakkha*) that knows how to 'cure' the suffering of all beings. See for instance *Theragāthā* 722 (*sabbaññū sabbadassāvī...*) and 1114 (*suyuttavādī dvipadānam uttamo...*) (Nālandā edn.); *Itivuttaka*, p. 101, paragraph 100 (PTS edn.); *Aṅguttara-Nikāya*, p. 340 (PTS edn.); *Saddharmapuṇḍarīka*, p. 140, verse 60 and p. 161, verse 8 (Kern-Nanjio edn.).

- Siṃha (25) ('Lion') is a term often used as an epithet of the Buddha. Cf. *Itivuttaka*, p. 123 (*sīho anuttaro*) (PTS edn.); *Saṃyutta-Nikāya* I, p. 28 (PTS edn.); *Aṅguttara-Nikāya* II, p. 24, and III, p. 122 (PTS ed.). Cf. also the name Śākyasiṃha, already mentioned (in *Saddharmapuṇḍarīkasūtra* I, verse 93, and in *Rājataraṅgiṇī* I, 172). And the expression *sīhanāda*, 'a lion's roar', is applied to the Buddha's preaching as in *Saṃyutta-Nikāya* II, p. 27 (PTS ed.); *Dīgha-Nikāya* I, p. 175 (PTS edn.).

- Mahāvikrāmin (15) ('He of great heroism'), Anantavikrāmin (16) ('He of limitless heroism') can also be considered as being related to the Buddha, since *vikrāma*: 'heroism', from which *vikrāmin* derives, could be taken as synonym of *viriya, vīrya*: heroism, heroic energy; and the Buddha is the Vīra, the Mahāvīra, the Vīravīra: the Hero, the Great Hero, the Hero of Heroes *par excellence*. See for instance, *Suttanipāta* 543 and 562 (PTS edn.), *Mahāvastu* III, p. 401 (Senart edn.).

It is possible to consider that these Bodhisattvas are only the result of the transformation of a quality, of an epithet, of a function of the Buddha, into an individual, a *Bodhisattva*.

A parallel situation is found in Roman Catholic Church. Virgin Mary, Christ mother of is believed to have been immune from original sin from the very first instant of her conception. She had what is called an 'Immaculate Conception', and this expression is engraved on images, which in fact represent Virgin Mary, the 'Mother of God', but which for many devotees represent a Divine Lady, whose name is 'Immaculate Conception', and who *prima facie* is not connected with Virgin Mary. Here we have the transformation of a fact related to a religious or holy personage into a different independent individual.

Names of the Bodhisattvas *with laudatory function*

Some of the names of the *Bodhisattvas* seem to be laudatory names, to have as function merely to extoll and glorify the personality of the bearer of the name in a metaphorical way, and to be the product of the devotees' admiration and respect.

Among these names we have Vyūharājan (10): 'King of magnificence, splendor or supernal manifestation', Ratnacandra (12): 'Jeweled or precious moon', Ratnaprabha (13): 'Jeweled or precious glow', Pūrṇacandra (14): 'Full moon', Padmaśrī (22): 'Glory of the lotus', Nakṣatrarājan (23): 'King of constellations'.

These names have no reference to any particular Buddhist virtue, attribute or quality; they point out the superior position, rank or status gained by the *Bodhisattvas* bearing them; moreover these names could be applied, as epithets, to any other *Bodhisattva*. It is to be noted that all these names are related to brightness, brilliancy, light, splendor, and beauty, which contribute to the magnificence that permeates the Mahāyāna.

Marvelous iconography of the Bodhisattvas

The iconographic representation of the *Bodhisattvas* contains many marvelous elements; it stands in contrast to that of the *Bhikṣus*. In general, the *Bodhisattvas* are represented under several forms to each of which corresponds a diverse name, with bodies possessed of different colours, provided with more than one head or more than two eyes or two arms, characterized by peculiar symbols, as swords, lotus etc., adorned with jewels, necklaces, precious stones, crowns etc. There is a rich literature that specifies how each *Bodhisattva* (as well as deities of the Buddhist pantheon) has to be represented by iconographic means, as the *Sādhanamālā* and other treatises mentioned by B. Bhattacharyya in his *Introduction* of *The Indian Buddhist Iconography*, pp. 1-7.

Let us take as example Avalokiteśvara. He is depicted under at least 15 different forms (as Saḍakṣarī-Lokeśvara, Siṃhanāda-Lokeśvara, etc.); the colour of his body can be white, red, blue, yellow etc.; he can have one, three, four, five, eleven heads or faces, and four, six, eight, twelve, eighteen, and even 1000 arms, and equal number of eyes; his symbols are rosary, lotus, sword, sword on lotus, *triśula* entwined by a snake, double lotus in all hands, bowl of jewels; he is richly and princely ornate. For detailed descriptions of Avalokiteśvara, see B. Bhattacharyya, pp. 124-144; Kirfel, *Symbolik des Buddhismus*, pp. 56-62; Haussig (ed.), p. 325, with bibliography; Schumann, pp. 121-133. As a magnificent example of the iconographic representation of the *Bodhisattva* Avalokiteśvara (Kannon) let us refer to the extraordinary temple popularly called Sanjūsangendo in Kyoto, with its sitting principal statue in the center of the hall and its 1000 standing statues on both sides of the central image, representing all of them the *Bodhisattva* of the Great Compassion.

Conceptual translation by Kumārajīva of the names of the Bodhisattvas

In a general way the names of the *Bodhisattvas* can be easily translated, because they have a clear etymological meaning. And in fact it is what Kumārajīva has done (see *Appendix* at the end of this article): while he *transliterates* all the *Bhikṣus*' names, giving their phonetical values, he *translates* into Chinese all the *Bodhisattvas'* names, giving their conceptual values, with the exception of Mañjuśrī and Maitreya. In other words, in relation to the majority of the names of the *Bodhisattvas* Kumārajīva has preferred the etymological (*yaugika*) meaning. And this is something that cannot be neglected. It reveals a different attitude of the great translator in face of the *Bhikṣus* and of the *Bodhisattvas*. The Japanese translators of the *Lotus Sūtra* (either from Sanskrit or from Kumārajīva's Chinese translation, either into Japanese or into English), and Hurvitz (who translates from Kumārajīva's version) follow Kumārajīva's procedure. Burnouf and Kern maintain the Sanskrit names, without translating them. Kubo and Yuyama in his English translation from Kumārajīva's version put the Sanskrit names of the *Bodhisattvas* instead of the conceptual translation given by Kumārajīva.

Why Kumārajīva gives a conceptual translation of the names of the Bodhisattvas *(*yaugika *meaning)?*

Kumārajīva belonged to a Buddhist culture, he had been educated in Buddhist faith, he was immersed in the Buddhist religious atmosphere of the *Lotus Sūtra*. The *Bodhisattvas* represented for him the personification of the great Buddhist values, and what they personified was expressed by their names. As such these *Bodhisattvas* were the sacred object of devotion and worship in the Buddhist world. For instance, Avalokiteśvara (= *Avalokitasvara* as he understands this name) was for Kumārajīva the archetype of Great Compassion, the highest virtue of a *Bodhisattva*; and this attribute manifests itself in his name as Kumārajīva understands it: "He who looks on (or regards) the sounds (the prayers) of the world". To give the conceptual translation (*yaugika* meaning) of the names of the *Bodhisattvas* was the only way to preserve all the treasures they possessed of religious significance, and it was also the only way to transmit to the Chinese readers this important contents of the names. Otherwise, if he had maintained the Sanskrit names of the Bodhisattvas in phonetical transliteration, the rich religious resonance of the names would have been lost; the names would have remained as mere collections of sounds without meaning.

The names of Mañjuśrī and Maitreya

The only *Bodhisattvas*' names that Kumārajīva does not translate are those of Mañjuśrī and Maitreya. He gives their phonetical transliteration as in the case of the proper names of the *Bhikṣus*: Wên-shu-shih-li (in Japanese Monjushiri or Monshushiri) and Mi-lê (in Japanese Miroku). Kumārajīva behaves thus in face of these two *Bodhisattvas* in the same way as he behaves in face of the *Bhikṣus*, whose realistic and historical characteristics we have already pointed out. Perhaps Kumārajīva was induced to treat the names of Mañjuśrī and Maitreya in the same way as he treats the names of the *Bhikṣus*, because in the biographies of these two *Bodhisattvas*, besides the supernatural elements, there are several elements that present them as real and historical personages.

For instance, in relation to Mañjuśrī: it was believed at least since the fourth century A.D. that he stayed in China in the mountain Wu-t'ai-shan (I-tsing, pp. 136 and 169; Lamotte, 'Mañjuśrī', p. 54); in *Vimalakīrtinirdeśa*, Chapter 4, it is said that Mañjuśrī went to the town of Vaiśālī in order to visit Vimalakīrti who was lying ill in bed, and with the same Vimalakīrti he went to Āmrapālīvana to pay homage to the Bhagavant; the *Gaṇḍavyūhasūtra*, Chapter 3, relates that Mañjuśrī left Śākyamuni and travelled south (*dakṣīṇāpatha*) to the town of Dhanyākara, where he preached the *Dharma* and was visited by Śāriputra; in the First Chapter of the *Lotus Sūtra*, Mañjuśrī (as well as Maitreya) is presented, and his behaviour is described, in terms that lack any supernatural, fantastic element: he is in Rājagṛha, in the Gṛdhrakūṭa, attending the Great Assembly that surrounded the Buddha Śākyamuni, he explains to Maitreya and the other followers of the Buddha what is going to happen.

As for Maitreya, among the realistic and historical elements connected with him, we have, for instance, the following ones: Maitreya, as already pointed out, was the name of a *gotra*, i.e., an historical family line; the sources indicate the concrete geographical place where he was born (Vārāṇasī kingdom, in the Kapāli village, in South India, in the Mālaṭa country, in the Kūṭagrāmaka village);

the names of his father, mother, wife, son, are mentioned; he was one of the disciples of the ascetic Bāvari, who were converted by the Buddha Śākyamuni (Lamotte, *Histoire*, pp. 775-783; Haussig (ed.), pp. 414-415). Besides the above mentioned biographical facts that could induce to consider Maitreya as having an historical existence, there is another important circumstance: many Mahāyanist Sanskrit works (as *Yogācārabhūmi*, *Abhisamayālaṃkāra* etc.) were attributed (even before Kumārajīva's time) to Maitreya, the *Bodhisattva*. If this attribution was so strong as to lead H. Ui ('Maitreya as an historical personage') and his followers to think that the *Bodhisattva* Maitreya was an historical personage, it could also have induced Kumārajīva to give to Maitreya the same real status, and therefore to behave in face of his name (in his translation into Chinese) as he did.

Why Burnouf and Kern did not translate the Bodhisattvas *'names?*

One may ask why Burnouf and Kern did not translate the names of the *Bodhisattvas*, while Kumārajīva and his followers did translate them. To answer this question we think it is necessary to have recourse to a cultural explanation. Contrarily to Kumārajīva, Burnouf and Kern, notwithstanding their profound and broad (academic) knowledge of Buddhism, did not participate of Buddhist Culture, education and belief; they were unable to grasp the religious resonance that the names of the Bodhisattvas carry with themselves; they did not feel the necessity to make evident the archetypal essence of the *Bodhisattvas* expressed by their names.

Conclusion

Bhikṣus and *Bodhisattvas* constitute two diverse worlds, each one with its own characteristic marks. The *Bhikṣus* belong to a common everyday, natural, concrete human reality; the *Bodhisattvas* belong to an extraordinary, supernatural, ideal, trascendent reality. For a historical scientific approach the *Bhikṣus* are the product of historical facts; the *Bodhisattvas* are the product of the devotees' religious imagination and aspirations. For Buddhist believers both, *Bhikṣus* and *Bodhisattvas*, are truly existent, although belonging each of them to two different levels of existence: the *Bhikṣus*, to human history, and the *Bodhisattvas*, to a spiritual realm, which is beyond that human history, although related in many aspects to it. We could say that the *Bhikṣus* are immersed in the empirical reality, while the *Bodhisattvas* dwell in a meta-empirical dimension.

These essential characteristic marks of *Bhikṣus* and *Bodhisattvas* are manifested in their biographies, in the iconography that represents them, and also in their names. And the attitude assumed by Kumārajīva in his translation into Chinese of the Sanskrit names of both, *Bhikṣus* and *Bodhisattvas*: i.e. the preference shown by him of the *rūḍha* meaning for the proper names of the *Bhikṣus*, and of the *yaugika* meaning for those of the *Bodhisattvas*, reveals on his part his vivid insight into the diversity of the two worlds, of *Bhikṣus* and of *Bodhisattvas*, which is an aspect of the structural differences between the two great periods of Buddhism, Hīnayāna and Mahāyāna.

APPENDIX

A. The Names of the Bhikṣus

In what follows we give the names of the *Bhikṣus* in Sanskrit (as they appear in the First Chapter of the *Lotus Sūtra*), Pāli (P), Chinese (Ch) (as they appear in Kumārajīva's translation of the *Lotus Sūtra*), Tibetan (T) (as they appear in the Tibetan translation of the *Lotus Sūtra)*, and Japanese (J), with some remarks on their connexion with the Indian onomastic tradition.

1. Ājñātakauṇḍinya
   - P Aññāta-Koṇḍañña
   - Ch A-jo-(to)-chiao-ch'ên-ju
   - T Kun-śes-Kauṇḍinya: 'Omniscient-Kauṇḍinya'
   - J Anyakyōjinnyo

Kauṇḍinya was the family name. "jñāta was an epithet added to the name. It means: "(The first) who knew or understood (the *Dharma*)."

Kauṇḍinya was the name of a *gotra* and it was common to *brāhmaṇas* and *kṣatriyas* (Malalasekera I, p. 683), and as such was applied to all the members of this *gotra.* Ājñātakauṇḍinya himself belonged to the *brāhmaṇa* branch of this *gotra.* We know several individuals who owned this name: Kauṇḍinya is the name of a grammarian quoted in *Taittirīya-Prātiśākhya* V, 38, XVIII, 3, XIX, 2; of an author on *Dharmaśāstra* quoted in *Baudhāyanagṛhyasūtra* III, 9, 6 (Kane, Vol. I, Part I, p. 39); of two Hindu kings (belonging to the *brāhmaṇa* caste) of Fou-nan (modern Cambodia) (Coedès, pp. 41, 75, 102 and 110); of a teacher mentioned in the *Bṛhadāraṇyaka-upaniṣad* II, 5, 20 and IV, 5, 26 (Mādhyaṃdina recension = II, 6, 1 and IV, 6, 1 Kāṇva recension); of the author of a commentary entitled *Pañcārthābhaṣya*, on the *Pāśupata-sūtra* (cf. Minoru Hara's review of the edition of this *Sūtra* by Chakroborti). Let us indicate two other teachers belonging to the same *brāhmaṇa gotra*: Kauṇḍinyāyana (*Bṛhadāraṇyaka-upaniṣad* II, 5, 20 and IV, 5, 26 Mādhyaṃdina recension) and

Vidarbhī-Kauṇḍineya (*ibidem* II, 55, 22 and IV, 5, 28 M = II, 6, 3 and IV, 6, 3 K).

2. Aśvajit

P Assaji

Ch —

T Rta-thul: 'Horse-Tamer'

J —

The name Aśvajit is used in the *Riǵ Veda* as an epithet of Indra (II, 21, 1) and of Soma (IX, 59, 1), and in the *Atharva Veda* (V, 3, 11) as an epithet of Indra.

Aśvajit (Assaji) was also the name of one of the leaders of the Assaji-Punabbasukā, a group of six Buddhist monks (*ṣaḍvārgika*, Pāli *chabbigga*) dedicated to evil doings (Malalasekera I, p. 226 and 926).

3. Bāṣpa

P Vappa

Ch —

T Rlaṅs pa: 'Vapour'

J —

He belonged to a *brāhmaṇa* family.

Bāṣpa was also the name of a Śākyan disciple of the Nirgrantha Jñātiputra (the founder of Jainism), and this Bāṣpa is said to have been the Buddha's uncle and a Śākyan *rājā* (Malalasekera II, p. 832).

4. Mahānāman

P Mahānāma

Ch —

T Mi-chen : 'Great-Name'

J —

Mahānāma (n) was born in a *brāhmaṇa* family.

Mahānāma(n) was also the name of several Buddhist monks; of a Śākyan *rājā*; of a Licchavī; of a king of Ceylon (409-431 A.D.) during whose reign Buddhaghosa arrived in Ceylon (Malalasekera II, pp. 514-516); of the author of the commentary entitled *Saddhammappakāsinī* upon the canonical treatise *Paṭisambhidāmagga*, which would have been written at the request of an *upāsaka* also named Mahānāma(n), in the first half of the 6th century A.D.; of the author of the *Mahāvaṃsa* (Norman, p. 132 and pp. 117-118).

5. Bhadrika

P	Bhaddiya
Ch	—
T	Bzaṅ po : 'Good'
J	—

He belonged to a family of the Śākyan *rājās* of Kapilavastu.

Bhadrika was also the name of an *anāgāmī* monk; of a *seṭṭhi*, father of a Buddhist monk; of a Buddhist monk who received the nickname of Lakuṇṭaka (the dwarf); of one of the four chief merchants of Ekarāja, king of Benares; and of a Licchavī, who visited the Buddha at the Kūṭāgārasālā (Malalasekera II, pp. 358-359, 764-766).

6. Mahākāśyapa

P	Mahākassapa
Ch	Mo-ho-chia-yeh
T	'od-sru-chen-po : 'Great Light-Protector'
J	Makakashō

Mahākāśyapa belonged to the ancient well-known *brāhmaṇa gotra*, Kāśyapa by name.

This *gotra* drew its origin from the sage Kāśyapa, who is mentioned once in the *Rig Veda* (IX, 114, 2). The members of this *gotra* bore the name Kāśyapa. To this *gotra* belonged many persons, who are mentioned since the earliest periods of Indian history and/or legend, sages, priests, ascetics, etc. We shall indicate some of them in the Brāhamaṇic tradition as well as in the Buddhist tradition.

Kaśyapa Naidhruvi is the name of a teacher who appears in the *Bṛhadāraṇyaka-upaniṣad* VI, 4, 33 (Mādhyaṃdina recension = VI, 5, 3 Kāṇva recension). The *Vaṃśabrāhmaṇa* II,

22-27, mentions several *ṛṣis* who were called Kāśyapa, as Agnibhū, Indrabhū, Mitrabhū, Vibhaṇḍaka, Ṛṣyaśṛṅga. Kāśyapī-bālākyā-māṭharī-putra appears in the list of teachers of *Bṛhadāraṇyaka-upaniṣad* VI, 4, 31 (Mādhyaṃdina recension). The *Mahābhārata* refers to several sages of the Kaśyapa's race (cf. Sörensen, p. 368 and Mani, p. 398). Kaśyapa was the name of an ancient authority on *Dharma* (cf. Kane, Vol. I, Part 1, pp. 274-276); of an ancient authority on grammar (referred to by Pāṇini, in I, 2, 25 and VIII, 4, 67); of an ancient authority on prosody whose opinion on *rāga* was cited and to whom a good number of verses that had been preserved are attributed (cf. Kane, *History on Sanskrit Poetics*, p. 2); of one of the 18 sages who promulgated the *Jyotiṣśāstra* (cf. Pingree, pp. 1, 72, 78), etc.

Passing to Buddhist tradition we have that Mahākāśyapa was also the name of an eminent monk of Ceylon during the reign of Parakkamabāhu I (Malalasekera II, p. 483); of the author of the commentary entitled *Mohavicchedanī* and of the author of the *ṭīkā Vimativinodanī* (Norman, pp. 147 and 172); of the author of the popular Pāli grammar *Bālāvabodhana* composed in 1200 A.D. (Scharfe, p. 164, note 14); of one of the six Non-Buddhist Teachers Purāṇa Kāśyapa (in Pāli Purāṇa Kassapa); of the monk surnamed Mātaṅga (Chia-she-mo-t'eng), who together with another monk (Dharmaratna) went to China to spread Buddhism at the invitation of Emperor Ming (reigned 58-76 A.D.) (Tsukamoto I, pp. 41 ff.; Bagchi I, pp. 4-5). And of course Uruvilvākāśyapa, Nadīkāśyapa and Gayākāśyapa belonged also to this same *gotra*. And in our time Bhikkhu J. Kashyap has been the General Editor of the Pāli Canon, edited in the Nālandā Devanāgarī-Pāli-Series, which renders so good services to Pāli research.

It is clear that the Tibetan translator has divided the Sanskrit word *Kāśyapa* into *kāśya* and *pa*, and derives *kāśya* from the root *Kāś-*, which means 'to shine, to be brilliant'. From this root comes the word *Kāśi*: 'shining, the sun' (Monier-Williams), 'light, splendour' (Apte). The Tibetan word *ḥod* is used to translate the Sanskrit words *jyotis*, *ābhā*, *ābhāsa*, *tejas* which among their meanings have that of 'light' (Lokesh Chandra). As for *pa*, it comes from the root *PĀ*- and means 'guarding, protecting, ruling'.

7. Uruvilvākaśyapa
   - P Uruvela-Kassapa
   - Ch Yu-lou-p'in-lo-chia-yeh
   - T Lteṅ-(ste)-rgyas-'od-sru: 'Light-Protector from the Great Pond'
   - J Urubinrakashō

8. Nadīkāśyapa
   - P Nadī-Kassapa
   - Ch Na-t'i-chia-yeh
   - T Chu-klu-od-sru : 'Light-Protector from the River'
   - J Nadaikashō

9. Gayākāśyapa
   - P Gayā-Kassapa
   - Ch Ga-yeh-chia-yeh
   - T Gayā-'od-sruṅ: 'Light-Protector from Gayā'
   - J Gayakashō

These names belong to three brothers of the Kāśyapa *brāhmaṇa* family. The first part of their names served to distinguish them from other members of the family.

Uruvilvākāśyapa lived and was ordained at the locality of Uruvilvā on the banks of the Nairañjarā river in the neighbourhood of the *Bodhi* tree at Buddhagayā. Nadikāśyapa is said to have received his name Nadī (river) from living on the bank of the Nairañjarā. And Gayākāśyapa, from living at Gayāśiras, a hill near the town known as Gayā on the road between the *Bodhi* tree and Benares.

10. Śāriputra
   - P Sāriputta
   - Ch Shê-li-fu
   - T Śāri'i-bu : 'Son-of-Śāri'
   - J Sharihotsu

His father and mother were of *brāhmaṇa* origin and the full name of his mother was Rūpaśārī. It was because of his mother's name that he was called Śāriputra: "the son of Śāri". In Sanskrit texts his name occurs as Śāriputra, Śāliputra, Śārisuta, Śāradvatīputra. He was originally named Upatiśya (Pāli: Upatissa).

Śāriputra was also the name of one of the sons of a king Buddhadāsa; of several Buddhist monks: a monk of Ceylon, who lived in the reign of Parakkamabāhu I, a monk of Dala in Burma, who was the author of one of the earliest law codes of Burma, a Choliyan monk (Malalasekera II, pp. 1108-1118); and of the author of a paraphrase of the *Abhidhammatthasaṅgaha* (Norman, p. 151).

The name Śāriputra was created to designate a specific person: the 'son of Śāri', and thus it is natural that it did not exist before the birth of that person and that afterwards it was not appropriate for other persons. This explains its scanty use. This does not happen with the name Upatiśya / Upatissa, the personal name of Śāriputra. Upatiśya / Upatissa was the name of several persons as can be seen in Malalasekera I, pp. 390-392: a *purohita* to Vijaya, king of Ceylon; two kings of Ceylon; a son of Silākāla, a member of the powerful *Lambakaṇṇa gotra* of Ceylon; and also of the author of *Vimuttimagga* (cf. Norman, pp. 113-114); of the author of *Mahābodhivaṃsa* (cf. Norman, pp. 141, 162), etc.

11. Mahāmaudgalyāyana
    - P Mahāmoggallāna
    - Ch Moho-mu-chien-lien
    - T Maud-gal-gyi-bu-chen-po: 'Great Son-of-Maudgal'
    - J Makamokkenren

He was born in Kolitagāma near Rājagṛha and was called Kolita after his village. The name of her mother was Maudgalyāyanī, Pāli Moggallānī (Malalasekera II, pp. 541-547). He belonged to the brahmanical *gotra* Maudgalya.

The Madgalya *gotra* sprung from the *ṛṣi* Mudgala, who is mentioned in a hymn of the Rig *Veda* X, 102. From Mudgala derives the patronimic Maudgalya (which appears in *Śatapathabrāhmaṇa*

XII, 5, 2, 1) and, at its turn, Maudgalyāyana derives from Maudgalya. This name was the name of many persons, who belonged to that *gotra*.

In ancient literature several persons belonging to this *gotra* are named: Nāka Maudgalya (*Bṛhadāraṇyaka-upaniṣad* VI, 4, 4; *Śatapatha-brāhmaṇa* XII, 5, 2, 1; *Taittirīya-upaniṣad* I, 9, 1); Śatabalākṣa (*Nirukta* XI, 6); Lāṅgalāyana Brahman Maudgalya (*Aitareya-brāhmaṇa* V, 3); an authority on *Dharma* quoted in *Baudhāyanadharmasūtra* II, 2, 8.

Moggallāna (in Pāli, equivalent to Maudgalya in Sanskrit) was the name of a king of Ceylon, Moggallāna I, during whose reign the Buddha's Hair-relic was brought to that island; of another king of Ceylon, Moggallāna II, known also as Culla-Moggallāna, who was a poet and who dammed the Kadamba River and constructed three tanks; of a third king of Ceylon, Moggallāna III, who reigned from 511 to 517 and built up some *vihāras*; of an eminent *thera* who participated in the Council of Pulatthipura which took place during the reign of king Parakkamabāhu in 1587; of a son of the Sinhalese princess Lokitā, who married Kāśyapa (Kassapa), who was later to become king Vikkamabāhu I (cf. for the preceding names Malalasekera II, pp. 666-669); of a celebrated grammarian, who wrote a Pāli grammar entitled *Māgadha Saddalakkhaṇa* in the second half of the 16th century (Scharfe, pp. 166, 195), etc.

12. Mahākātyāyana

P	Mahākaccāyana
Ch	Mo-ho-chia-chan-yen
T	Kā-tyā-hi-bu-chen-po : 'Great Son-of-Kātyā'
J	Makakasennen

His father belonged to the brahmanical *gotra* called Kātyāyana.

This *gotra* was issued from the *ṛṣi* Kati. As the name of any *gotra* it was applied to numerous persons. We have thus, in the Hindu tradition, that Kātyāyana was the name of the founder of a ritual school of the *White Yajurveda*, to which belong the *Kātyāyanaśrautasūtra* and the *Kātīyagṛhyasūtra*, better known under the name of *Pāraskaragṛhyasūtra*; of the author of the celebrated *vārttikas* on Pāṇini's grammatical *sūtras* and of the *Vājasaneyi Prātiśākhya* (Scharfe, pp. 129 and 135-148); of the author of a *Dharmaśāstra,* verses of which have been preserved in quotations (Kane, Vol. I, Part 1, pp. 496-507).

In the Buddhist tradition, Kātyāyana / Kaccāyana was the name of the author of the *Kaccāyanavyākaraṇa*, the oldest of the Pāli grammars we have (Scharfe, p. 194); of the author of the *Peṭakopadesa*; of the author of the *Nettippakaraṇa.* For the two last authors, see Norman, pp. 108-110. Many other historical persons bore the name Kātyāyana, as for instance Kakuda Kātyāyana, in Pāli Pakudha Kaccāyana (one of the six famous heretical teachers of Śākyamuni's days) and several monks mentioned by Malalasekera I, p. 476.

13. Aniruddha

P	Aniruddha, Anuruddha
Ch	A-ni-lou t'o
T	Ma-'gags-pa: 'Unobstructed'
J	Anuruda

Aniruddha (or Anuruddha) belonged to a *Śākyan* family. In Mahāyāna texts Anuruddha's name appears as Aniruddha.

Aniruddha or Anuruddha was a common name. The *New Catalogus Catalogorum* I, pp. 197-199, enumerates many authors who owned this name, among whom the principal are: an inscriptional poet under Dharmapālavarmadeva, a King of Assam; a writer on *Dharma*, who assisted Ballālasena, king of Bengal, in the compilation of his *Dānasāgara*; the author of the celebrated commentary on the *Sāṃkhyapravacanasūtra* (cf. Garbe, p. 74), etc.

Aniruddha was the name of the parricide king of Magadha who killed his father Udayabhaddaka; and of several monks (Malalasekera I, pp. 85-91); of a great king of Burma also called Anōratha, who reigned 1044-1077 and converted Burma to Theravāda Buddhism (Coedès, pp. 273-278). The author of the celebrated *Abhidhammatthasaṅgaha*, a manual on *Abhidharma* and of the *Nāmarūpaparicchedа,* a poem containing 1845 verses dealing on *abhidharmic* subjects (Norman, pp. 151-153) was called Anuruddha.

Aniruddha appears also in several compound names of authors with -Jhā, -Dviveda, -Paṇḍita, -Bhaṭṭa, -Bhaṭṭācārya, -Miśra, -Sarasvatī, -Sūri (cf. *New Catalogus Catalogorum* I, pp. 198-199).

14. Revata

P Revata

Ch Li-p'o-to

T Nam-gru : 'The Revatī-Constellation'

J Rihata

Revata was the youngest brother of Śāriputra.

Many persons bore the name Revata: Soreyya Revata, one of the Elders who had a prominent part in the Second Council (Bareau, pp. 39-40); an Elder of Ceylon who was a *Majjhimabhāṇaka*; and another Elder of Ceylon who met and advised the previous one (Malalasekera II, pp. 751-755). Revata was, according to tradition, the name of the monk who met Buddhaghosa and converted him into Buddhism (Law, pp. 2-9, including the text of Dhammakitti's account of Buddhaghosa's life, cf. Andersen, pp. 113-114).

The Tibetan translator has interpreted Revata, *masculine noun* in Sanskrit, as Revatī, femenine noun. Revatī is the name of a constellation in Indian astrology, cf. Kirfel, *Die Kosmographie der Inder,* pp. 138-139, 288-289. The Tibetan name of the Revatī constellation is Nam-gru.

15. Kapphina

P (Mahā) Kappina

Ch Chieh-pin-na

T Kab-pi-na

J Kōhinna

He probably belonged to a *kṣatriya* family. This name is also written Kapphiṇa.

Kapphiṇa is also the name of the king, hero of the *Kāvya Kapphiṇābhyudaya* by Śivasvāmin, edited by Gauri Shankar in the University of the Panjab, 1937.

16. Gavāṃpati

P Gavampati
Ch Ch'iao-fan-po-t'i
T Ba-lan-bdag : 'Lord-of-Cows'
J Kyōbon-hadai

Gavāṃpati was the son of a *seṭṭhi* of Benares.

Gavāṃpati is one of the names of Śiva (*Mahābhārata* XIII, 17, 70, *Śivasahasranāma*, Poona ed.). Under its form *Gopati*, this name appears more frequently. It is a name of Viṣṇu (*Viṣṇusahasranāma* 495 and 592); of a Gandharva; of a demon killed by Kṛṣṇa; of Sūrya; of Varuṇa; of a son of king Śibi (cf. Sörensen, p. 312, Hopkins, pp. 153, 217, Mani, p. 295).

17. Pilindavatsa

P Pilinda
Ch Pi-ling-ch'ie-p'o-ts'uo
T Pi-lin-dai-bu: 'Son-of-Pilinda'
J Hitsuryōgabasha

He was a *brāhmaṇa*. Pilinda was his personal name, Vatsa his family name.

Vatsa is a name frequentely found in the Hindu area. It is the name of a *ṛṣi*, son of Kaṇva mentioned in *Rig Veda* VIII, 8, 8, and of the poet author of the hymm X, 187 of the same *Veda*. *Manusmṛti* VIII, 116 (cf. Kullūka commentary) mentions this same *ṛṣi* Vatsa as submitting himself to the fire-ordeal in order to prove that he was, as he affirmed, of brahmanical origin (Macdonell and Keith II, p. 238). Vatsa is the name of two characters in the *Kathāsaritsāgara:* a *brāhmaṇa* (I, 6, Story of Guṇāḍhya), and an ascetic (VI, 2, Story of Suṣeṇa and Sulocanā). It is also the name of a prince, the son of king Pratardana (*Mahābhārata* XII, 49, 71).

18. Bakkula

P Bakkula, Bākula, Vakkhula
Ch Po-chü-lo
T Ba-kku-la, Bag-ku-la, Ba-ku-la, Bag-kul
J Hakura

His name was interpreted as meaning 'two-families', and derived from the fact that, according to a legend about him, he was held by two families.

Bakula (with one *k*) is the name of a tree; it is also one of the 1000 names of Śiva, *Mahābhārata* (Poona edn.) XIII, 17, 107 (*varia lectio*, in note).

19. Mahākauṣṭhila

P	Mahākoṭṭita
Ch	Mo-ho-chü-ch'ih-lo
T	Gsus-po-che : 'Great Belly'
J	Makakuchira

Mahākauṣṭhila was born in a wealthy *brāhmaṇa* family of Śrāvastī. The name of his father was Āśvalāyana and he gained great proficiency in the *Vedas* (Malalasekera II, pp. 485-487). Very probably Mahākauṣṭhila was a member of a branch of the well-known *Āśvalāyana gotra*.

Many persons belonged to this *gotra*. The most conspicuous member of this family was Āśvalāyana, the founder of a Vedic School, to which belonged two important Vedic texts: *Āśvalāyana-śrautasūtra* and *Āśvalāyana-gṛhyasūtra* (Gonda, *The Ritual Sūtras, Index*).

The Tibetan translator has interpreted *kauṣṭhila* as deriving from *koṣṭha*, 'stomach, belly, abdomen', and consequently has translated Mahākauṣṭhila as Gsus-po-che: 'Great-belly'. Let us remark that Tao-sheng in his commentary of the Sūtra indicates that the equivalent Chinese word for Mahākauṣṭhila is *Ta-hsi*: 'Great Knee' (Young-ho Kim, p. 165). Perhaps Mahākauṣṭhila was only a nick-name of this disciple of the Buddha.

20. Bhāradvāja

P	Bhāradvāja
Ch	—
T	Ba-ra-dhva-tsha
J	—

Bhāradvāja was a *brāhmaṇa* of Rajagṛha, who belonged to the ancient and numerous *Bharadvāja gotra*.

The name Bhāradvāja frequently occurs in Indian tradition. The Sixth Book of the *Rig Veda* was composed, according to tradition, by a *ṛṣi* named Bhāradvāja. Bhāradvāja was the name of the founder of a Vedic School to which were attached a *Śrautasūtra* and a *Gṛhyasūtra* (Gonda, *The Ritual Sūtras, Index*); of a foremost teacher of Political Science, quoted several times by Kauṭilya (Kangle III, p. 46). Bhāradvāja was also the family name of the great Nyāya master Uddyotakara (Matilal, p. 85). Mention is made of a *Bhāradvājavṛtti*, an old commentary on the *Vaiśeṣikasūtra*, that has not come down to us, but is often mentioned by Śaṇkara Miśra in his *Upaskāra* (Faddegon, pp. 34-40 and p. 17); and also of a *Bhāradvājaśīkṣā*, a work on Phonetics (Subhadra Jhā, in Winternitz III, 2, p. 465).

The Pāli Canon mentions several persons bearing the name of Bhāradvāja, living in Rajagṛha, Veṇuvana, Śrāvastī, Kosala, etc. Many of them joined the Buddhist Order as monks or as lay disciples (Malalasekera II, pp. 372-374).

21. Mahānanda or Nanda

P	Nanda
Ch	Nan-t'o
T	Dga-bo : 'Enjoyment'
J	Nanda

Nanda was the half brother of Buddha Śākyamuni.

Nanda has been a common name in India. In the *Mahābhārata* Nanda was the name of a son of Dhṛtarāṣṭra; of a cowherd; of a serpent; of two warriors of Skanda (Sörensen, p. 503). Viṣṇu was also called Nanda (*Viṣṇusahasranāma* 528). Nanda is the name of a dynasty that reigned in Northern India for about 30 years and was overthrown by Chandragupta Maurya in about 322 B.C. (*The History and Culture of the Indian People* II, pp. 31-35).

Many persons in the Buddhist texts bear this name: the disciple of the *brāhmaṇa* ascetic Bāvarī; a cowherd of Kosambī; a herdman living in Śrāvastī; a slave; a *brāhmaṇa* living in Takṣaśilā learned in the *Vedas* etc. (Malalasekera II, pp. 10-17). According to *Mahāvyutpatti* 9471, a monk named Nanda was one of the *ṣaḍvārgika* (Pāli *chabbaggiya*) group of monks, but not so according to Pāli tradition. These monks in Pāli texts were given as examples of trespassing the rules of *Vinaya* (Malalasekera I, p. 926). It does not seem that this *ṣaḍvārgika* Nanda was the same as Mahānanda or Nanda, the half-brother of the Buddha.

In compounds with other words, Nanda occurs in many names of persons, as for instance: Nanda Vatsa was an Ājīvika leader predecessor of Maskarin Gośāla (Pāli Makkhali Gośāla) (Basham, pp. 27-29); Nandagopa was the name of Kṛṣṇa's foster-father, and Nandabhadra, of a religious *vaiśya* (Mani, p. 524); Nanda Paṇḍita in the 16th century is a writer on *Dharma* (Kane, Vol. I, 2, section 110). Nanda Kumar was a Bengali *brāhmaṇa* who had political activity in India during the second half of the 18th century (S. Bhattacharya, pp. 633-634). Cf. *New Catalogus Catalogorum*, Vol. IX, pp. 326-327, and Aufrecht, I, pp. 275-276, for other compound names with Nanda.

22. Upananda

P	Upananda
Ch	—
T	Ñe-dga': 'Near-Joy'
J	—

He was of the *Śākyan* clan. He is mentioned several times in the *Vinaya* as a vicious monk, especially characterized by his greediness. According to *Mahāvyutpatti* 9472, Upananda was also one of the *ṣaḍvārgika* (Pāli: *chabbaggiya*) group of monks, but not so according to Pāli tradition (Malalasekera I, p. 926). In the *Mahābhārata* Upananda is the name of a son of Dhṛtarāṣṭra; of a serpent; and of a warrior of Skanda (Sörensen, p. 692; Mani, p. 808).

Upananda was also the name of a commander-in-chief of the Magadha kingdom, of a Nāga-king, etc. (Malalasekera I, pp. 393-396).

23. Sundarananda

P	Sundarananda, Nanda
Ch	Sun-to-lo-nan-to
T	Mdzes-dga': 'Handsome-Joy'
J	Sondarananda

Sundarananda seems to be another name for Nanda, who was celebrated for his beauty.

24. Pūrṇa Maitrāyanīputra
P Puṇṇa-Mantānīputta
Ch Fu-lou-na-ni-to-lo-ni-tzu
T Byams-ma'i-bu-gan-po: 'Full, Son-of-Maitrī'
J Furuna

Pūrṇa Maitrāyanīputra belonged to a *brāhmaṇa* family of Donavastu near Kapilavastu. He received the name Maitrāyanīputra because of his mother. The *Mahāvastu* III, 380-382 (Senart ed.) contains twenty verses attributed to Pūrṇa Maitrāyanīputra.

In the *Mahābhārata Pūrṇa* occurs as the name of a serpent and of a gandharva (Sörensen, p. 567). It is also one of the thousand names of Viṣṇu (*Viṣṇusahasranāma* 685). Pūrṇaka was the name of the general of the Yakṣas army; of a minister of Vesamuṇu or Kubera, the god of riches and treasures; of the father of Dāḍimuṇḍa, a deity that accompanies Viṣṇu (Haussig (ed.), pp. 631 and 572).

At the Buddha's time the name Pūrṇa belonged to a person born in the family of a householder. Pūrṇa or Pūrṇaka was also the name of a *śreṣṭhin* of Rājagṛha; of a slave; of a naked ascetic; of several disciples of the Buddha; of one of the sixteen disciples of the *brāhmaṇa* ascetic Bāvarī, etc. (Malalasekesa II, pp. 220-224).

Kumārajīva transliterates Pūrṇa and Maitrāyanī and translates *putra* by its Chinese equivalent *tzu.* The Tibetan translator renders Pūrṇa by its Tibetan equivalent *gan-po*: 'full', and Maitrāyanīputra also by its Tibetan equivalent words *Byams-ma:* 'Maitrāyanī', and *bu:* 'son'. *Byams-pa* in Tibetan, like *maitrī* in Sanskrit, means 'love', 'kindness'.

25. Subhūti
P Subhūti
Ch Sü-p'u-t'i
T Rab-'byor :'Welfare'
J Shubodai

Subhūti was the younger brother of Anāthapiṇḍika, a banker of Śrāvastī, famous because of his generosity to the Buddha.

Subhūti was also the name of a character of *Kathāsaritsāgara* (a *brahmāṇa* bandit), XII, 6, p. 186, Patna edn.).

Subhūti in composition with *candra* (Subhūticandra) was the name of a lexicographer (Vogel, p. 314).

26. Rāhula

P Rāhula

Ch Lo-hou-lo

T Sgra-gcan-dzin : 'Eclipse-of-Moon'

J Ragora

Rāhula was the only son of the Buddha Śākyamuni.

Rāhula was also the name of one of the four monks who accompanied Saddharmajyotiṣpāla (generally known as Chapaṭa) on his return from Ceylon to Burma, where he founded the Sīhalasaṅgha (a sect) in Pagan in the twelfth century. Saddharmajyotiṣpāla was the author of several Buddhist works (Norman, pp. 153, 164, 171, and Malalasekera II, pp. 737-740 and 1016). The *Sīmāsaṅkarachedanī*, a work about boundaries between Buddhist communities, is ascribed to an author named Śrī Rāhula, who wrote in the fifteenth century (Norman, p. 172). Rāhula was also the name of a *cakravartin* king (*Mahāvyutpati* 3611). There was a Prakrit lexicographer called Rāhulaka (Vogel, p. 344). In our own days Rāhula is a common Buddhist name, as for instance of the well-known author Walpola Rahula.

The Tibetan translator translated the name Rāhula of the son of the Buddha by *Sgra-gcan-dzin*, which in this case must be taken as meaning 'an eclipse of moon', on account of the tradition that an eclipse of the moon took place at his birth.

27. Ānanda

P Ānanda

Ch A-nan

T Kun-dga' bo: 'Joy'

J Anan

Ānanda was a first cousin of the Buddha and one of his most important disciples.

On the Hindu side many authors have had this name as it can be seen in Aufrecht's *Catalogus Catalogorum* and in the *New Catalogus Catalogorum sub* 'Ānanda', as for instance: the father of the Kashmir Śaiva Ācārya Somānanda; an ancestor of the *Dharma* author Gadādhara; a younger brother of Bilhaṇa, the author of the *Vikramāṅkadevacarita*; a great physician; a *naiyāyika*; several *kavis*; the author of the treatise on Erotics, *Kokamañjarī*, etc.

In the Pāli texts the name Ānanda is also the name of a *kṣatriya* king of Haṃsavatī; of a banker of Śrāvastī; of a *brāhmaṇa* youth, a cousin of the *therī* Uppalavaṇṇā, etc. (Malalasekera I, pp. 249-272). Another of the four monks that accompanied Saddharmajyotiṣpāla (Chapaṭa) on his return from Ceylon to Burma was called Ānanda (see the preceding section on Rāhula). Ānanda was the name of the author of the *Mūlaṭīkā*, a commentary on the *Abhidhammapiṭaka* (Norman, p. 148). This Ānanda probably was the teacher of Culla Dhammapāla, author of the *Saccasaṅkhepa* (Norman, p. 152). Furthermore Ānanda was also the name of a teacher of Buddhappiya, author of several works (Norman, pp. 159, 164, 173). According to its commentary entitled *Saddhammopāyanaviggaha*, the *Saddhammopāyana* has as its author a certain Abhayagiri Kavicakravarti Ānanda Mahāthera (Norman, pp. 159-160). The author of the *Upāsakajanālaṅkāra*, a systematic treatise on the conduct of a layman, is stated in its colophon to be Ānanda, a *sīhalācariya* who lived in the 12th century (Norman, p. 170).

In compound with other words, the name Ānanda is frequently used, as for instance in Ānandagarbha, in Ānandavardhana, both Buddhist authors (Naudou, pp. 124-125, 100 and 103) and in many others, as can be seen in Aufrecht I, pp. 46-49, and *New Catalogus Catalogorum*, pp. 97-119 (as for instance Ānandakanda, Ānandakavi, Ānandagajapati, Ānandagiri, Ānandacaitanya, Ānandatīrtha, etc.). Ānandaśrāvaka is the name of the eighth Jain Tirthaṅkara (Stevenson, p. 276). Ānandapāla was a king of the Hindu Shahiya dynasty of Udbhandapur (Bhattacharya, pp. 44-45).

B. The Names of the Bodhisattvas

In what follows we give the names of the *Bodhisattvas* in Sanskrit (as they appear in the First Chapter of the *Lotus Sūtra*), in Chinese (Ch) (as they appear in Kumārajīva's translation of the *Lotus Sūtra*), in Tibetan (T) (as they appear in the Tibetan translation of the *Lotus Sūtra*), and in Japanese (J).

1. Mañjuśrī: "(Possessing) beautiful (sweet etc.) splendour (glory, auspiciousness etc.)".
   Ch Wên-shu-shih-li
   T Ḥjam-dpal
   J Monjushiri (or Monshushiri)

2. Avalokiteśvara: "Lord gazed upon (i.e. revered by others)".
   Ch Kuan-shi-yin
   T Spyan-ras-gzigs-dbaṅ-phyug: 'Lord seeing with penetrating vision'.
   J Kanzeon

3. Mahāsthāmaprapta: "He who gained a great power".
   Ch Tê-ta-shih
   T Mthu-chen-thob
   J Tokudaisei

4. Sarvārthanāman: "Whose name is 'Benefit of all' " (?).
   Ch —
   T Don-thams-cad-ces-bya-ba
   J —

5. Nityodyukta : 'Always energetic'.
   Ch Ch'ang-ching-chin
   T Rtag-tu-brtson
   J Jōshōjin

6. Anikṣiptadhura: "He who does not reject the burden."
   Ch Pu-hsiu-hsi
   T Brtson-pa-mi-gtoṅ-ba
   J Fukusoku

7. Ratnapāṇi: 'Jeweled hand'.
Ch Pao-chang
T Lag-na-rin-chen
J Hōshō

8. Bhaiṣajyarāja: 'King of medicines'.
Ch Yo-wang
T Sman-gyi-rgyal-po
J Yakuō

9. Bhaiṣajyasamudgata: 'Excellent in medicines'.
Ch —
T Sman-yaṅ-dag-'phags
J —

10. Vyūharāja: 'King of magnificence'.
Ch —
T Bkod-pa'i-rgyal-po
J —

11. Pradānaśūra: 'Hero in donations'.
Ch Yung-shih
T Rab-tu-sbyin-dpa'
J Yuze

12. Ratnacandra: 'Jeweled moon'.
Ch Pao-yüeh
T Dpa'-rin-chen-zla-ba
J Hōgachi

The Tibetan translator adds to this name and the next one the epithet *dpa'*: *śūra, vīra*, perhaps by influence of the preceding name.

13. Ratnaprabha: 'Jeweled glow'.
Ch Yüeh-kuang
T Dpa'-rin-chen-'od
J Gakkō

Kumārajīva has translated *ratna* in this name by the Chinese sign *yüeh* (moon) instead of the sign *pao* (treasure, jewel), which he uses in the case of Ratnapāṇi (7) to translate the same word *ratna*.

14. Pūrṇacandra: ‘Full moon’.
    Ch Man-yüeh
    T Dpa‘-zla-gaṅ
    J Mangachi

15. Mahāvikrāmin: ‘He of great heroism’.
    Ch Ta-pi
    T Gnon-pa-chen-po
    J Dairiki

16. Anantavikrāmin: ‘He of limitless heroism’.
    Ch Wu-liang-li
    T Mtha‘-yas-gnon
    J Muryōriki

17. Trailokyavikrāmin: ‘He who possesses heroism in the Three Worlds’.
    Ch Yüeh-san-chiai
    T Ḥjig-rten-gsum-gnon
    J Ossangai

18. Mahāpratibhāna: ‘He of great eloquence’.
    Ch —
    T Spobs-pa-chen-po
    J —

19. Satatasamitābhiyukta: ‘Always continually diligent’.
    Ch —
    T Rtag-par-rgyun-tu-brtson
    J —

20. Dharaṇīṃdhara: ‘Sustainer of the earth’.
    Ch —
    T Sa-‘dsin
    J —

21. Akṣayamati: 'He whose intelligence is not exhausted'.

Ch	—
T	Blo-gros-mi-zad-pa
J	—

22. Padmaśrī: 'Lotus-glory'.

Ch	—
T	Pad-ma'i-dpial
J	—

23. Nakṣatrarāja: 'Constellations king'.

Ch	—
T	Skar-ma'i-rgyal-po
J	—

24. Maitreya: 'Benevolent'.

Ch	Mi-lê
T	Byams-pa
J	Miroku

25. Siṃha: 'Lion'.

Ch	—
T	Sems-dpa'
J	—

C. Names of the Bodhisattvas Exceptionally Inserted in the Onomastic Indian tradition

Mañjuśrī(1), in the list included in the second part of this *Appendix*), for instance, was the name of the *paṇḍit* who collaborated in the translation of the *Tārāstotra* and the *Karmasaṃkṣepa* and of one of the translators of the *Āryavajracchedikāprajñāpāramitaṭīka* of Kamalaśīla (Naudou, pp. 66 and 89).

The name Mañjuśrī is also used in compounds to form proper names, as Mañjuśrī-varman, translator of Śūra's *Jātakamālā*; Mañjuśrī-sattva, translator who collaborated with Marpa (Naudou, pp.194 and 174); Mañjuśrī-kīrti, author of the commentary *Kīrtimālā* on the *Samādhirājasūtra* (cf. Cüppers, p. 110).

As for *Avalokiteśvara* (2), it is the name of a Buddhist writer to whom are attributed two works: *Kālacakratantrahṛdayavṛtti-Vimalaprabhānāma* and *Tārāpārājikā (New Catalogus Catalogorum* I, p. 424). The first part of the name Avalokiteśvara also appears in the name Avalokita-vrata, the author of a very extensive and detailed *ṭīkā* on Bhāvaviveka's *Prajñāpradīpa* (Ruegg, p. 67) and in the name of a poet mentioned in the *Subhāṣitāvali* of Vallabhadeva (1088): Bhaṭṭāvalokita. Avalokita alone was the name of the *guru* of Vāgbhaṭa, author of the medical treatise *Aśṭaṅgahṛdayasaṃhitā* (Vogel, p. 7).

Maitreya (24) has some connexion with the onomastic tradition of India. It is the name of a brahmanical *gotra* (Macdonell-Keith II, p.180). It appears several times alone or in compound names, as for instance: Maitreya, the founder of the Yogācāra school; Paṇḍit Maitreyanātha, the author of a *ṭīkā* on the *Bhavasaṅkrānti* (Sastri ed., pp. 31-42), attributed to Nāgārjuna; Maitreya(rakṣita), who composed a commentary on the *Dhātupāṭha*, called *Dhātupradīpa* (Vogel, p. 101, note 63).

Siṃha (25) is frequently used as a proper name in Hindu tradition as well as in Buddhist tradition. Let us mention some of the persons that bore that name: an astronomer (Aufrecht I, p. 716 b); a relative of Pṛthvīhara, a feudal land-holder of Kashmir (*Rājataraṅginī* VIII, 957 and 1006); a brother of Simba, who was commander-in-chief of Sussala, a king of Kashmir (*Rājataraṅginī* VIII, 1045); a king of the Gohila dinasty of Mewar (*The History and Culture of the Indian People, The Age of Imperial Kanauj*, p. 108); a *paṇḍit* from Kashmir mentioned in *Annals of Ladakh* (Naudou, p. 45); a general (*senapati*) in Vaiśālī (*Mahāvastu* I, 288); a merchant (*Divyāvadāna*, p. 523, line 22), etc.

Siṃha appears as a member of compound proper names: Siṃhagupta, father of Vāgbhaṭa (Vogel, p. 7); Siṃhatilaka Sūri, a Jaina; Siṃhadatta, a poet (Aufrecht I, p. 716 b); Amarasiṃha, the author of the *Amarakośa*; Siṃharāja, Siṃharatha, Vijayasiṃha, Tilakasiṃha, Udayasiṃha, Thakkanasiṃha, etc., who are historical personages (politicians, warriors, kings, etc.) mentioned in *Rājataraṅginī* (VI, 176; VII, 82; VIII, 184; VIII, 184,

430, 573, 592, 632, 713; VII, 581, 1054, 1299; VIII, 1045); Jayasiṃha, king of Kashmir of the second Lohara ynasty (1128-*circa* 1154); the kings Pañcamasiṃha, Siṃhacandra, Siṃhadeva (Naudou, pp. 58, 202, cf. Tāranātha in Schiefner's translation, p. 158); Jñānasiṃha, another name of Nāropā; Vidyākarasiṃha or Vidyāsiṃha, translator of the *Jātakamālā*; Devasiṃha, who together with Vidyākarasiṃha introduced Dharmakīrti's logic in Kashmir; Devavitsiṃha, master of 'Thon-mi Saṃbhoṭa, the famous envoy of the Tibetan king Sroṅ-bcan-sgam-po who went to India to learn the Indian alphabet in order to adapt it to Tibetan language (Naudou, pp. 147, 194, 43, 45, 61), etc. It is noteworthy to observe that in *Saddharmapuṇḍarīka-sūtra* I, verse 93, and in *Rājataraṅginī* I, 172, the Buddha is called Śākyasiṃha.

It is necessary to remark in relation to the name Siṃha (the more often used among the names of the *Bodhisattvas*) that, more than a proper name, it seems to be an honorific appellative as *śrī, svāmin, ācārya, paṇḍita*, etc. added to the real proper name, in order to extoll the excellence of the owner of the name. It is specially applied to rulers and warriors, whose valour, courage, and prowess it intends to point out. The examples of the use of the name Siṃha belong in general to a later period, as it also happens with Mañjuśrī, Avalokita-īśvara and Maitreya.

REFERENCES

Aufrecht, Th., *Catalogus Catalogorum*, Wiesbaden, F.Steiner, 1962.

Bagchi, P.Ch., *Le Canon Bouddhique en Chine*, Tome 1er, Paris, P. Geuthner, 1927.

Basham, A.L., *History and Doctrines of the Ājīvikas*, London, Luzac & Company Ltd., 1951.

Bhattacharya, S., *A Dictionary of Indian History*, Calcutta, University of Calcutta, 1967.

Bhattacharyya, B., *The Indian Buddhist Iconography, Mainly Based on the Sādhanamālā and Cognate Tāntric Texts of Rituals*, Calcutta, K.L. Mukhopadhyay, 1968.

Buddhism, Art and Faith, edited by W. Zwalf, London, British Museum, 1985.

Burnouf, E., *Le Lotus de la Bonne Loi*, Paris, Maisonneuve, 1973.

Coedès, G., *Les États hindouisés d'Indonchine et d'Indonésie*, Paris, E. de Boccard, 1964.

Cüppers, Ch., *The IXth Chapter of the Samādhirājasūtra*, Stuttgart, F. Steiner, 1990.

Daijō Butten, Vol. IV, Japanese translation of the *Lotus Sūtra* by Nagao, G., and others, Tokyo, 1976.

de la Vallée Poussin, L., "Avalokiteśvara", in *ERE*, 2, pp. 256-261.

—, L., "Mañjuśrī", in *ERE*, 8, pp. 405-406.

De Silva-Vigier, A., *La Vie du Bouddha*, Londres, Phaidon Press, 1955.

Edgerton, F., *Buddhist Hybrid Sanskrit Grammar and Dictionary*, Volume II: *Dictionary*, New Haven, Yale University Press, 1953.

Encyclopaedia of Buddhism, edited by G.P. Malalasekera, Ceylon (Sri Lanka), Government of Ceylon (Sri Lanka), 1961 and ff. up to Vol. VII, Fasc. 1, 2003.

ERE = *Encyclopaedia of Religion and Ethics*, ed. J. Hastings, Edinburgh, T. & T. Clark, 1964.

Faddegon, B., *The Vaiçeṣika-System*, Wiesbaden, M.Sändig, 1969.

Garbe, R., *Die Sâṃkhya-Philosophie*, Leipzig, H.Haessel, 1894.

Gonda, J., *The Ritual Sūtras*, Wiesbaden, O.Harrassowitz, 1977.

—, J., *The Vision of the Vedic Poets*, The Hague, Mouton & Co, 1963.

Hallade, M. and Hinz, H., *Gandharan Art of North India*, New York, Harry N. Abrams, 1968.

Hara, M., Review of *Pāśupata Sūtram with Pañchārtha-Bhāsya of Kauṇḍinya*, by Haripada Chakraborti, Calcutta, Academic Publishers, 1970, in *Indo-Iranian Journal*, XVI, 1, 1974, pp. 57-80.

Haussig, H.W., (ed.) *Götter und Mythen des indischen Subkontinents*, Stuttgart, Klett-Cotta, 1984.

Hopkins, E.W., *Epic Mythology*, Strassburg, Karl J. Trübner, 1915.

Hurvitz, L., *Scripture of the Lotus Blossom of the Fine Dharma (The Lotus Sūtra), trans. from Chinese of Kumārajīva*, New York, Columbia University Press, 1976.

I-Tsing, *A Record of the Buddhist Religion as practised in India and the Malay Archipelago (A.D. 671-695)*, Delhi, Munshiram Manoharlal, 1966.

Iwanami Series, No. 33-304-1, Japanese translation of the *Lotus Sūtra* by Sakamoto Yukio and Iwamoto Yutaka, Tokyo, 1988.

Kane, P.V., *History of Dharmaśāstra*, Vols. I-V, Poona, Bhandarkar Oriental Research Institute, 1968 ff.

—, P.V., *History of Sanskrit Poetics*, Delhi, Motilal Banarsidass, 1961.

Kangle, R.P., *The Kauṭilīya Arthaśāstra, Part III. A Study*, Bombay, University of Bombay, 1965.

Katō, Bunnō, *The Threefold Lotus Sūtra*, Tokyo, Kosei Publishing Co., 1988.

Kern, H., *The Saddharma-puṇḍarīka or The Lotus of the True Law*, Delhi, Motilal Banarsidass, 1968.

Kirfel, W., *Die Kosmographie der Inder*, Darmstadt, Wissenschaftliche Buchgesellschaft, 1967.

—, W., *Symbolik des Buddhismus*, Stuttgart, Hiersemann, 1959.

Kubo, Tsugunari and Yuyama, Akira, *The Lotus Sūtra. The White Lotus of Marvelous Law*, translated from the Chinese of Kumārajīva, Tokyo, The Reiyukai, 1991.

Kunjunni Raja, K., *Indian Theories of Meaning*, Adyar, The Adyar Library and Research Centre, 1969.

Kurita, Isao, *Gandhāran Art*, Tokyo, Ancient Buddhist Art Series, 1988.

Lamotte, É., *Histoire du Bouddhisme Indien. Des Origines à l'ère Śaka*, Louvain, Institut Orientaliste, 1958.

—, "Mañjuśrī", in *T'oung Pao* 48, 1960, pp. 1-96.

Law, B.C., *The Life and Work of Buddhaghosa*, Delhi, Nag Publishers, 1976.

Macdonell, A.A., and Keith, A.B., *Vedic Index of Names and Subjects*, Delhi, Motilal Banarsidass, 1967.

MacQueen, G., "Inspired speech in early Mahāyāna Buddhism I and II", in *Religion*, London, Vol. 11, October 1981, pp. 303-319, and Vol. 12, January 1982, pp. 49-65.

Malalasekera, G.P., *Dictionary of Pāli Proper Names*, London & Company (PTS), 1960.

Mani, Vettam, *Purāṇic Encyclopaedia*, Delhi, Motilal Banarsidass, 1979.

Mochizuki, Shinko, *Bukkyō Dai Jiten*, Tokyo, Sekai Seiten Kankō Kyōkai, 1960-1963.

Murano, Senchu, *The Lotus Sutra, The Sūtra of the Lotus Flower of the Wonderful Dharma*, Tokyo, Nichiren Shu Shimbun Co., 1991.

Naudou, J., *Les Bouddhistes Kaśmīriens au Moyen Age*, Paris, Presses Universitaires de France, 1968.

New Catalogus Catalogorum, ed. V.Raghavan, Madras, University of Madras, 1968 ff.

Norman, K.R., *Pāli Literature*, Wiesbaden, O. Harrassowitz, 1983.

Pingree, D., *Jyotiḥśāstra*, Wiesbaden, O. Harrassowitz, 1981.

PTS = Pali Text Society.

Ruegg, D.S., *The Literature of the Madhyamaka School of Philosophy in India*, Wiesbaden, O. Harrassowitz, 1981.

Sastri, N.A., *Bhavasaṅkrānti Sūtra and Nāgārjuna's Bhavasaṅkrānti Śāstra, with the Commentary of Maitreyanātha*, Adyar (Madras), Adyar Library, 1938.

Scharfe, H., *Grammatical Literature*, Wiesbaden, O.Harrassowitz, 1977.

Schumann, H.W., *Buddhistische Bilderwelt. Ein ikonographisches Handbuch des Mahāyāna- und Tantrayāna-Buddhismus*, Köln, Diederichs, 1986.

Seckel, D., *The Art of Buddhism*, London, Methuen, 1964,

Śivasvāmin, *Kapphiṇābhyudaya*, Lahore, The University of the Panjab, 1937.

Solmsen, F., *Germanische Eigennamen als Spiegel der Kulturgeschichte*, Heidelberg, C. Winter, 1922.

Soothill, W.E. and Hodous, L., *A Dictionary of Chinese Buddhist Terms*, Taipei, Ch'eng Wen Publishing Company, 1972.

Sörensen, S., *An Index to the Names in the Mahābhārata*, Delhi, Motilal Banarsidass, 1963.

Stevenson, S., *The Heart of Jainism*, London, Oxford University Press, 1915.

Tao-sheng, see Young-ho Kim.

The History and Culture of the Indian People. The Age of Imperial Unity, Vol. II, Bombay, Bharatiya Vidya Bhavan, 1960.

The Sacred Art of Tibet, ed. M.M. Rhie, R.A.F. Thurman, London, Thames and Hudson, 1991.

The Way of the Buddha, Delhi, Publications Division, Ministry of Information and Broadcasting, Government of India, 2500 B.E. (= 1956).

Tsukamoto, Zenryū, *A History of Early Chinese Buddhism*, Vol. 1, Tokyo, Kodansha, 1985.

Ui, Hakuju, "Maitreya as an Historical Personage", in *Indian Studies in Honor of Charles Rockwell Lanman*, Cambridge Mass., Harvard University Press, 1929.

Viṣṇusahasranāma, ed. R.A. Sastry, Adyar (Madras), The Adyar Library and Research Centre, 1980.

Vogel, C., *Indian Lexicography*, Wiesbaden, O. Harrassowitz, 1979.

Winternitz, M., *History of Indian Literature*, Vol. III, Part II (*Scientific Literature*), Delhi, Motilal Banarsidass, 1967.

Young-ho Kim, *A Study and Translation, Tao-sheng's Commentary on the Lotus Sūtra*, Albany, State University of New York Press, 1990.

X

Buddhist Spirituality: Positiveness in the *Lotus Sūtra*

His Holiness Pope John Paul II, in his recent book *Varcare la soglia della Speranza*,[1] considers (I) that Buddhism is only a negative soteriology; (II) that the Buddha's Enlightenment is nothing else than the conviction of the world being evil and a source of suffering; (III) that, for Buddhism, the way to free oneself from suffering, i.e., from the evil that has its origin in the world, is detachment from the world and, as an effect of detachment, indifference in regard to the world; (IV) that of course Buddhism cannot admit that Liberation comes from God, who represents the good, since Buddhism does not accept the existence of God; (V) that salvation, *Nirvāṇa*, is nothing else than indifference to the world, and (VI) that this is the culmination of the spiritual process.

On reading this text I had the idea to study whether the Lotus Sūtra teaches a negative soteriology or not. This study led me to examine the other assertions contained in the text. This have I done with due respect for the author of the book, without any polemical intention, and only with the desire to clarify the issues raised by the text I am commenting. I think these assertions are worthy to be elucidated by persons who study Buddhism, and especially by those who consider it not only as a collection of texts with a mere linguistic interest, but also as a treasure of thought and feeling, that has guided the life of many millions of human beings during many centuries, that has produced marvelous works of intelligence and beauty, that has propounded a way of life that inspires admiration and respect, and that presents as its founder a man of extraordinary personality.

---

[1] Milano: Arnoldo Mondadori Editore, 1994 (Spanish edition: *Cruzando el umbral de la Esperanza*, Barcelona: Plaza y Janés Editores, 1994, p. 100).

1. Is Buddhism a negative soteriology?

1. This question should be approached from two points of view: from the point of view of Early and 'Hīnayāna' Buddhism, the first stage in the history of Buddhism, and from the point of view of Mahāyāna Buddhism, its last stage.

2. Early and 'Hīnayāna' Buddhism on one side preached a kind of moral conduct in this life, which emphasized non-violence, compassion, peace and personal development, and on the other side offered *Nirvāṇa* / *Nibbāna*, 'extinction of existence' - existence always conceived under the form of reincarnations - as the supreme goal, to whose attainment all human efforts should be directed. This message had a broad range of acceptance and a powerful attraction; it was accepted by millions of persons who converted to it and have lived with this faith for many centuries until our days, in India where it originated, and in Sri Laṅka and in South East Asia where it was propagated. Considering its great acceptance, it is difficult to admit that the Buddhist message of Early and Hīnayāna Buddhism was felt as something negative. *Prima facie* we must think that it was not taken for a negative message.

To appreciate in a correct way the attraction that *Nirvāṇa* conceived as extinction could offer to Indians, it is necessary to see it from the perspective of Indian culture, which believed that man is enchained to an eternal and painful transmigration. To get free from it was something to be desired as it was the only way to put an end to recurrent pain and suffering. Any teaching which offered a path for deliverance from transmigration, as the Buddhist did, could be looked upon as something positive, to be well received and adhered to. The exalting terms applied to *Nirvāṇa* like *śānti* / *sānti* (tranquillity), *śiva* / *siva* (auspiciousness), *sukha* (happiness),[2] and the *Theragāthās* and *Therīgāthās*, where monks and nuns express

[2] Cf. P. Oltramare, *L'Histoire des idées théosophiques dans l'Inde, La Théosophie bouddhique*, Paris: P. Geuthner, 1923, pp. 450-453.

their joy because they are certain that they are ready for entering *Nirvāṇa*, give us an idea of the positive feeling that the notion of *Nirvāṇa* awoke in them.

3. Mahāyāna Buddhism preached also a noble ethic message, in which compassion occupied the central place. Supreme Perfect Enlightenment was the great goal it offered. With Mahāyāna, Buddhism was transformed from a religion aiming at *Nirvāṇa* into a religion aiming at Enlightenment.

Buddhism in its Mahāyānist form from India reached China, Tibet, Mongolia, Korea, Japan and in these regions, as it had happened in Sri Lanka and South East Asia, Buddhism was also accepted by millions of persons who converted to it and have maintained their Buddhist faith for many centuries until now. The great acceptance Buddhism enjoyed in these regions is also proved by the great number of translations of Buddhist texts done in China and Tibet during several centuries and the huge amount of manuscripts and printed copies of these texts and of their translations that have been found there. Thus we must think *prima facie* here also that the spread of Mahāyāna Buddhism in North Asia can only be explained if we accept that it was not considered as a negative message.

4. We shall examine a Mahāyānist text, which was and is very much appreciated in Buddhist countries and which is the object of great veneration by Buddhist people, in order to find whether its salvific message is to be described either as negative or as positive and capable by its nature of attracting the adherence of people to which it is transmitted. This text is the *Lotus Sūtra* (*Saddharmapuṇḍarīkasūtra*) as edited by Kern-Nanjio, and which has been translated into several Asian and Western languages ancient and modern.

5. The *Lotus Sūtra* preaches a generous universalistic message. All people will reach Supreme Perfect Enlightenment (*anuttarasamyak-saṃbodhi*), the highest form of Intelligence, Knowledge, Consciousness; every person will thus become a *Buddha*, will be omniscient, will obtain the supreme degree of

spiritual development. This destiny is open to everybody. In the *Lotus Sūtra*, the Buddha predicts the Supreme Perfect Enlightenment to His old disciples who adhered to the overcome forms of Buddhism, to millions of new disciples, to women and even to Devadatta, who attempted against His life.

To attain this goal is not an easy task.[3] To obtain the Supreme Perfect Enlightenment one has to become a *Bodhisattva*, "a being who aspires to Enlightenment", and as such has to submit himself to a strict discipline. This discipline is called *Bodhisattvacaryā*: "Bodhisattvas' course of conduct". If one decides to follow this course of conduct, one must first of all take the vow (*praṇidhāna*) to attain Enlightenment, making it the sole aim of all his efforts, of all his wishes, of all his actions. Consequently one must realize in himself the *Pāramitās* or Perfections of several moral virtues, carrying them to their supreme degree; one must respectfully serve the Buddhas he encounters and hear their Teachings; one must plant roots of merit (*kuśalamūla*); one must study and master the Doctrine (*Dharma*). A human existence is not enough to attain the lofty goal of the Supreme Perfect Enlightenment; innumerable reincarnations, innumerable lives are necessary to progress in the *Bodhisattvas'* course of action and to get nearer to the desired aim, accumulating moral merits and knowledge. If man perseveres and exerts himself with unfailing constancy, after an infinitely long chain of reincarnations he will get the experience of the Supreme Perfect Enlightenment.

Once he attains the Supreme Perfect Enlightenment, the *Bodhisattva* becomes a *Buddha*, a *Tathāgata*. He will exist in a Buddha-world. All the Buddha-worlds are magnificent

---

[3] Basic texts on the *Bodhisattvacaryā* are Śāntideva's *Bodhicaryāvatāra* and Asaṅga's *Bodhisattvabhūmi*. Cf. Har Dayal, *The Bodhisattva Doctrine in Buddhist Sanskrit Literature*, Delhi: Motilal Banarsidass, 1975; L. de la Vallée Poussin, 'Bodhisattva', in J. Hastings (Editor), *Encyclopaedia of Religion and Ethics*, Edinburgh: T. and T. Clark, 1964, Vol. II, pp. 739-753; A.G.S.K., 'Bodhisattva', in G.P. Malalasekera (Editor), *Encyclopaedia of Buddhism*, Vol. III, Fascicle 2, Ceylon: Government Press, 1972, pp. 224-233.

paradises, with level ground, full of flowers, jewels, gold; all in them is beauty, happiness, glory. Nothing in these worlds is ugly or disagreeable or painful. The new *Tathāgata* in his Buddha-world will be accompanied by millions of *Bodhisattvas* and Disciples, who will venerate him, follow him, hear his teachings. And during infinite millions of years, being in full possession of the most excellent virtues and qualities, he will preach the Doctrine to innumerable communities of beings, leading them towards Enlightenment.[4]

After an infinite existence of bliss, during which he deploys an intense compassionate activity, on the moment he chooses, with full consciousness and freedom, the *Tathāgata* will enter into *Nirvāṇa*, will extinguish himself.[5]

It is not being just with Buddhism to affirm that this message is a negative one. On the contrary it could be thought that few religious Masters discovered and offered to their followers a more magnificent destiny, more in harmony with deep human aspirations.

6. In accordance with the *positiveness* of its message, the world of the *Lotus Sūtra* is not gloomy at all. On the contrary, in general, it is full of light, color and beauty. Let us mention for instance:

- the miracles of the rays of light emitted from Śhākyamuni's and Candrasūryapradīpa's foreheads, which illuminate the whole universe and reveal all that exists in them (Chapter I, p. 6, line 6, and *passim* for Śākyamuni, and p. 20, lines 8-9, and *passim* for Candrasūryapradīpa. See also Chapter VII, p. 263, line 5-p. 264, line 2);

---

[4] On the Buddha-worlds see next paragraph 6; on the existence of a *Tathāgata* in a Buddha-world see the story of Candrasūryapradīpa in Chapter I of the *Lotus Sūtra*.

[5] The entrance in the *nirvāṇadhātu* of the *Tathāgata* is always very briefly described. Candrasūryapradīpa's *parinirvāṇa* is referred to in two lines: *atha khalvajita sa bhagavāṃś Candrasūryapradīpas tathāgato 'rhan samyaksaṃbuddhas tasyām eva rātryāṃ madhyame yāme 'nupad hiśeṣe nirvāṇadhātau parinirvṛtaḥ* (I, p. 21, lines 15-16).

- the marvelous and colorful Buddha-worlds (as for instance Chapter III, p. 65, lines 8-11, the Buddha-world Viraja, 'Pure'; Chapter VIII, p. 202, line 1-p. 203, line 2, the Buddha-world Suviśuddha, 'Completely Purified');

- the divine flowers that rain form the space (as for instance Chapter I, p. 5, line 11-p. 6, line 1; p. 20, lines 1-3);

- the millions of lotuses that are offered to the Buddha by the *Bodhisattva* Gadgadasvara with golden stalks and silver leaves and splendorous colors (Chapter XXIII, p. 426, lines 11-12);

- the rich thrones of the Buddhas (as for instance Chapter XI, p. 245, lines 3-5);

- the lavishly decorated *stūpas* or 'funeral monuments' and *vihāras* or 'monasteries' (as for instance Chapter I, verse 38 and verses 44-47; Chapter XI, p. 239, line 1-p. 240, line 4, the *stūpa* of Prabhūtaratna);

- the valuable jewels offered as a mark of respect and veneration (as for instance Chapter XI, p. 264, lines 14-16; Chapter XXIII, p. 428, line 12-p. 429, line 1);

- the embellishing canopies and garlands, bells, banners, etc. (as for instance Chapter I, verse 17; Chapter XI, p. 239, line 1-p. 240 line 2; p. 243, lines 3-7; Chapter XX, p. 390, lines 1-10);

- the profusion of precious stones mentioned *passim* (as for instance Chapter XI, pp. 239-240);

- the delicious perfumes and incenses (as for instance Chapter XI, p. 260, line 3);

- the splendent carriages of the Gods (Chapter VII *passim*).

All this contributes to the splendour of the scenery in which the preaching of Lord Buddha takes place.

7. In the *Sūtra* predominate the positive feelings of optimism and happiness, the desire to collaborate and help, the *positive* attitudes:

- the *Bodhisattvas* and Disciples contemplate the Buddha in meditation or predicting the Supreme Perfect Enlightenment to his followers, with veneration, with eyes fixed on their Master, blooming with admiration and joy (Chapter I, p. 6, lines 2-5);

- the *Bodhisattvas*, whom the ray of light emitted by

Śhākyamuni shows in the infinite number of universes, eagerly practice the virtues prescribed by the Buddhist Discipline (Chapter I, verses 13-40);

- Śāriputra (Chapter III, p. 60), Subhūti, Mahākātyāyana, Mahākāśyapa, Mahāmaudgalyāyana (Chapter IV, p. 100), Pūrṇa (Chapter VIII, p. 199), Great Disciples of the Buddha manifest their joy and admiration after hearing the Buddha's message;

- all the *Bodhisattvas* and Disciples that gather in the Assembly, after hearing the Buddha's words, are sure that they will attain the supreme goal of Enlightenment, they are sure that this is their preeminent and auspicious destiny. They cannot doubt, since the Buddha has declared that all human beings will become *Buddhas* (Chapter I, verse 82; Chapter II, verse 145) and has predicted to many of his Disciples, in an individual way, their future Enlightenment (as for instance Chapter III, p. 65: Śariputra; Chapter VI: Kāśyapa and other Great Disciples; Chapter VIII, p. 201: Pūrṇa; Chapter X, p. 224: all who revere the *Lotus Sūtra* ;

- monks, Disciples, *Bodhisattvas* express their decision to preach the *Lotus Sūtra* overcoming all the difficulties they may face (Chapter XII, pp. 267-268; Chapter XIV, p. 297);

- the *Bodhisattvas*, the Great Kings Vaiśravaṇa and Virūḍhaka and even the Rākṣasīs or 'female demons' grant *dhāraṇīs* to the Preachers of the *Dharma* for their protection and guard (Chapter XXI);

- the *Bodhisattvas* express that they are ready to patiently tolerate insults, affronts, abuses, attacks from the ignorant and from the false monks and heretics, while preaching the *Lotus Sūtra* (as for instance Chapter XII, verses 2-21);

- Gods, *Bodhisattvas*, Disciples, deliver hymns of praise in honour of the Buddhas, eulogies referring to their virtues, powers, accomplishments, teachings (as for instance Chapter VII *passim*).

8. The great majority of the names of the *Buddhas* and the *Bodhisattvas*, of the *Buddha-worlds*, of their *kalpas* or 'cosmic periods' of duration are brilliant epithet-like names similar to those that are so frequent in the Indian epics, in the Homeric

poems, in Milton's *Paradise Lost.* Many of these names express that their possessor is preeminent in some particular Buddhist virtue or praiseworthy quality, like Nityodyukta, Pradānaśura, Mahāsthāmaprāpta, Mahāpratibhāna. Some of them are laudatory names, whose function is merely to extol and glorify the personality of the bearer of the name in a metaphorical way, like Candrasūryapradīpa, Nakṣatrarāja, Ratnacandra, Ratnaprabha, Padmaśrī. These names constitute also a positive element of the *Sūtra.*[6]

9. In the *Sūtra* are found a good number of stories that could be considered as parables. A common trait of them all is that they have a 'happy end'. The old father saves his sons from the burning house (Chapter III); the physician restores to health his sons that are ill (Chapter XV); the rich father recovers the son that had abandoned the paternal house (Chapter IV); the leader of the caravan, overcoming the dangers of the forest, saves the merchants and guides them to success (Chapter VII); the blind man gets his vision restored and can enjoy looking at the diversity of the world (Chapter V).

10. Another element, which enhances the impression of *positiveness* created by the already mentioned elements, is the imposing grandeur of the reality where occurs all that is referred to or is described in the *Lotus Sūtra*: a reality composed of an infinite number of worlds, located in an infinite space, inhabited by numberless millions of beings,[7] and which has had no beginning in time (*anādi*). (Cf. for instance Chapter XV, p. 317, lines 5-9).

11. The assemblies that surround Śhākyamuni partake of this imposing grandeur. They are composed of innumerable beings, Gods, human beings, *Bodhisattvas*, Disciples,

---

[6] Cf. F. Tola and C. Dragonetti, "On the names of Bhikṣus and Bodhisattvas in the *Lotus Sūtra*", in *Hokke Bunka Kenkyu* N° 24, March 1998, pp. 95-123, included in this book.

[7] The conception of reality of the *Lotus Sūtra* is the standard Buddhist conception. See F. Tola and C. Dragonetti, "Buddhist Conception of Reality", in *Journal of the Indian Council of Philosophical Research,* Vol. XIV, N° 1, 1996, pp. 35-64.

extraordinary non human beings as *yakṣas*, *gandharvas*, *asuras*, etc., united and identified in their veneration and admiration for the Buddha, which they express by their attitudes and gestures (for instance Chapter I, pp. 1-6; Chapter XI *passim*).

The nature of the message of the *Lotus Sūtra*, the reality where it was delivered and the form how it was delivered make it difficult to declare that it is a *negative* salvific message.

2. Is Enlightenment only the conviction that the world is evil and a source of suffering?

Enlightenment (*bodhi*) according to Buddhism is an extraordinary experience, beyond speech and reason, where verbalization and conceptualization have no entrance, and where it is believed that one attains a *sui generis* knowledge, that cannot be attained in another different situation. After the experience has ceased, the person, who had that experience, is able, resorting to a verbalizing and conceptualizing process, to inform about the knowledge he has obtained.

It can be said that the knowledge, reached at in the course of the Buddhist Enlightenment experience, is a knowledge that, even before the experience, one *already* possessed, and that one had obtained thanks to personal reflexion or reasoning, thanks to tradition or thanks to the teachings of some Master. Anyhow, the Enlightenment experience confirms, in the enlightened person, the knowledge he already possessed. This remark is also valid for the Enlightenment in any other religion.

1. First of all let us say that to attain Enlightenment (*bodhi*) according to Buddhism is not an easy task. To attain it requires the firm decision to dedicate all one's efforts and energy to that purpose. And this exertion must be maintained during an infinite number of reincarnations. In each one of them one has to acquire, practice and lead to perfection many virtues, venerate innumerable *Buddhas*, hear their preaching and follow their example; one has also to submit to a strict intellectual discipline in order to acquire the Buddhist teachings, centered around the

knowledge of the true nature of reality, and one must master the meditation technic systematized by Yoga. Thus one prepares oneself to the Enlightenment experience.

The Buddha prepared Himself for such an experience and, in a memorable night, according to the whole of the Buddhist traditions, expressed in numerous texts, He obtained the *bodhi.*

2. Which knowledge did the Buddha obtain in His *bodhi* experience? He perceived the Four Noble Truths (cf. *Saṃyutta Nikāya* V (for the Pāli texts I quote the PTS edition], p. 420 (*Dhammacakkappavattanasutta*): 1. the Noble Truth about Suffering (*dukkha*), 2. the Noble Truth about its Origin (*dukkha-samudaya*), 3. the Noble Truth about its Cessation (*dukkha-nirodha*), and 4. the Noble Truth about the Eightfold Path that leads to Cessation (*aṭṭhaṅgikā dukkha-nirodhagāminī paṭipadā*). Each of these Four Noble Truths covers a very complex set of truths, principles, laws, norms, rules, etc.[8] The totality of the truths, etc., that constitute each of these sets, is nothing else than the Buddha's Doctrine.

The Buddha perceived the Doctrine of the Four Noble Truths *tota et simul* in its complete fullness and astonishing richness. The Masters that came after Him in the following centuries gradually unfolded, unveiled, disclosed all the contents of the Buddha supreme intuition.

3. The First Noble Truth asserts that man is subject to suffering, which adopts manifold forms: birth, old age, sickness, death, to be together with what one dislikes (*appiya*), to be separated from what one likes (*piya*), not to get what one wants – all this are human experiences imposed on us by our human nature and all this is cause of suffering. The words *piya* and *appiya* cover persons, things, ways of life, experiences, etc. that one cherishes or that one abhors, that produce positive feelings or that produce negative feelings, the bright or the

[8] See É. Lamotte, *Histoire du Bouddhisme Indien, Des origines à l'Ère Śaka,* Louvain: Institut Orientaliste, 1958, pp. 29-52, where he briefly explains "*le sens et la portée de ces quatre vérités*".

dark aspects of life. All these forms of suffering are *dhammas / dharmas* (factors, elements, constituents of existence) or *saṅkhāras / saṃskāras* (aggregates of *dharmas*). And *dhammas / dharmas* and *saṅkhāras / saṃskāras* – all things – are impermanent (*anicca / anitya*), painful (*dukkha / du'kha*) and without an own self (*anatta / anātman*). See *Majjhima-Nikāya* I, p. 435 (*Mahāmāluṅkyasutta*); *Dhammapāda* 277-279; *Aṅguttara Nikāya* I, p. 286 (*Uppādāsutta*); *Saṃyutta Nikāya* III, p. 21 (*Aniccasutta, Dukkhasutta* and *Anattasutta*), pp. 66-68 (*Anattalakkhaṇasutta*), etc. Suffering is inherent in every thing that compose our reality; it is a part of its nature.

4. The Second Noble Truth points out the cause of suffering: desire (*taṇhā*). The principle that underlies this assertion is that everything that exists has a cause (*imasmiṃ sati idaṃ hoti imass' uppādā idam uppajjati*) (*Udāna*, p. 1). A strict determinism reigns in our reality; nothing is left to chance or hazard; nothing can be produced if the adequate causes are not present. Upon this principle are built the great philosophical Buddhist systems: the *śūnyatā* or Voidness or lack of an own being Philosophy and the *vijñānavāda* or Idealistic Philosophy; this principle is the foundation of the negation of substance and the proclamation of phenomenalism that characterize Buddhism. Suffering as anything else has a cause. Its production is the effect of a chain of causes, the *paṭiccasamuppāda* / *pratītyasamutpāda.* See *Dīgha Nikāya* II, p. 55 ff. (*Mahānidānasuttanta*); *Saṃyutta Nikāya* II, p. 1 ff. (*Paṭiccasamuppādasutta*), and p. 2 ff. (*Vibhaṅgasutta*); *Udāna*, pp. 1-3; *Lalita Vistara*, Chapter XXII; *Śālistambasūtra.*

5. The Third Noble Truth deals with the end of *desire*, the elimination of *suffering*, the cessation of *reincarnations*, the suppression of *existence*, since existence is possible only under the form of reincarnations. The state in which all these facts are given is called *nibbāna / nirvāṇa, nibbuti / nirvṛtti*, whose basic meaning is extinction. Cf. *Majjhima Nikāya* I, p. 436 (*Mahāmāluṅkyasutta*) (*sabbasaṅkhārasamatho sabbūpadhi-*

paṭinissaggo taṇhākkhayo virāgo nirodho nibbānan ti = *Mahāniddesa*, p. 20, line 11; *Mahāvagga*, p. 5, lines 2-4 (*Brahmayācanakathā*); *Saṃyutta Nikāya* I, p. 88, verse 210 (*Saññojanasutta*) (*taṇhāya vippahānena nibbānam iti vuccati ti*); II, p. 117, §§ 26-27 (*Kosambisutta*) (*bhavanirodho nibbānaṃ ti*), p. 278 (*nibbānaṃ ... sabbadukkhappamocanam*); III, p. 190, § 15 (*Sattasutta*) (*taṇhākkhayo hi Rādha nibbānam ti*); *Aṅguttara Nikāya* V, p. 9, § 3 (*Sāriputtasutta*) (*bhavanirodho nibbānaṃ bhavanirodho nibbānam*); *Udāna* III, 10 (*bhavataṇhā pahīyati vibhavataṇhā abhinandati / sabbato taṇhānaṃ khayā asesavirāganirodho nibbānaṃ / tassa nibbutassa bhikkhuno anupādā punabbhavo na hoti /*); VIII, 1 (*atthi bhikkhave tad āyatanaṃ, etc.*) and 3 (*atthi bhikkhave ajātam, etc.*); and also P. Oltramare, *op. cit.*, pp. 441-460. In the preceding section on Buddhist soteriology paragraphs 2 and 5 we have referred to *Nirvāṇa* and its *positiveness.*

Nibbāna / nirvāṇa is an Absolute. It does not belong to our empirical reality, it is something completely different from all that exists in this reality, it is transcendent and heterogeneous, beyond words and reason. Cf. the celebrated *Udāna* VIII, 1-4.

6. The Fourth Noble Truth is the Eightfold Path that leads to suppression of suffering. It is a moral Path. It establishes the rules that must guide the actions of the persons that wish to get rid of suffering. The Eightfold Path is constituted by right views (*sammādiṭṭhi*), right intentions (*sammāsaṅkappa*), right speech (*sammāvācā*), right action (*sammā-kammanta*), right living (*sammājīva*), right effort (*sammāvāyāma*), right mindfulness (*sammāsati*) and right mental concentration (*sammāsamādhi*). Many texts of Hīnayānist and Mahāyānist inspiration contain numerous norms on moral conduct that make more explicit the items of the Noble Eightfold Path. As examples of these texts we mention *Dīgha Nikāya* I, 1 (*Brahmajālasutta*), §§ 7-27; XXXI (*Siṅgālovādasuttanta*), *Dhammapāda*, *Udāna*, *Jātakas* of Hīnayānist inspiration, and *Ratnāvalī*, *Suhṛllekha*, *Sūtra-samuccaya*, *Bodhisattvacaryā* of Śāntideva, *Bodhisattvabhūmi*

and *Śrāvakabhūmi* of Asaṅga, etc. of Mahāyānist inspiration. On the basis of these texts it is possible to construct a Buddhist moral system characterized as a lofty, complete, subtle set of moral rules.[9]

7. The *Lotus Sūtra* in its Second Chapter refers to what the Buddhas have attained in their Enlightenment experience: the Supreme Knowledge, Omniscience.

The Chapter starts expressing that the knowledge (*jñāna*) of the *Buddhas* is profound, difficult to be understood, difficult to be comprehended, difficult to be conceived by anybody except the *Tathāgatas* (p. 29, lines 2-3); it is immeasurable (verse 11). Even if all the most intelligent Disciples, if all the *Śrāvakas*, *Pratyekabuddhas* and *Bodhisattvas* came together and reflected on the Buddha's Knowledge, they could not comprehend that knowledge (verse 9).

The *Buddhas* have been able to get that knowledge because they have revered many millions of *Buddhas*, because they have followed the true Buddhist course of life under the discipline of many millions of *Buddhas* during many millions of Cosmic Periods, because they have advanced from afar

---

[9] On Buddhist Ethics see: A.G.S.K., 'Bodhisattva', cf. note 3; M. Anesaki, 'Ethics and Morality (Buddhist)', in J. Hastings (Editor), *Encyclopaedia of Religion and Ethics*, Vol. V, pp. 447-455; L. de la Vallée Poussin, 'Bodhisattva', cf. note 3; R. Spence Hardy, *Manual of Buddhism in its Modern Development*, Varanasi: Chowkhamba, 1967, Chapter 10, reprint of the edition of London, 1853. This work was praisefully commented by A. Weber, *Indische Streifen*, Osnabrück: Biblio Verlag, 1983, reprint of the edition of 1869, volume II, pp. 188-190; É. Lamotte, *op. cit.*, pp. 73-82; H. Oldenberg, *Buddha, Sein Leben, Seine Lehre, Seine Gemeinde, Herausgegeben von Helmuth von Glasenapp*, München: Wilhelm Goldmann Verlag, 1961, pp. 267-306; Bhikkhu Pāsādika, "Early Mahāyāna Lay Ethics in Nāgārjuna", in *The Tibet Journal*, Vol. XXI, N° 1, 1996, pp. 3-18; H. Saddhatissa, *Buddhist Ethics, Essence of Buddhism*, London: G. Allen and Unwin, 1970; L. de la Vallee Poussin, *La morale bouddhique*, Paris: Nouvelle Librairie Nationale, 1927; and F. Tola and C. Dragonetti, "El Budismo frente a la justificaciól©n de la violencia en la India Antigua", in *Pensamiento* (Madrid), Vol. 55, N° 211, 1999, pp. 105-126, "Buddhism and Justification of Violence", in *Hokke Bunka Kenkyū*, No. 27, Tokyo, Marzo 2001, pp. 63-100.

towards the Supreme Perfect Enlightenment, displaying energy, possessed of admirable, wonderful qualities, possessed of qualities difficult to be conceived (p. 29, lines 4-6). Thanks to their effort, energy, constancy during many millions of reincarnations they have succeeded, and they have attained the knowledge that is proper of the *Buddhas* and only of them and of nobody else.

This *Buddha* knowledge is the knowledge of Laws (*dharma*) difficult to be understood (*durvijñeya*, p. 29, line 6), Laws that have their causes in themselves (*svapratyaya*, p. 29, line 8). These laws are profound and subtle, they are beyond reasoning (*atārkika*, verse 18). And these Laws constitute the Doctrine of the *Buddhas* (p. 30, lines 2-3, verse 15). Among these Laws the *Sūtra* mentions the Four Noble Truths (p. 17, line 13, p. 18, line 11, p. 80, line 6); the Dependent Origination (p. 17, line 14, p. 18, line 11, p. 179, line 4, p. 376, line 6); the moral retribution of actions (*karman*) (p. 9, verse 6, p. 354, line 9); Voidness (p. 101, line 1, p. 117, verse 45 a-b, p. 136, line 13- p. 137, line 2, p. 138, verse 51, p. 139, verse 53 a-b, p. 142, verses 75-77, pp. 142-143, verses 79-83, p. 234, line 10, p. 236, verse 24 c-d, p. 262, line 2), etc.

According to what has been expressed in the previous lines Enlightenment is something *hard to attain*, it grants *knowledge* and that *knowledge is knowledge of something much more precious and rich* than the mere conviction that our world is bad and a source of suffering.

Is the world really evil, and a source of suffering?

1. The Buddha declares that the world is evil and a source of suffering and he points out the reasons for this affirmation.

In the *Dhammacakkappavattanasutta* (*Saṃyutta Nikāya* V, p. 420 ff., and *Vinaya* I, *Mahāvagga*, p. 10), his first sermon, he affirms that man is submitted to suffering. See in the preceding section on Enlightenment the paragraph 3.

2. It is also necessary to have in mind that, according to Buddhism, man is dominated by three *kilesas* / *kleśas* (moral

impurities): *rāga, dosa / dveṣa* and *moha. Rāga* means desire: greed, covetousness, avarice, lubricity, gluttony; *dosa / dveṣa*, ill-will: aggressivity, dislike, hatred, malevolence, enmity, etc.; *moha*, error: not to see things *yathābhūtam* (as they are in reality), but as our emotions induce us to see them or as we are interested to see them or as it has been inculcated in us how to see them. These *kilesas / kleśas* generally bring about actions, attitudes, and behaviours that always provoke suffering in others and often in the persons who are captured by them.

3. Owing to the mentioned reasons, we live in a world of painful existence, the *Sahā* world. In Chapter III of the *Lotus Sūtra* there is the celebrated parable of the burning house, the sinister, ruinous and decaying dwelling of ferocious, cruel, aggressive, or suffering, hungry and destitute beings. The *Sahā* world is compared to that house (Chapter III, p. 77, line 4-p. 78, line 5): it burns by a mass of suffering; beings living in it are subject to birth, old age, disease, death, grief, wailing, pain, dejectedness, mental disturbance, to the covering of the veil of blindness produced by the darkness and obscurity of ignorance; the Buddha appears in that world to deliver beings from the impurities of *rāga, dosa / dveṣa* and *moha*; He sees beings burning, tormented, vexed, distressed by birth, old age, disease, grief, wailing, pain, dejectedness, mental disturbance, for the sake of enjoyments and sensual pleasure they experience multifarious pains; owing to their desire to gain and keep in this life they experience diverse pains in their next life; they suffer poverty provoked by Gods and men, union with what they detest and separation from what they cherish.

It is because of His great compassion that the Buddha has chosen to appear in this *Sahā* world instead of in some more fortunate Buddha-world. This is the central theme of the *Karuṇāpuṇḍarīkasūtra*.

4. Which person born in this 20th century could not agree with the Buddha's idea about our world and human condition? Our century has seen terrific events: world wars, local conflicts,

cruel dictatorships, terrorism, genocides, racial, religious, political persecutions, huge communities submerged in poverty, fear, injustice, ignorance, which increase the suffering proper of human nature. There has been great technological and scientific progress not accompanied by moral progress: solidarity, compassion, benevolence are at a very low level. Many persons live in abundance and among pleasures in face of many more who suffer and are deprived of all hope and opportunities, and who have neither present nor future.

It is difficult to declare that this world is good, unless one adopts the point of view of the happy few.

3. The Buddhist Salvific Path

The doctrine of the Four Noble Truths is the basic doctrine of Buddhism. The Fourth Noble Truth, the Eightfold Path that leads to the suppression of suffering, is the Buddhist system of Ethics. See the preceding section on Enlightenment, paragraph 6. What Buddhism intends to do with its remarkable system of Ethics, is to make man a moral being who submits himself to a severe discipline of Ethics, in order to reach the Buddhist goal.

Detachment and indifference

1. The elimination of desire, considered as the cause of suffering, must necessarily produce a sentiment of detachment. Detachment means the weakening, limitation or elimination of greediness, covetousness, avarice, ambition, gluttony, inordinate desire of sexual pleasure, etc. that enchain man to worldly objects and submits him to them. Detachment on its turn gives rise to sentiments of serenity and of emotional and mental peace. The Buddhist detachment is basically similar to the stoic detachment (cf. W. Windelband, *Storia della Filosofia*, Milano: R. Sandron Editore, Vol. I, pp. 213 ff.) or to the detachment arrived at by members of several Catholic religious orders. Of course, in Buddhism, detachment practiced by the

monk is more complete and profound than the one practiced by lay people.

2. The case of indifference is not the same. Indifference means not having any emotional connection with other people's destiny, not worrying about what happens to them, not feeling any desire to reduce their misery or to increase their happiness, being without the consciousness of the ties that link human beings among themselves and give rise to duties of solidarity. We think that it cannot be said that Buddhism preached *indifference* to the world in the indicated sense. Let us examine this question looking at some virtues taught by Hīnayāna and Mahāyāna Buddhism that regulate one's own relation with other beings.

3. The three first *Brahmavihāra* are *mettā* (in Pāli, for Sanskrit cf. *mitra*): 'love, amity, sympathy, friendliness, active interest in others' (*The Pali Text Society Pali English Dictionary*), *karuṇā*: 'pity, compassion' (*ibidem*), and *muditā*: 'soft-heartedness, kindliness, sympathy' (*ibidem*). Buddhaghośa in his commentary on *Sutta Nipāta* I, p. 128, taking as a criterion the well known utterance of the Buddha: *sabbe sattā bhavantu sukhitattā*: 'May all beings be happy' (*Sutta Nipāta* 145) defines *mettā* as 'the desire of bringing (to one's fellow-men) what is good and agreeable' (*hitasukhūpanayanakāmatā*), *karuṇā* as 'the desire of removing (from one's fellow-men) what is bad and disagreeable' (*ahitadukkhāpanayanakāmatā*) and *muditā* as 'the desire that there be no separation' (of one's fellowmen) from the good and agreeable (they have) (*hitasukhāvippayogakāmatā*). The Buddha in *Dīgha Nikāya* I, pp. 250-251, §§ 76-78 (*Tevijjasutta*) expresses that a *bhikkhu* is possessed of moral discipline (*sīla*) when his mind pervades the whole world with a heart of love (*mettā*), of compassion (*karuṇā*), of sympathy (*muditā*), 'great, very great, beyond measure, friendly, peaceful'.

4. Mahāyāna Buddhism praises *karuṇā* (compassion) in the highest terms. Har Dayal[10] indicates the great importance that

---

[10] Har Dayal, *The Bodhisattva Doctrine in Buddhist Sanskrit Literature*, Delhi: Motilal Banarsidass, 1975, pp. 178-181.

karuṇā has in Mahāyāna and the various forms under which *karuṇā* manifests itself (I quote him, giving in note the texts he adduces in each case in his notes): "*No one word can convey an adequate idea of what* karuṇā *means. It is mentioned in an enormous number of passages in all the principal treatises.*[11] *It is perhaps the word that occurs most frequently in Mahāyānist literature. According to the* Śata-sāhasrikā Prajñāpāramitā, *a* bodhisattva *shows his* karuṇā *chiefly by resolving to suffer the torments and agonies of the dreadful purgatories during innumerable aeons, if need be, so that he may lead all beings to perfect Enlightenment.*[12] *He desires Enlightenment first for all beings and not for himself.*[13] *He is consumed with grief on account of the sufferings of others, and does not care for his own happiness.*[14] *He desires the good and welfare of the world.*[15] *All his faults and sins are destroyed, when his heart is full of* karuṇā.[16] *He loves all beings, as a mother loves her only child.*[17] *This famous simile sums up a* bodhisattva*'s ideal of*

---

[11] *Lalita Vistara*, S. Lefmann ed. (1902-8), 352.11, 162.6, 180.6. *Mahāvastu*, É. Senart ed. (1882-97), I, 78.16; II, 340.22. *Jātaka-Mālā*, H. Kern ed. (1991), 41.1, 238.22, 2.18, etc. *Śikṣāsamuccaya*, C. Bendall ed. (1897-1902), 8.2, 232.10, 184.12, etc. *Daśa-bhūmikasūtra*, J. Rahder ed. (1926), 11.13, 13.13, 18.17, 19.8, 43.8, 42.12, 46.3, 47.23, 52.10, 52.14, 60.7, 63.24, 70.24, 71.2, 73.16, 78.19, 82.6, 88.12, 90.1, etc. *Śata-sāhasrikā Prajñāpāramitā*, P. Ghosa ed. (1902-1913), 1455.8, 282.11, 1461.8, etc. *Mahāyāna-sūtrālaṅkāra*, S. Lévi ed. (1907, 1911), 11.5, 14.3, 31.14, 33.22, 167.42, 84.24, 124.30, 167.39, 172.67, 174.74, etc. Kṣemendra, *Bodhisattvāvadanakalpalatā*, S.C. Das and H.M. Vidyābhūṣaṇa ed. (1888), II, 57.42, 831.6, 909.1, etc.

[12] *Śata-sāhasrikā Prajñāpāramitā*, 1461.8 ff.

[13] *Śikṣāsamuccaya*, 146.10.

[14] *Jātaka-Mālā*, 41.1.

[15] *Lalita Vistara*, 180.18.

[16] Kṣemendra, *Bodhisattvāvadanakalpalatā*, 1.1.

[17] *Laṅkāvatārasūtra*, B. Nanjio ed. (1923), 244.8. *Mahāyāna-sūtrālaṅkāra*, 123.28. *Avadānaśataka*, J.S. Speyer ed. (1906, 1909), I, 184.12, I, 209.12. *Saddharmapuṇḍarīka*, H. Kern and B. Nanjio ed. (1912), 136.4. *Lalita Vistara*, 280.7. *Śikṣāsamuccaya*, 287.9. Cf. *Sutta-nipāta*, 149-150 (p. 26): *mātā yathā niyaṃ puttaṃ*, etc.

karuṇā. *He loves all creatures more than he loves himself or his wife and children.*[18] *He does not love his own children more that other children, as his love is the same for all.*[19] *He is like a mother, a father, a relative, a friend, a slave and a teacher for all beings*".[20]

In the *Bodhisattvabhūmi*, p. 4, lines 11-13 and 15-18 (N. Dutt ed., Patna: K.P. Jayaswal Research Institute, 1966) there is an important passage on this matter. The text indicates the duties of a true *Bodhisattva*: he collaborates in the accomplishment of meritorious actions done by others, giving them preference over actions that he is doing; he suffers with the suffering of others, when others are killed, imprisoned, wounded, menaced or insulted, either when he sees or he hears about that suffering; he helps other beings in the various tasks they have to perform, doing his best in order that persons for whom the task is done be satisfied and pleased.

The *karuṇā* is practiced and developed chiefly by *dāna* (giving, generosity, liberality), the first of the *pāramitās* (perfections) that the *Bodhisattva* has to cultivate in itself to its foremost degree.

5. That the preoccupation for others' welfare, happiness, safety, salvation is a duty of the Buddhist is clearly shown in several chapters of the *Lotus Sūtra*, which describe as a model for beings the behaviour of *Buddhas* and *Bodhisattvas*. For instance in Chapter I the Buddha emits a ray of light from His forehead; this ray illuminates the universe and shows the *Buddhas* fully dedicated to their task of helping people to reach a better destiny, revealing and preaching the salvific *Dharma* (verse 7) and announcing the calm extinction (*praśāntanirvṛti*) to people oppressed by suffering and distressed in their minds by birth and old age (verse 9). The *Bodhisattvas* on their turn practice the *dāna-pāramitā*, giving all their goods to needy

---

[18] *Mahāyāna-sūtrālaṅkāra*, 161.6.

[19] *Śikṣāsamuccaya*, 19.

[20] *Mahāyāna-sūtrālaṅkāra*, 162-4.

persons and even generously sacrificing their own bodies and lives for other beings' sake (verses 14-19).

Chapter XXIV of the same *Sūtra* is consecrated to *Bodhisattva* Avalokiteśvara, the most important and beloved *Bodhisattva* of the Mahāyāna. He is the incarnation of compassion (*karuṇā*), which he manifests in multifarious ways in his actions towards other beings and which many texts enjoy describing.[21]

Buddhists must be detached from worldly goods and free from worldly feelings in the degree allowed to them by their progress in the spiritual path and by their karmic history, but at the same time it is their duty to feel solidarity with their fellow men / women, to be always ready to help them and to procure them welfare and safety, avoiding to be indifferent to them.

4. God

It is obvious that Buddhism cannot expect that salvation come from God as Christianity thinks, since Buddhism is atheistic. It is not our task to discuss whether Christianity or Buddhism is right regarding the belief in God's existence; our task is only to establish if the opinion we are commenting agree or do not agree with the Buddhist texts and teachings.

5. Is salvation, nibbāna / nirvāṇa, nothing else than indifference to the world?

In the previous section on Enlightenment it has been said that salvation, *nibbāna / nirvāṇa*, is the elimination of suffering, the cessation of reincarnations, the suppression of existence, and that it is conceived as transcendent and heterogeneous, as an Absolute. It is not solely an attitude of indifference to the world; it is a richer and more complex notion. Moreover it is necessary to take into account that indifference to the world is not a Buddhist teaching.

[21] Cf. H.W. Haussig and others (eds.), *Götter und Mythen des indischen Subkontinents*, Stuttgart: Klett-Cotta, 1984, pp. 322-326, with bibliography.

6. Is the culmination of the Buddhist spiritual process nothing else than indifference to the world?

The culmination of the Buddhist spiritual process is, from a Hīnayānist perspective, the Ar(a)hantship (*arahatta / arhattva*) or condition of an *ar(a)hant* and, from a Mahāyānist perspective, the Buddhahood (*buddhatā / buddhatva*) or *condition of a Buddha*.

1. An *ar(a)hant* is a man who has arrived to the highest degree of spiritual perfection. He has reached the end of the Noble Eightfold Path realizing in himself the ideals of right views, right intentions, right speech, right action, right living, right effort, right mindfulness and right mental concentration i.e., realizing in himself the most complete ideal of the morally perfect man. He is described as possessing lofty moral qualities. The *ar(a)hant* obtains the *bodhi*, becomes a *Buddha*, and is ready to enter in *nirvāṇa*, but in the most ancient Buddhist texts the arhantship is more emphasized as the final attainment of the *ar(a)hant* than the condition of a *Buddha* that he also obtains. The arhantship is the last stage of the Hīnayānist spiritual course of action, attained by means of a strenuous and long effort. Cf. on the *arahant* for instance *Dīgha Nikāya* I, p. 177 (*Kassapa Sīhanāda Sutta*), III, p. 97, § 31 (*Aggañña Suttanta*), *Dhammapada*, Chapter VII; *Lotus Sūtra*, p. 1, *Avadānaśataka* N° 17, p. 96, lines 4-9, J.S. Speyer ed. (formula repeated many times, as for instance pp. 207, lines 9-14, 262, lines 8-13, 284, line 12-285, line 4), and also P. Oltramare quoted in section on Enlightenment § 5, pp. 336-337 and pp. 376-379; T.W. Rhys Davids, 'Arhat', in J. Hastings (Editor), *Encyclopaedia of Religion and Ethics* (quoted in note 9), Vol. I, pp. 774-775, and the article 'Arahant' by W.G.W. and others, in *Encyclopaedia of Buddhism*, quoted in note 3, Vol. II, Fascicle 1, pp. 41-54.

2. We have already referred in the previous section on Enlightenment to the richness of contents of the *bodhi* experience, which transforms a being into a *Buddha*. The texts

quoted in that section reveal the broad knowledge the Buddha got on having that experience.

3. One passage, that is repeated several times in the *Avadanaśataka* as for instance pp. 16, line 9-17 line 4, 30, line 7-31 line 4, 72, lines 3-14, 78, line 13-79, line 10, etc.), enumerates some of the virtues and accomplishments of the *Buddhas*:

- their omniscience (*nāsti kiñcid buddhānāṃ bhagavatām ajñātam adṛṣṭam aviditam avijñātam*);
- they are full of compassion (*mahākāruṇikānām*) and kindness for the world (*lokānugrahapravṛttakānām*);
- they have a single protector (mindfulness) (*ekārakṣāṇām*);
- they possess tranquillity and insight (*śamathavipaśyanāvihāriṇām*);
- they are skilled in the three-fold self-control (of thoughts, words and acts) (*tridamathavastukuśalānām*);
- they have traversed the four floods [of desire (*kāma*), existence (*bhava*), ignorance (*avidyā*), wrong views (*dṛṣṭi*)] (*caturoghottīrṇānāṃ*);
- they are well established on the ground of the four bases of supernatural powers necessary for gaining proficiency in meditation [desire (*chanda*), energy (*vīrya*), (composed) mind (*citta*), inquiry (*mīmāṃsā*) based on correct knowledge, all directed towards the mastery of meditation] (*caturṛddhipādacara-ṇatalasupratiṣṭhānām*);
- they have practiced during long time the four items of attraction or means by which a *Buddha* attracts creatures leading them to a moral form of life [and which are liberality (*dāna*), affability (*priyavacana*), action for the benefit of others (*arthakriyā*) and having the same joys and sorrows with others i.e., sympathy] (*samānasukhaduḥkhatā*)] (*caturṣu saṃgrahavastuṣu dīrgharātrakṛtaparicayānām*);
- they have given up the five hindrances (*nīvaraṇa*) [i.e., desire for lusts (*kāmacchanda*), malice (*vyāpāda*), torpor and drowsiness (*styāna-middha*), flurry and worry (*auddhatya-kaukṛtya*), doubt (*vicikitsā*)] (*pañcāṅgaviprahīṇānām*);

- they have gone beyond the five *gatis* or forms of existence (as god, as man, as animal, as ghost, as infernal beings) (*pañcagatisamatikrāntānām*);

- they possess a sixfold attitude of indifference to the objects of each of the six senses (*ṣaḍaṅgasamanvāgatānām*);

- they have fully realized the six Perfections (*Pāramitā*) [giving, generosity, liberality (*dāna*), morality (*śīla*), forbearance or patience (*kṣānti*), energy (*vīrya*), mental concentration (*dhyāna*) and wisdom (*prajñā*)] (*ṣaḍpāramitāparipūrṇānām*);

- they are richly endowed with the seven "flowers" of Enlightenment [which are mindfulness (*smṛti*), investigation of the *Dharma* (*dharmapravicaya*), energy (*vīrya*), happiness (*prīti*), calmness (*praśabdhi*), concentration of mind (*samādhi*), equanimity (*upekṣā*)] (*saptabodhyaṅga-kusumāḍhyānām*);

- they teach the Eightfold Path (*aṣṭāṅgamārgadeśikānām*);

- they are skilled in the nine successive states or stages of mental concentration [which are the four concentrations of mind described in *Dīgha Nikāya* I, pp. 73-76, §§ 75-82 (*Samaññaphalasutta*), the four concentrations of mind and the total *nirodha* described in *Aṅguttara Nikāya* IV, pp. 412-414 (*Anupubbavihārasutta* and *Anupubhavihārasamāpattisutta*)] (*navānupūrvavihārasamāpattikuśalānām*);

- they possess the ten powers [of distinguishing right from wrong (*sthānāsthānajñānabala*), of knowing the consequences of actions (*karmavipāka°*), the different dispositions (of men) (*nānādhimukti°*), the different elements (*nānādhātu°*), the degree of the mental powers (of men) (*indriyavarāvara°*), the course of conduct that leads everywhere (*sarvatra gaminīpratipadā°*), all the meditations, liberations, concentrations of mind, *samāpattis* and the rising up and the elimination of impurities (*sarvadhyānavimokṣasamādhi-samāpattisaṃkleśavyavadānavyutthāna°*), of remembering former abodes (in the reincarnations' series) (*pūrvanivāsānusmṛti°*) and of knowing the fall (from one existence) and the rebirth (in another) (of all men) (*cyutyutpatti°*)];

- they enjoy a complete glory in the ten directions of space (*daśadiksamāpūrṇayaśasām*);

- they are the (most) eminent among ten hundred all-powerful persons (*daśaśatavaśavartiprativiśiṣṭānām*);

- they have obtained the knowledge very soon after their birth, looking at the world with their *Buddha's* eye (*trīrātres trirdivasasya buddhacakṣusā lokaṃ vyavalokya jñānadarśanaṃ pravartate*).

The passage ends pointing out the preoccupation of the *Buddha* for the woes of the suffering beings and His desire to help them: "Who is deficient (*hīyate*)? Who succeeds (*vardhate*)? Who is affected by pain (*kṛcchraprāpta*)? Who is affected by difficulties (*saṃkaṭaprāpta*)? Who is affected by distress (*saṃbādhaprāpta*)? Who is affected by pain, difficulties, and distress? Who is sinking into an evil state of existence (*apāyanimna*)? Who is propense to an evil state of existence (*apāyapravaṇa*)? Who is inclined towards an evil state of existence (*apāyaprāgbhāra*)? Whom shall I rescue from an evil state of existence and establish in heaven (*svarga*) and in Liberation (*mokṣa*)? To whom fallen into the mire of desire shall I give my hand to deliver him? Whom deprived of the Treasure (*dhāna*) of the Nobles (*ārya*: the Buddhists) shall I establish in the Treasure, the Sovereignty and the Overlordship of the Nobles? Of which being, whose eye is covered by the mass of darkness of ignorance, shall I purify the vision? Whose roots of merit, not yet planted, shall I plant? Whose roots of merit, already planted, shall I bring to maturity? Whose roots of merit, fully developed, shall I bring to Deliverance?"

Such are the *Buddhas* and such are their attainments, accomplishments, and attributes. And all that is truly *the culmination of the Buddhist spiritual progress*, which they incarnate, and not merely the conviction that world is evil.

XI

Buddhism and Family

When *circa* 500 B.C. [1] Buddhism appears and spreads in India, family was already organized according to old traditions. Family was then basic unity in society. Due to the economic and social changes ocurred in the 6th century B.C., monogamy was appearing together with poligamy. *Family* covered a greater number of persons than the number it covers today: husband, his father and mother, his wife, his married sons together with their wives, and even his servants. Relations among the members of the family were already regulated in the ethic and legal realms.[2]

In the huge Buddhist literature, in Pāli as well in Sanskrit, which comes from around 500 B.C., numerous references to the family are found. Much of these references have to do with the relations, which have to exist among members of a family. Because of the

---

[1] This date is according to the Theravāda's tradition that fixes as the limits of the life of the Buddha the years 566 and 486 B.C. The date of the *parinirvāṇa* (death) of the Buddha is a subject of research and discussion, as it can be seen in the work *The Dating of the Historical Buddha*, edited by H. Bechert: Abhandlungen der Akademie der Wissenschaften in Göttingen, 1991, 1992 and 1997 (three volumes). See F. Tola and C. Dragonetti, "Fecha del *Parinirvāṇa* de Buda", in *Revista de Estudios Budistas*, México-Buenos Aires, 1994, Number 7, pp. 89-106. Many scholars are inclined to put the date of the *parinirvāṇa* between the years 420 and 350 B.C. Cf. Volume III, p. 13, of the work edited by Bechert.

[2] About the family in Ancient India see P.V. Kane, *History of Dharmashāstra*, Poona: Bhandarkar Oriental Research Institute, 1941, Vol. II, Part 1, Chapter IX; A.S. Altekar, *The Position of Women in Hindu Civilization from Prehistoric Times to the Present Times*, Delhi: Motilal Banarsidass, 1962; and Veda Mitra, *India of Dharma Sutras*, New Delhi: Arya Book Depot, 1965, Third Part. See also R.K. Mookerji and R.C. Majumdar "Social Condition", Chapter XXI in R.C. Majumdar (Editor), *The History and Culture of the Indian People*, Bombay: Bharatiya Vidya Bhavan, 1960, Vol. II (*The Age of Imperial Unity*); S.K. Nanayakkara, "Family", in G.P. Malalasekera (Editor), *Encyclopaedia of Buddhism*, Sri Lanka: Government of Sri Lanka, 1961 ss., Vol. V, Fasc. 2, pp. 218-220; and T.W. Rhys Davids, "Family (Buddhist)", in J. Hastings (Editor), *Encyclopaedia of Religion and Ethics*, Edinburgh: T. and T. Clark, 1964, Vol. V, pp. 727-728.

great emphasis Buddhism always put in the moral aspect of conduct, the texts, in which are found those references, constitute –it may be say– manuals of family ethics. The ethics of familiar relations are their fundamental subject.[3]

The moral norms in the Siṅgālovādasuttanta *relative to family*

Among these Buddhist texts there is one extremely beautiful, the *Siṅgālovādasuttanta*, [4] which belongs to the *Dīgha-Nikāya* (N°. XXI, XXXI, Pali Text Society ed., in what follows PTS), a collection of texts which preserve the Teachings of the Buddha, written in Pāli language, one of the sacred languages of

[3] Cf. on this subject R. Spence Hardy, *Manual of Buddhism in its Modern Development*, Varanasi: Choukhamba, 1967, Chapter 10 (reprint of the London edition, 1853. This work was favourably commented by A. Weber, *Indische Streifen*, Osnabrück: Biblio Verlag, 1983, reprint of the edition of 1869, Volume II, pp. 188-190); É. Lamotte, *Histoire du Bouddhisme Indien, Des origines à l'Ère Śaka*, Louvain: Institut Orientaliste, 1958, pp. 73-82; M. Anesaki, "Ethics and Morality (Buddhist)", in J. Hastings (Editor), *Encyclopaedia of Religion and Ethics* (see note 2), Vol. V, pp. 447-455; H. Saddhatissa, *Buddhist Ethics. Essence of Buddhism*, London: George Allen & Unwin, 1970; L. de la Vallée Poussin, *La morale bouddhique*, Paris: Nouvelle Librairie Nationale, 1927; H. Oldenberg, *Buddha, Sein Leben, Seine Lehre, Seine Gemeinde, herausgege ben von H. von Glasenapp*, München: W. Goldmann Verlag, 1961, pp. 267-306; Bhikkhu Pāsādika, "Early Mahāyāna Lay Ethics in Nāgārjuna", in *The Tibet Journal*, Vol. XXI, N° 1, 1996, pp. 3-18; F. Schäfer, *Der Buddha sprach nicht nur für Mönche und Nonnen. Die ganze Lehre erstmals nur nach seinen Reden für Nichtasketen*, Heidelberg (Leimen): Werner Kristkeitz Verlag, 1995.

[4] It is also called *Sigālovāda*. In the *Cullavagga* LIV it receives the name of *Gihivinaya* or " *Vinaya* (Discipline) of the lays". It is a basic work for the exposition of the mutual duties of the members of the family in relation to themselves and in relation to others. There is an English translation in *Dialogues of the Buddha*, by T.W. and C.A.F. Rhys Davids, edition of the PTS. Cf. also Bhadanta Pannasiri, *Sigālovāda-sutta*, in *Visva Bharati Annals*, Vol. III (Santiniketan), 1950, pp. 150-228, which gives the English translation of the Chinese version of the Pāli text. The Volume 45, 2, of *BDK English Tripiṭaka*, Berkeley: Numata Center for Buddhist Translation and Research, 1994, gives the English translation by the Bhikṣuṇī Shih Heng-ching of *Yu-p'o-sai-chieh ching* (*Upāsakaśīla-sūtra*) that is a Chinese version of three Pālis *suttas* that are related to the Ethics of the family.

Buddhism. The Pāli *Dīgha Nikāya* belongs to the Theravāda school of Buddhism. In this text (N° XXXI) the Buddha meets the young Siṅgāla, who, standing and putting his hands together as a sign of respect, is paying homage to the regions of the space. The Buddha asks him what is he doing, and the young Siṅgāla answers that, when his father died, he asked him not to stop paying homage to the regions of the space. Then the Buddha tells him that this is not the way of paying homage to the regions of the space, and at the request of the young Siṅgāla the Buddha impart him His Teaching.

First of all the Buddha explains to the young Siṅgāla which are really the ten regions of the space:

> "*You should know, O young householder, that these are the six regions of the space. The region of the Orient is your father and your mother; the region of the South, your Masters; the region of the West, your wife and your children; the region of the North, your friends and companions; the region of the Nadir, your servants and employees; and the region of the Zenit, the ascetics and brahmans.*"

Then the Buddha points to young Siṅgāla that the right way of paying homage to the regions of the space is complying with the obligations and duties concerning oneself in regard to each one of the indicated categories of persons. We briefly indicate those duties.

Duties of the son in relation to his parents : to support them in old age; to do the tasks they have to accomplish; to do all what is necessary for the permanence of the family and for the lineage not to be extinguished; to show oneself worthy of the received inheritance; to offer to his dead parents the funerary cult that correponds to them.

On their turn the parents will show their affection[5] for the son keeping him apart from what is evil, teaching him what is

---

[5] The word used by the text is '*anukampanti*' from the root *anu-KAMP-*, which means 'to have compassion', 'to feel sympathy' according to the *Critical Pāli Dictionary* and besides that 'to sympathize with' according to the *Pali-English Dictionary* of the PTS.

good, making him learn a trade, searching for him an appropriate wife, giving him at the right time the inheritance that corresponds to him.

Duties of the disciple in relation to his masters : to stand up from the seat when the master is coming, to pay attention to him, to obey him, to serve him, to learn earnestly the master's teachings.

The masters will show affection for their disciples, guiding them as is proper, they will make them understand the teachings they transmit, they will teach all the knowledge they possess, they will praise their abilities among friends and companions, they will protect them in every occasion.

Duties of the husband in relation to his wife : to show respect to her, to avoid any act of disrespect, to keep fidelity to her, to impart authority to her, to give beautiful ornaments to her.

The wife will show affection for her husband, being careful with her tasks and domestic duties, welcoming with courtesy her husband's relatives, being faithful, taking care of the familiar possessions, being active and industrious.

Duties of the friend in relation to his friends and companions : generosity, cordiality, will to help, constancy on his feelings and behaviour, loyalty.

The friends and companions will show affection to the friend who treats them in that way, and who has for them such feelings, taking care of him and his possessions, when he is in a bad situation, protecting him whenever he is in danger, not leaving him in misfortune, showing respect for his family.

Duties of the masters in relation to their servants : to give them a job according to their strength, to provide them with food and to pay them as it corresponds, to heal them when they are sick, to give them part of the tasty food they enjoy, and to grant them an appropriate rest.

The servants will show affection for their masters, getting up before them, going to bed after them, taking only what their masters give to them, making earnestly their tasks, not speaking ill of them.

Duties of the householder in relation to the ascetics and brahmans : to have a good behaviour, nice words and good intentions towards them, to keep his house open for them, to give them food.

The ascetics and brahmans will show at their turn their affection for the householders, removing them from evil, inculcating in them what is morally good, teaching them what they do not know, rectifying what they wrongly know, showing them the way that leads to a happy destiny *post-mortem.*

It must be remarked that the norms of behaviour pointed by the *Siṅgālovāda* prescribe the realization of certain *acts* and not to experience certain *feelings.* For instance, it is not said that the son should *love* his father, but that he should *support him at old age*, etc. Likewise, it is not said that the husband should *feel love* for his wife, but that he should *behave in a correct way* with her. Generally the Buddhist Ethics is interested in remarking the kind of behaviour that must be avoided.

The norms of the *Siṅgālovāda* should be complemented by the norms of morality that are valid for every Buddhist, especially those that constitute the *dasa-sīla* (ten moralities), which are the following ones: not to kill, not to steal, not to commit adultery, not to lie, not to slander, not to use rough words, not to have frivolous conversations, not to feel greed, not to feel malevolence, to avoid wrong points of view,[6] and those that constitute the three first *brahmavihāras* (selected states): benevolence, love, friendship, sympathy or active interest for others, compassion and smoothness of heart, kindness and affection. In the *dasa-sīla* predominates the references to acts that should not be done, in the *brahmavihāras* those related to positive and moderate feelings that one should develop in onself.[7]

---

[6] See *Saṃyutta Nikāya* IV, pp. 342-343, PTS edition.

[7] Cf. *Dīgha Nikāya* I (*Tevijjasutta*), pp. 250-251, §§ 76-78.

Presence of positive feelings in the Buddhist texts

The feelings that link or should link the members of a family are very much present in the Buddhist texts. Through the description shown in those texts it can be seen the high valuation that Buddhism had for the positive feelings of sympathy or affection. We refer to some cases.

The *Lotus Sūtra*,[8] an important text of Mahāyāna Buddhism, exposes a salvific, generous and universal message, and for that reason their principal themes are of doctrinaire contents. Anyhow we find in it several passages related to family affections.

In Chapter III (pp. 72-76 and verses 40-84 of the Sanskrit text edition of Kern-Nanjio) it is narrated the parable of the children saved by their father from the burning house at risk of his own life. When he realises that the house, where his little children are playing, is burning and they do not notice the risks they are running, "*he was full of fear, fright and terror*" (p. 72, line 10); he suffers imagining the danger his children are exposed to (verse 69), he wants to enter the burning house and take his children to his breast to effect their escape out of the fire (p. 73, line 2); he knows the inclinations and tendencies of his children (p.73, lines 14-15), and thanks to that knowledge a devise occurred to his mind in order to make them go out of the house. When the children are safe, the father feels great joy and happiness and gets rid of anxiety and worry (p. 75, lines 2-3 and verse 76).

---

[8] The *Lotus Sūtra* has been translated several times from its original Sanskrit text as well as from its Chinese translation by Kumārajīva (406 A.D.). There are translations into Chinese, Tibetan, Mongol, Turkish, Tangut, Japanese, English, French, and German. F. Tola and C. Dragonetti have published a translation of this *Sūtra* into Spanish from the Sanskrit original text: *El Sūtra del Loto de la Verdadera Doctrina, Saddharmapuṇḍarīkasūtra*, México: El Colegio de México-Asociación Latinoamericana de Estudios Budistas, 1999. A Portuguese translation from the Spanish version by Tola and Dragonetti done by Professor Carlos Alberto Da Fonseca from Sao Paulo University will be published in this year in New Jersey, USA, by Primordia editions. The texts quoted in this article are easy to locate in the edition of the Sanskrit text done by Kern-Nanjio.

On Chapter IV (pp. 101-108 and verses 3-35) we find the parable of the son that because of his low disposition leaves his father's house and lives in poverty, roaming from one place to another, during fifty years. The father, a rich and opulent man, "*remembered permanently that missing son*" and "*remembering his son, without telling anyone, he suffered within his heart*" (p. 102, lines 7-9; cf. verse 4) and "*with pain, he spent his nights and days thinking of his son all the time*" (verse 9). Looking for his son (verse 5) the father arrives to another city where he settles down. On one occasion, by chance, the son arrives to that city where his father lives. His father seeing him recognizes him immediately, and so "*that man, who had suffered from the desire of having his son with him*" (p. 104, line 1), "*felt happy, fortunate, lucky, pleased, full of joy and hapiness on seeing his son,*" (p. 103, lines 13-14, verse 18). Then the father, "*thirsty of love for his son*" (p. 107, line 6), in a clever, considered and affectionate way gets the trust of his son, and at the moment of his death, before the notables and the people of the town, declares with pride "*He is my son, I am his father*" (p. 108, lines 10-11).

Chapter XV presents the parable of a physician-father who had many children; they were all them affected by a terrible pain, but they did not want to take the remedy offered to them by the father, which would heal and save them; to make them change their mood, he leaves to a foreign country and lets them belief that he is dead. The children '*felt great sorrow, and lamented extremely*' the death of their father who was their '*protector*', who '*had affection for them*'. They felt themselves '*without protection*' and were '*permanently grieving*'. Thus they react, and start taking the medicine that heals and saves them. The father, that with his clever stratagem, had healed their children, shows himself again and joins them.

It is remarkable that, with the aim of exalting the feelings of affection, compassion and benevolence that the Buddha feels for the beings sunk in ignorance and in suffering, the *Lotus*

Sūtra many times introduces the Buddha as the *Father* of beings.[9] Aśoka, the great Buddhist Emperor of India (272-232 B.C.), in his edict of Kalinga [10] declares likewise that *all men are his children.*

In the *Jātakas* (more than 500 texts that deal with the previous lives of the Buddha) are found many narrations that exalt the feelings of affection, benevolence, loyalty, fidelity between wife and husband, among relatives, among friends, and that condemn the opposite feelings.[11]

Finally, we quote verse 7 of *Mettasutta* of *Khuddakapāṭha* relative to a mother's love:

> "*As a mother would protect her son with her own life,*
> *so let one produce in oneself,*
> *with regard to all living beings,*
> *a mind of benevolence that does not know limits.*"

Family conflicts in Ancient India

But things were not always as the Buddha would have expected, and there were people who did not follow His norms of behaviour. The *Suttanipāta*, verse 106, refers to men addicted to women, to alcohol, to gambling, who provoke the ruin of their families; the *Aṅguttara-Nikāya* IV (*Bhariyāsutta*), pp. 223-225, mentions diverse kinds of women of wrong, blamable and disagreeable conduct, which can only do harm to their families.

---

9 Cf. Jesús López-Gay, "Buda como Padre en el *Hokekyō* (El Sūtra del Loto)", in *Revista de Estudios Budistas*, México-Buenos Aires, N° 8 (1994), pp. 41-63. The Italian original of this article was published in *Studia Missionalia*, Roma, Vol. 33 (1984), pp. 127-144.

10 J. Bloch, *Les inscriptions d'Asoka*, Paris: Les Belles Lettres, 1950, p. 142.

11 See L. Grey, *A Concordance of Buddhist Birth Stories*, Oxford: The Pali Text Society, 1994. Excellent work that indicates the content of each *Jātaka* and the moral norm illustrated, besides of useful references to other texts of similar contents. A simple perusal of their pages gives an idea of the richness of subjects that are developed in these narrations and of the moral values that they propose. There is an English translation of the *Jātakas* by E.B. Cowell and others, edited by the PTS.

And in the *Jātakas* already quoted there are references to the wrong behaviour of family members. In India, at the Buddha's epoch, there could be family crises as in every epoch, like in ours – but perhaps without the intensity and frequency they have now due to several causes as economic, social and cultural factors that foment them.

What did Buddhism offer to avoid these conflicts?

What did Buddhism offer to beings suffering those crises? What does Buddhism offer to beings suffering those crises today? From a *strictly* Buddhist perspective, one has to answer: the only thing that Buddhism could and can offer is *its Doctrine*. That is why we shall refer to some aspects of the Doctrine that could contribute to hinder the rise of family conflicts and to solve them when they appear, or at least to alleviate them.

Importance of mind

Buddhism has always exalted the importance of mind in the conformation of human destiny. Mind is the cause of success in this life and also the cause of a happy destiny after death; mind is the cause of failure in this life and also the cause of an unhappy destiny after death.[12] Mind for Buddhism has two principal levels: the conscious level and the sub-conscious level. The sub-conscious level receives the name of *ālayavijñāna*, "receptacle-consciousness", which is constituted by the subliminal impressions that are left in it - as in a deposit - by every experience, every cognition, every feeling, that are kept in it in a latent state, and that, under the appropriate circumstances pass from the subliminal level to the conscious level, provoking in man experiences, cognitions,

[12] About the importance of mind in Buddhism, see C. Dragonetti, "The origin of the Buddhist conception of *cittamātra* (only-mind)", in *Journal of the International Association of Buddhist Studies*, Vol. 23, N° 1, 2000. Cf. F. Tola and C. Dragonetti, *Being as Consciousness. Yogācāra Philosophy of Buddhism*, Delhi: Motilal Banarsidass, 2004.

feelings [13], whose origin he does not know and which impel him to actions whose sense or purpose he does not perceive.

State of alert and vigilance

Man should protect his mind, take care of it, defend it, and for that he must always make it the object of an inteligent and lucid awareness. As the Japanese *samurai*, always alert to dangers and traps around him, thus man should keep alert and vigilant in relation to his own mind, to know what happens in it. Buddhism recommends as one of its highest virtues the state of *alert and vigilance.*[14] Keeping alert and vigilant, man will be able to notice what kind of impulses, inclinations, are appearing in him, to handle them as it is right, and, in each case, to destroy them *in ovo*, or to foment them and make them prosper or let them follow their natural and healthy process.

Cultivation of positive feelings

Moreover, man should foster and cultivate in himself several positive feelings that counteract negative feelings, as hatred,

[13] About the structure of mind in Buddhism, see F. Tola and C. Dragonetti, "La estructura de la mente según la escuela idealista budista (Yogāchāra)", in *Pensamiento*, Vol. 46, N° 182 (Madrid), 1990, pp. 129-147, also published in *Revista de Estudios Budistas REB*, N° 4, Octubre 1992, México-Buenos Aires, pp. 51-73. Cf. the text "Estrofas acerca de las Tres Naturalezas", by Vasubandhu, also published in this same number of *REB*, pp. 139-160, and in English (together with its Sanskrit original) in the book *Being as consciousness* mentioned in the previous note.

[14] Cf. C. Dragonetti and F. Tola, *Dhammapada. La esencia de la sabiduría budista*, 8th edition, New Jersey, USA: Primordia, 2004, specially Chapter II: *El estado de alerta y vigilancia* and the Introduction, pp. 52-53. Cf. *Satipaṭṭhāna. Der Heilsweg buddhistischer Geistesschulung*, Text und Kommentar ... von Nyanaponika, Konstanz: Verlag Christiani, 1950 (English translation: *The Heart of Buddhist Meditation*, Kandy, Sri Lanka: Buddhist Publication Society, 1996) and the articles "Appamāda" and "Indriya-saṃvara", in the *Encyclopaedia of Buddhism* quoted in note 2.

selfishness, lust, ambition, pride, a disorderly sensuality, idleness, lack of strength that usually, as experience shows, are the causes of wrong behaviour, which destroy the harmony in oneself and the harmony that should reign in the relations among human beings.[15] In the following paragraphs we mark some of that positive feelings.

Tolerance

Tolerance is an attitude that Buddhism earnestly advises to cultivate in oneself [16] – it allows others to have different ideas, and also to believe that those ideas are the true and the best ones.

Buddhism was tolerant by nature, because in its conception truth has multiple aspects, but generally man sees only one of those aspects, considers it to be the only truth, clings to it, and to defend it, adopts aggressive attitudes. Besides that, intolerance authoritatively imposes itself to make the others think, feel and act as the intolerant does.

If it is great the evil that intolerance causes among human communities in the field of religion and politics, the damages that it causes in the relation among persons and among the members of a family are equally great, creating in all of them resentful feelings: in the intolerant, because his will of power is not realized or it is refused, and in those persons who are submitted to him, because they feel that their personality - their

---

[15] The *sūtra* (aphorism) I, 33 of the *Yogasūtras* de Patañjali, the basic treatise on the theory of Yoga, also recommends in order to promote the serenity of mind to cultivate in oneself feelings of "benevolence, compassion, satisfaction, indifference in regard to (respectively) happiness, misfortune, merit and demerit (of somebody else)". See the commentary of Vācaspati Miśra *ad locum*.

[16] Cf. F. Tola, "Budismo y Humanismo", in *Revista de Estudios Budistas REB*, N° 9, Abril 1995, México-Buenos Aires, specially pp. 76-78, and in F. Tola and C. Dragonetti, *Budismo: Unidad y Diversidad*, New Jersey: The Buddhist Association of the United States, 2004, pp. 55-89.

ideas and feelings - is not respected. These kinds of reactions destroy the harmonious relations among people.

Kṣānti

As in the case of tolerance, Buddhism also gives great importance to *kṣanti*,[17] one of whose most interesting meanings is to be open-minded to any new theory, doctrine or idea, which comes to our knowledge, i.e., to examine it, to evaluate it, to take from it what is valuable, to reject it, if it is found to be defective, even if it comes from one's own Master, or to accept it and integrate it into our own system of thought - even if it contradicts inveterate convictions - if it is found to be positive and possesses intellectual or moral values.

Kṣānti also means 'patience' in face of offences, humiliations or menaces; it hinders thus the arising in oneself of feelings of resentment and of desires of revenge.

Moderation

Moderation [18] is another virtue that Buddhism recommends to cultivate. Buddhism received the designation of 'Middle Path' in order to point out, in the metaphysical level, its position equally far from *being* and *not-being* and, in the ethical level, its equal rejection of the exacerbated *ascetism* and the disorderly *sensuality*.

Compassion

Buddhism rests on two pillars: the *knowledge of the true nature of things*, the only antidote for ignorance - root and source of all evil according to Buddhism - and *compassion* [19] that, on

---

[17] See Alex Wayman, "La teoría budista de la paciencia (*kshānti*) del rey como creadora de paz", in *Revista de Estudios Budistas REB*, N° 12, Octubre 1996, México-Buenos Aires, pp. 23-41.

[18] Cf. C. Dragonetti and F. Tola, *Dhammapada*, quoted in note 13, pp. 83-86, and F. Tola and C. Dragonetti, *Las actitudes frente al alimento en la India Antigua*, Buenos Aires: Fundación Instituto de Estudios Budistas FIEB, 1999, pp. 14-15, included in this book in its English version.

[19] Cf. F. Tola, "Positiveness in the Lotus Sūtra", in revista *Hokke Bunka Kenkyū*, N° 26, Tokyo, 2000, whose English version is also included in this book.

one side, induces to abstain from any act of violence, from any agressive attitude, which leads to avoid with horror causing pain to others for whatever reason, motive, or pretext it may be, and that imposes as a norm of conduct not to do to others what one does not want others to do to oneself, and that, on the other side, leads to mitigate the suffering of others, to give them strength when they weaken, to advise them when they hesitate on the decision they must take, not to condem them for a fault, to transmit them the knowledge of the Doctrine, to show them the Path that will lead them to happiness and to spiritual progress.

Unavoidable consequences of every action

Buddhism advises to keep always in mind that every corporal, vocal or mental action has unavoidable consequences, because, as everything has a cause, so everything produces effects. Action is dangerous. Once action is set in motion, one never knows to which remote or close, harmful or beneficial effects can it give origin.[20]

Universal interdependence

Buddhism also has the conviction of the absolute interdependence of all beings and things.[21] All beings and the reality in which they exist constitute a great whole, as a living organism; what affects one of its parts may affect, and as a matter of fact actually effects, the whole and the other parts; there is a *solidarity* that links every thing with every thing else. This interdependence is also valid in the case of the family; the behaviour, feelings, ideas, words of one of its members may affect the family as a whole or individually the persons that constitute a part of it.

---

[20] The law of *karman* is a basic principle in Indian thought. See F. Tola and C. Dragonetti, "Buddhist Conception of Reality", in *Journal of Indian Council of Philosophical Research*, Vol. XIV, N° 1, 1996, pp. 52-56.

[21] Cf. F. Tola and C. Dragonetti, "Buddhist Conception of Reality", quoted in the previous note, pp. 49-52.

Being conscious that every action has effects, and being conscious of the universal interdependence, man must take care not to do, impelled by disorderly feelings, in a state of excitation, without previous reflection, precipitately, irrecoverable actions that could damage family relations for ever. Caution in reactions and the wise control of them avoid the coming forth of any disturbing process of unthinkable consequences.

The state of alert and vigilance, tolerance, *kṣānti* (open-mindedness and patience), moderation, compassion, self-control in the reactions – these are some of the virtues or qualities that Buddhism exalts and could be considered as means that serve to avoid conducts that threaten the family harmony or that contribute to solve conflicts caused by the broken harmony.

Yogic meditation

Beside these mentioned means that are part of the Buddhist Ethics, Buddhism offers another means that could be considered as a technique, as a way of therapy. It receives the name of *dhyāna* in Sanskrit, *jhāna* in Pāli, *ch'an* in Chinese, *zen* in Japanese; it is nothing else than '*yoga*' that sinks its roots in the most ancient stages of Indian culture.[22] Yoga presents two aspects: a first aspect is that of a relaxation technique; a second aspect, which has the first one as its foundation or basis, is that of a method for reaching the mystic ecstasy or trance. Concerning the subject we are dealing with, only the mentioned first aspect interests us. This aspect is beyond any religious, mystic or spiritual connotation. Through appropriate respiratory, postural, and mental concentration practices, yoga allows to reach - as it is shown by experience - relaxation states characterized by tranquillity and quietness, and by the lack of

[22] On Yoga and Buddhist meditation see F. Tola and C. Dragonetti, *The Yogasūtras of Patañjali. On Concentration of Mind*, Delhi: Motilal Banarsidass, 2005, 5th edition, and Amadeo Solé-Leris, *Tranquillity & Insight. An Introduction to the oldest form of Buddhist Meditation*, Kandy, Sri Lanka: Buddhist Publication Society, 1992.

emotional tensions. The practice of yoga allows to live moments of calmness and peace, which strengthen and train those who have recourse to it to face the turbulences of life with a peaceful and calm mind, and with more mastery over themselves.

XII

Attitudes in regard to Food in Ancient India

A. Vedism, Brahmanism and Hinduism

Today in our culture the attitude in regard to food is not at all complicated, it is a simple attitude without any complexity. We could say that the expression '*fast-food*' is its symbol. Was it different in the past? We could answer *a priori* in an affirmative way, taking into account that generally all the attitudes change in the course of time – for example the attitude in relation to sex, to religion, to parents, etc. In India were given several attitudes in regard to food in the course of the evolution of its rich and manifold culture. We shall refer here to some of these attitudes in ancient India.

The food as a gift of the Gods

We could say that in the Vedic epoch (*circa* 1500-800 B.C.) the attitude that predominates in relation to food is inspired by the idea that food is produced, possessed and given by the Gods or Goddesses in general or by some of them in particular. For this reason man has to venerate the Gods, must flatter them, and beg them to grant him the desired food, necessary for the prolongation of life. Man depends on an abundant harvest for his food, depends also on the generous reproduction of the livestock; and the abundance of the sown field and the fertility of the herds depend in their turn on the rains, on the air, on the ground, on the sun, and all this is under the sway of Deities. Although techniques are progressing, they have not replaced yet the good divine favour. The prayer of man to God: "*Give us the bread of every day*" still resounds with force from the bottom of the hearts.

One of the Goddesses related to food is *Pṛthivī*, the Earth, who is not completely personified and whose attributes are fundamentally those of the physical earth. To her is dedicated a beatiful hymn of the *Atharva Veda* (XII, 1). In this hymn many stanzas express *Pṛthivī*'s function as possessor, producer and giver of food. We quote some verses of this hymn.

> *... yasyā udvataḥ pravataḥ samaṃ bahu /*
> *nānāvīryā oṣadhīr yā bibharti ...* 2 b-c
> Hers are the heights, the slopes, the great plains;
> She bears the herbs of manifold powers.
>
> *yasyāṃ samudra uta sindhur āpo*
> *yasyām annaṃ kṛṣṭayaḥ saṃbabhūvuḥ...* / 3 a-b
> In Her are the ocean, the rivers, the waters;
> in Her food and ploughing lands came into being.
>
> *yasyāś catasraḥ pradiśaḥ pṛthivyā*
> *yasyām annaṃ kṛṣṭayaḥ saṃbabhūvuḥ /*
> *yā bibharti bahudhā prāṇad ejat ...* 4 a-c
> Hers, *Pṛthivī*'s, are the four quarters of the space,
> in Her food and ploughing lands came into being;
> She bears what manifoldly breathes and moves.
>
> *... gavām aśvānāṃ vayasaś ca viṣṭā*
> *bhagaṃ varcaḥ pṛthivī no dadhātu* // 5 c-d
> Let *Pṛthivī*, the abode of cows, of horses, and birds
> procure for us fortune and splendor!
>
> *yāṃ rakṣanty asvapnā viśvadānīṃ*
> *devā bhūmiṃ pṛthivīm apramādam /*
> *sā no madhu priyaṃ duhām*
> *atho ukṣatu varcasā* // 7
> The Gods, whom never does sleep submit,
> carefully protect the all-giving Earth, *Pṛthivī*.

Let Her yield to us honey that we love!
Let Her besprinkle us with splendor!

... sā no bhūmir bhūridhārā payo
duhām atho ukṣatu varcasā // 9 c-d
Let the Earth, abundant in streams,
yield to us milk!
Let Her besprinkle us with splendor!

... sā no bhūmir vi sṛjatāṃ
mātā putrāya me payaḥ// 10 c-d
Let the Earth pour forth milk for us –
She, a Mother, for me, Her son!

... mātā bhūmiḥ putro ahaṃ pṛthivyā' /
parjanyaḥ pitā sa u naḥ pipartu // 12 d-e
The Earth is the Mother,
I am the son of *Pṛthivī*;
Parjanya[1] is the Father.
Let him protect us!

pṛthivīm ā vadāmi ...
ūrjaṃ puṣṭaṃ bibhratīm annabhāgaṃ
ghṛtaṃ tvābhi ni ṣīdema bhūme // 29 a, c-d
The Earth do I invoke ...
who bearest force, prosperity, food
and clarified butter.
May we settle down upon Thee, O Earth!

yat te bhūme vikhanāmi
kṣipraṃ tad api rohatu /
mā te marma vimṛgvari
mā te hṛdayam arpipam // 35
What of Thee, O Earth, I dig out

[1] God of the rain, sometimes considered in the *Vedas* as the husband of the Earth.

let that quickly grow again:
may I not pierce Thy vital parts, O Pure!
may I not hurt your heart!

yasyām annaṃ vrīhiyavau ... // 42 a
On whom is food, rice and barley ...

... *prajāpatiḥ pṛthivīṃ viśvagarbhām*
āśām āśāṃ raṇyāṃ naḥ kṛṇotu // 43 c-d
Let Prajāpati [2] make *Pṛthivī* pleasant to us
in every one of Her regions
– She is the Universal Womb!

... *yac chivaṃ tena no mṛḍa* // 47 d
Be Thou gracious to us
with what in Thee is auspicious and good.

bhujiṣyaṃ pātraṃ nihitaṃ guhā
yad āvir bhoge abhavan mātṛmadbhya // 60 c-d
The vessel destined to nourrish
was deposited in a secret place;
and, for being enjoyed
by those who have a mother,
it became manifest.

tvam asy āvapanī janānām
aditiḥ kāmadughā ... 61 a-b
Thou are the benefactor of men,
Aditi, the wish-fulfilling cow.

bhūme mātar ni dhehi mā
bhadrayā supratiṣṭhitam /
saṃvidānā divā kave

---

[2] Protector and Creator God, sometimes presented, in the *Vedas* and regularly in the *Brāhmaṇas*, as a Supreme God.

śriyāṃ mā dhehi bhūtyām // 63
O Mother Earth,
kindly set me down well established,
and, associated with Heaven,
do set me in happiness, in prosperity,
O Thou wise one.

Food identified with the principle of life

In the Vedic and Brahmanic epoch (*circa* 800-500 B.C.) we also find other texts that do not indicate where food comes from, but express the importance that food has: food is identified with an entity that possesses a superior status: *the principle of life.*

The hymn 107 of Book X in the *Rig Veda* is dedicated to extol the *dakṣhiṇā*, i. e. the donation that the patron of a rite gives to the persons that perform it: the poet who writes the verses that are recited in the rite, and the priests who accomplish the rite process. As it frequently happens in the *Rig Veda* the *dakshiṇā* is personified. In the stanza 7 of the mentioned hymn it is said that the *dakshiṇā* "brings the food (*anna*)", and that this one is the *ātman* of man (*yo na ātmā*). In the *Rig Veda* the term *ātman* designates the breath that is conceived as *the principle of life.* The idea is not that we breathe because we live, but that we live because we breathe, since in us dwells the *ātman*, the vital breath, *the principle of life*, a subtle and mysterious entity, to which we owe the life and the existence.

After several centuries, thanks to the brahmanical especulation, the term *ātman* comes to designate the spiritual individual principle, identical in essence and exalted qualities with *Brahman*, the Absolut. But in this hymn, as generally in the *Rig Veda*, *ātman* designates only the vital breath, motor of life; the term is still in the beginning of its brilliant semantic career, similar to the Greek term *psyché*, and the Latin terms *spiritus*, *anima*, *animus* in the West.

We find similar ideas expressed in other texts. In the *Śatapathabrāhmaṇa* IV, 3, 4, 25, food is identified with *prāṇa*, term that can be considered as a synonym of *ātman*. And in the *Aitareya Brāhmaṇa* VII, 13, 8, we have the following stanza that we must not forget was written more than twenty-five centuries ago:

> *annaṃ ha prāṇaḥ śaraṇaṃ ha vāso*
> *rūpaṃ hiraṇyaṃ paśavo vivāhāḥ* /
> *sakhā ha jāyā kdṛpaṇaṃ ha duhitā*
> *jyotir ha putraḥ parame vyoman* //
> "Food is *prāṇa*, clothing a protection,
> gold an ornament, cattle marriage vehicles,
> a wife a companion, a daughter a misfortune,
> and a son a light in the highest heaven".

Food identified with Brahman, *the Absolute*

In the *Upanishads*, texts later than the mentioned *Brāhmaṇas*, many references to food (*anna*) are found, and many of them exalt it in a remarkable way. The *Chandogya-Upanishad* I, 3, 6 expresses that all is established upon food (*anne hīdaṃ sarvaṃ sthitam*); the *Bṛhadāraṇyaka-Upanishad* V, 12, 1, that all beings rest in food (*anne hīmāni sarvāṇi bhūtāni viṣṭānī*); the *Taittirīya-Upanishad* II, 2, 1, that food is the eldest born of beings (*annaṃ hi bhūtānāṃ jyeṣṭham*), that beings are born from food and grow up by food (*annād bhūtāni jāyante, jātāny annena vardhante*), and nobody should speak ill of food or despise food (*annaṃ na nindyāt, annaṃ na paricakṣīta, annaṃ bahu kurvīta*) (III, 7, 1; 8, 1); the *Maitrī-Upanishad* VI, 11, that food is the highest form of Self (*param vā etad ātmano rūpam yad annam*).

The exaltation of food reaches its highest point when it is identified with *Brahman*, the Supreme Principle, wherefrom beings come forth when they are born, wherein they have their support as long as they live, where they enter when they die (as it is defined in the *Taittirīya-Upanishad* III, 1, 1). In the *Chāndogya-Upanishad* VII, 9, 2 are pointed out the benefits that get those who venerate *Brahman* as food (*sa yo 'nnaṃ brahmety upāste*). The *Taittirīya-Upanishad* II, 2, 1 expresses a similar idea in relation to the veneration of *Brahman* as food. And, finally, the same *Upanishad* III, 2, 1 tells how Bhṛgu Vāruṇi, son of God Varuṇa, after practising asceticism, reached the knowledge that food is *Brahman*, the Absolut (*annaṃ brahmeti vyajānāt*).

The exaltation of food expressed in the indicated identifications corresponds not only to the importance food has in relation to the individual, as means of conservation of life, health, and capacity of action, but also to the importance it had and has still in regard to the history of nations as a factor of migrations, revolutions and wars.

Food as source of impurity

In India is also found another attitude, very different from the previous ones in relation to food: the attitude that establishes differences among foods, considering some of them pure, and some others impure. Impure food makes impure those who consume them and compels them to submit themselves to a purification rite. Members of the highest castes, who are considered to be pure, are not allowed to eat impure food; for the pariahs, considered to be impure by nature, this prohibition is not applicable. Moreover it is also believed that pure food can become impure depending on the person that offers it, etc.

Among the forbidden foods meat coming from living beings is considered impure. In the legal treatises, as *Manusmriti* V, 48 and *Viṣṇusmriti* 51, 71, there is a famous stanza that forbids eating meat from living beings and at the same time gives the reason of the prohibition:

nākṛtvā prāṇināṃ hiṃsāṃ
māṃsam utpadyate kvacit /
na ca prāṇivadhaḥ svargyas
tasmān māṃsaṃ vivarjayet //

"Meat can never be obtained
without inhuring a living creature;
to kill a living being does not lead to Heaven;
therefore everybody should avoid eating meat".

The attitude of Brahmanism was equally severe regarding alcohol. Its prohibition is very strict and its use is considered as the gravest fault. Cf. *Manusmriti* IX, 235 and XI, 54.

Little by little the norms of legislators opposed to the use of meat coming from living beings as food, and to the use of alcoholic beverages, were imposed in Brahmanic and Hindu India, converting vegetarianism and abstention from alcohol in important moral laws.

Legal literature (*Dharma-sūtras*, *Dharma-smṛtis*; *Dharma-śāstras*) dedicates many of its commandments to the theme of food from the point of view of their purity or impurity. So, for instance, the *Manusmriti*, already quoted, in verses 205-225 of Chapter IV points out the persons from whom a Brahmin should not receive food; and in verses 5-56 of Chapter V it enumerates all the foods that are forbidden to him. The *Vishnusmriti*, also quoted, in Chapter LI has prescriptions similar to those of the *Manusmṛti*. And in a general way these norms are found in all the legal treatises.[3]

Tantrism in relation to food

Tantrism (from *circa* 500 B.C.onwards) has in relation to meat and alcohol a disconcerting attitude that stands in contrast with that of the legal texts that express the strict puritanic feeling of Brahmanism. The Tantric texts prescribe the use of meat and

[3] Cf. Chapter XXII of the second part of Volume II of P.V. Kane, *History of Dharmashāstra*, Poona: Bhandarkar Oriental Research Institute, 1941, and L. Alsdorf, *Beiträge zur Geschichte von Vegetarismus und Rinderverehrung in Indien* en sus *Kleine Schriften*: Stuttgart: Franz Steiner, 1998, pp. 831-899. This article studies the texts that express opposite opinions to that of Manu, and make think that at the beginning of the history of Indian Culture the use of meat as food was not forbidden.

wine and the realization of the sexual act in the *cakrapujā* ceremony, typical of Tantrism, as a means that allows man to approach divinity. Meat and wine not only are not considered impure, nor the sexual act inmoral, but on the contrary they are conceived as a means of spiritual realization.

This attitude is in agreement with the basic Tantric philosophy. The Tantric texts (as the *Kulārṇavatantra* II, 23-24) say that "the soul" of Tantrism "is pleasure" and that in it "pleasure has become Yoga, and sin a meritorious action". According to Tantrism Gods enjoy when the man, who pays homage to them, enjoys; ascetism, suffering and pain are not necessary to get close to them; Liberation, *mukti*, i.e., identification and unification with Divinity, is obtained together with *bhukti*, joy, not being necessary to separate one from the other or to confront them".[4]

B. Buddhism and The Lotus Sūtra

Buddhism in relation to food
Food as something essential to life.
Food as an instrument of wrong behaviour

Buddhism received among others the name of 'Middle Path', *majjhimā paṭipadā*, that keeps away - on the Ethics area - from ascetism, as "a life of self-torture, painful, ignoble, that leads nowhere (*attakilamathānuyogo dukkho anariyo anatthasaṃhito, Saṃyutta-Nikāya*, V, p. 421, PTS edition)", and from sensuality, "common, vulgar, ordinary, ignoble devotion to sensual pleasure that leads nowhere (*kāmasukhallikānu-yogo hīno gammo pothujjaniko anariyo anatthasaṃhito, ibidem*)".

Buddhism was thus a system of conduct characterized by its sense of moderation, the *Middle Way*, which considers that

[4] On Tantrism see F. Tola, "El hombre en la cultura de la India", in F. Tola and C. Dragonetti, *Yoga y Mística de la India*, Buenos Aires: Kier, 1978, pp. 9-74.

moderation is the right attitude in order to reach the spiritual perfection, the supreme goal of the Buddhist effort.

So Buddhism adopted also in regard to food an attitude of moderation (*bhojane mattaññutā*) that is very much praised in the ancient texts. In that attitude is also manifested the typical tendency to pragmatism of Buddhist Teaching. The *Majjhima-Nikāya* I, p. 10 (PTS edition) and the *Visuddhimagga* of Buddhaghosa, pp. 26-27 (H.C. Warren and Dh. Kosambi edition) expose the basic idea of Buddhism in regard to this subject.[5]

To keep body alive man must eat; man has to keep body healthy, able to realize its functions, full of strength and energy in order that it be not afflicted by pain, discomfort, and weakness, and become thus an obstacle. A healthy body will collaborate, in an efficient way, in the intellectual search of the knowledge of truth that the Buddha discovered, and in the realization of the noble virtues that He preached. The Buddha is not in favour of ascetic hunger, or of the ascetic starvation, to which so many mystic and religious persons submitted in their search of spiritual perfection and truth. Food is considered as a necessary instrument to be able to achieve a superior aim.

But to avoid extreme ascetism is not the whole thing. Extreme sensuality must also be avoided. Food must not be taken for the sake of fun (*na davāya*), as children do; or for the sake of vanity (*na madāya*), as the boxers and fighters do to obtain strenght, vigour and courage; or for the sake of embellishment (*na maṇḍanāya, na vibhūsanāya*), as the harem's women and the courtesans, actors and dancers do; or to satisfy an overflowing anxiety of sensual pleasure (*kāmasukhallikānuyoga*). Food can become in this way also an instrument of wrong behaviour.

---

[5] On the food in Buddhism see the articles "Āhāra" of H.G.A. van Zeyst, "Bhojana" of H.R.P., "Fasting" of S.K. Nanayakkara, and "Food" of H.G.A. van Zeyst, in *Encyclopaedia of Buddhism*, G.P. Malalasekera ed., Vol. 1, Fasc. 2, pp. 280-283, Vol. 3, Fasc. 1, pp. 64-66, and Vol. 5, Fasc. 2, p. 255, respectively.

Vegetarianism and the use of meat as food

The attitudes regarding the use of meat as food changes in the Buddhist countries according to the Buddhist moral discipline codes (*vinaya*) they follow.

In the countries of South East Asia, i.e., Thailand, Cambodia, Laos, Burma and Sri Lanka that belong to 'Hīnayāna' Buddhism, the use of meat as food is not forbidden. This attitude comes from the *Vinaya* of the Theravādin Buddhist Canon that is adopted in these regions. This *Vinaya* allows, for instance, the ill monk to eat meat and fish (*Pāṭimokkha, Pācittiyā* N° 39); and in a general way allows every monk, without taking into account his health, to eat meat and fish they receive by begging, only when that meat does not come from an animal specially sacrified *for him* and is not from special indicated animals: horses, elephants, snakes, tigers, panthers, hyenas, dogs. In the just indicated cases meat is considered to be pure (*Mahāvagga*, pp. 216-220 and 237-238, *Cullavagga*, p. 197, *Suttavibhaṅga*, pp. 171-172, PTS editions).

In China, a country which adhered to Mahāyāna Buddhism (at least until the arrival of the Communist Revolution), fish and meat were forbidden to monks, because a good number of Mahāyānist *sūtras* forbid it, as for instance the *Laṅkāvatārasūtra*, Chapter VIII, and specially the *Fang Wang King* (Third secondary norm: *About the use of meat*), p. 42, J.J.M. de Groot's edition,[6] the most important treatise of monastic Discipline in Chinese Buddhism. The prohibition was also extended to the lay devotees. In Japan and Korea, countries that belong also to Mahāyāna Buddhism, the attitude in relation to meat and fish was similar to that of Buddhist China.

In Tibet the situation was different. Although in Tibet predominated Mahāyāna Buddhism (at least until it was occupied by the Communist China), nevertheless monks

---

[6] *Le Code du Mahâyâna en Chine. Son influence sur la vie monacale et sur le monde laïque* par J.J.M. De Groot, Wiesbaden: Dr. Martin Sändig, oHG, 1967.

adopted the *Vinaya* of the Hīnayānist sect of the Mūlasarvāstivādins that does not forbid the use of meat. So in Tibet eating meat is not forbidden to Buddhists, monks as well as lay devotees.

Several factors have determined the prohibition of eating meat: the will to comply with the norm of *ahiṃsā* (non-violence) (cf. the stanza quoted in section *Food as a source of impurity*), the doctrine of the *tathāgatagarbha* (Buddha Nature present in all beings, that must be respected), and the belief in reincarnations, according to which a beloved being can reincarnate as an animal, depending on his conduct.[7]

If the attitude of Buddhism in regard to food was enough permissive, it did not happen the same in relation to alcohol: it was strictly prohibited in Hīnayāna (cf. *Kuddakapātha* 2, *Fifth sikkhāpada*, PTS edition) as well as in Mahāyāna Buddhism. Cf. *Fang Wang King* (Fifth principal norm), p. 35, and (Second secondary norm), p. 41 (J.J.M. de Groot edition).

Food considered from an aesthetic point of view

We find in Buddhism a very peculiar practise regarding food: to control in monks the attachment to food and to inculcate in them moderation in relation to it, Buddhism resorts also to an aesthetic measure. The Monastic Discipline recommends the monk meditation on the disagreeable and painful aspects that imply the search and preparation of food, the ingredients that it contains, the origin of these ingredients, the act of masticating and swallowing it, the physiological process of digestion, the transformations that food suffers inside the body, etc.[8]

---

[7] Cf. the article of David Seyfort Ruegg, "Ahiṃsā y el vegetarianismo en la historia del Budismo", in *Revista de Estudios Budistas*, México-Buenos Aires, N° 6, 1994, pp. 47-62. English version of this article: "Ahiṃsā and Vegetarianism in the History of Buddhism", included in *Buddhist Studies in honour of Walpola Rahula*, London: Gordon Fraser, 1980, pp. 234-241.

[8] Buddhaghosa in *Visuddhimagga*, Chapter XI, pp. 285-290, H.C. Warren and Dh. Kosambi edition, Cambridge (Mass.): Harvard University Press, Harvard Oriental Series, 1950.

The Buddha and food

In many episodes of the Buddha's life important aspects of His Doctrine manifest themselves. Two of these episodes are related to food.

When the Buddha leaves the Royal Palace of his father in search of Truth, he retires to a forest where he practises painful and severe austerities, thinking that the ascetic path, very much appreciated in India, would lead Him to the aim He is looking for. But, after some time, "with his body tormented, clearly to no purpose, by severe austerities" (*kaṣṭatapaḥspaṣṭa-vyarthakliṣṭatanuḥ*), the Buddha, thanks to His wisdom, discovers that "it is not the path that will lead Him to emotional serenity, to Enlightment, to Liberation" (*nāyaṃ dharmo virāgāya na bodhāya na muktaye*) (Ashvaghosha, *Buddhacarita* XII, 100-101). He renounces the ascetic path and, afterwards as Aśvaghośa describes:

snāto nairañjanātīrād uttatāra śanaiḥ kṛśaḥ /
*bhaktyāvanataśākhāgrair dattahastas taṭadrumaiḥ//*108

108. "He bathed in the Nairañjanā river
and, due to His weakness,
He painfully went out from its waters,
while the trees of the shore for helping Him
bent down the tips of their branches,
inspired by a feeling of veneration."

atha gopādhipasutā daivatair abhicoditā /
udbhūtahṛdayānandā tatra nandabalāgamat // 109

109. "Then Nandabalā,
the daugthet of the cowherd chief,
instigated by the Gods,
came there with the joy of her heart bursting."

sā śraddhāvardhitaprītir vikasallocanotpalā /
śirasā praṇipatyainaṃ grāhayām āsa pāyasam // 111

111. "Her gladness was increased by faith,
the blue lotus of her eyes blossomed,
doing homage with her head,
she made him accept rice boiled in milk."

kṛtvā tadupabhogena prāptajanmaphalāṃ sa tām /
bodhiprāptau samartho 'bhūt saṃtarpitaṣaḍindriyaḥ //112

112. "Eating that food,
He made her obtain the fruit of her birth,
and, his sense faculties invigorated,
He became capable of obtaining Enlightenment."

The Buddha accepts the simple food that the shepherd's daughter offers to Him and in this way He contributes to make her gather merits, and at the same time He recovers His strength what allows Him to continue the hard search of Truth.

The second episode regarding food takes us to the last days of the Buddha's life. It is narrated in Chapter VIII, Section ṇ, of the *Udāna.*[9] When the Buddha was travelling through the country of the Mallas, He was invited by Cunda, the son of the goldsmith, to take food with him. Cunda served Him with a dish of pork meat. Due to that food, and being weakened owing to His eighty years, the Buddha got ill, but he did not say anything in order not to cause Cunda's remorse, since Cunda could feel guilty for the aches and pains of the Master. Due to that illness the Buddha died soon afterwards, entering *Supreme Nirvāṇa* without return.

The Buddha ate the food prepared with meat by a devotee that offered it. It was not from an animal specially killed for His meal, and because of that it was licit for the Buddha to eat it. Moreover the Buddha, in His great compassion, could not refuse that food-offering, depriving Cunda of the merit that he could obtain through it.

The Buddha never denied His human condition. He was only a Master who had conquered the Truth with His effort, His errors, His achievements, and who guided others to Salvation, Liberation, *Nirvāṇa,* which He Himself had reached. His death occurs in a human way: old, He got sick and died. The First

---

[9] C. Dragonetti, *Udāna, la Palabra de Buda,* New Jersey, USA: Yin-shun Foundation-Fundación Instituto de Estudios Budistas, 2002, 5th edition.

Noble Truth, that states that suffering is the unavoidable heritage of man, points out among its causes old age, illness and death. The Buddha, a man, did not escape the common human destiny: He was born as a man, lived as a man, made efforts as a man, and as a man He died.

Food in the Lotus Sūtra

The *Lotus Sūtra*, a very important text of Mahāyāna Buddhism, is dedicated to the exposition of the generous doctrine that every man can become a *Buddha* and that the *Buddha* during all His life preached only One and the same doctrine, revealing it according to the intellectual, psychological and spiritual abilities of His audience. In this *Sūtra* are found two interesting references to food that constitute a special attitude in regard to it.

Food and the burning house

In Chapter III of the *Lotus Sūtra* there is the famous parable of the burning house, also known as the parable of the children saved from fire by their father. The *Sūtra* describes (see specially III, verses 39 ss.) the old house, with its columns rotten at their basis, with its decaying walls, with its wholly ruined roofs, with its rooms and corridors full of rubbish. In that house lived not only several human being, but also beings not belonging to the human race: hyenas, owls, vultures and other birds of prey, and besides them demoniacal beings such as *yakshas* and *pretas* (starving ghosts). And the old house catches fire, becomes a blazing mass of fire and smoke, where the inhabitants are imprisoned, unable to escape, running terrified from one side to another, and dying burnt.

The old burning house is the symbol of our world, a cruel and heartless world, where men suffer and die, consumed by the flames of their numerous passions, desires, and hatred, always threatened by old age, illness and death.

The text makes references to food, when it describes the old house. It mentions the hyenas devouring corpses, while the dogs and jackals wait them to move away for satisfying at their turn their own hunger, which tortures them; and the *yakshas* tearing to pieces corpses, as the hyenas, or devouring the breedings of disgusting beings or feeding on other living beings. And in all the house, among the hyenas, jackals, dogs and *yakshas* that consume their ignoble food, wander the *pretas*, condemned to the punishment of a permanent hunger.

The vision of food in the burning house (symbol of our world) is in agreement with the conditions that reign in it: it is sinister. In our world, the *Sahā World*, the reality of food is also sinister although we do not perceive it. To get food means destroying trees, plants, vegetables and seeds, and, what is more serious, the suffering and death for many beings, cruelly slaughtered and unscrupulously consumed. And near those who satisfy their hunger are those who suffer hunger for not having anything to eat. This situation is against the basic Buddhist principles of compassion, non-violence, interdependence, solidarity and harmony that must reign in our world.

Food in the Buddha's Worlds

But the *Lotus Sūtra* does not leave us with this deplorable vision of food. Although Buddhism considers that this world is a 'valley of tears', a place of suffering and frustration, it cannot be accused of being pessimistic; its inspiration is rather optimistic, because it knows there is a 'escape' (*nissaraṇa*, *Udāna* VII, 3), discovered by the Buddha that leads man beyond suffering. To the depressing vision of food in the description of the burning house, the *Lotus Sūtra* opposes the vision of food in the Buddha's Worlds.

The Buddha's Worlds are scattered in the limitless space and are lofty paradises built with jewels, silver and gold; beautified with trees full of flowers and fruits; perfumed with incense and aromatic powders; where hundreds of hundreds of small bells resound shaken by the breeze; with ornaments of flags and banners; over which hang precious canopies. All evil is unknown there: illness, pains, sorrow, death, and ignorance.

Māra, the Evil, the Lord of sensuality, has not entrance there, or evil and perverted creatures. There are reborn, adorned with the most excellent virtues, beings who reached their spiritual perfection, and with it Enlightenment, the supreme form of Consciousness, Inteligence and Knowledge. There they will exist for millions of millions of Cosmic Periods, preaching the Doctrine of the Buddha to millions of millions of beings that have not yet reached Enlightenment, guiding and helping them to reach it and to become themselves *Buddhas*, who on their turn will obtain their own *Buddha's World* and will guide millions of millions of beings. And after an almost infinite existence in one of these Worlds, the being, the *Buddha*, who obtained that World, when he desires and determines it, will extinguish himself in *Nirvāṇa*, the place of happiness, peace, silence - as the flame of a lamp when its oil comes to an end. Magnificent destiny for those who exerted themselves and with their human effort, without the help of a divine grace, have reached the aim!

We wonder: Which is the food taken by these fortunate beings in their *Buddha's Worlds*? The *Lotus Sūtra*, p. 202, lines 7-9, Kern and Nanjio edition, gives the answer to us:

> *tena khalu punar bhikṣavaḥ samayena tasmin buddhakṣetre teṣāṃ sattvānāṃ dvāv āhārau bhaviṣyataḥ /*
> *katamā dvau / yaduta dharmaprītyāhāro dhyānaprītyāhāraś ca.*
> Cf. p. 206, stanza 19.
>
> "And at that time, O monks, in this *World of Buddha* two kinds of food will exist for the beings that dwell in it. Which two? The food constituted by the happiness that the Doctrine produces, and the food constituted by the happiness that Meditation produces."

The *Karuṇāpuṇḍarīkasūtra* II, p. 16, lines 15 and 16, Isshi Yamada edition,[10] mentions as typical food of the *Worlds of*

[10] *Karuṇāpuṇḍarīka*, ed. by Isshi Yamada, London: School of Oriental and African Studies, 1968.

Buddha the food constituted by the happiness that Meditation produces and the happiness that the Doctrine produces, adding to them the food constituted by the aroma flowers and the perfumes.

Food as a symbol of the present and the future destiny of man

The food in the *Sahā World*, where we live, and the food in the *Worlds of Buddha*, to which the Buddhist should aspire, are radically opposite. The food in the *Sahā World* is rough, in some way disgusting, can be used in an unappropriate way and become an instrument of wrong behaviour; many people suffer for not having it, and the food is some times the product of destruction and some other times of suffering and death. The food in the *Worlds of Buddha* is subtle, of spiritual nature or of the finest essence; it does not harm anything or anybody, and everyone who intends to do it, can have access to it, and that food due to its special essence elevates those who take it.

The food in the *Sahā World* and the food in the *Worlds of Buddha* are presented as symbols, the first one of the present destiny of man, enchained to evil and pain, and the latter of the future and unavoidable destiny of man, beyond the dark aspects of life.

XIII

Reviews Concerning the *Lotus Sūtra*

The Lotus Sūtra, The White Lotus of Marvelous Law, Translated from the Chinese of Kumārajīva, by Tsugunari Kubo and Akira Yuyama, Tokyo: The Reiyukai, 1991, XIII, 332 pp.

The *Lotus Sūtra* (*Saddharmapuṇḍarīka* in Sanskrit) was translated six times from Sanskrit into Chinese, in the years 255, 286, 290, 335, 406 and 601 A.D. This gives an idea of the acceptance it had in the Buddhist world. Only three of these translations have been preserved, that of the year 290 by Dharmaraksha, that of the year 406 by Kumārajīva, and that of the year 601, which is only a revision of the translation of the year 406. The translation by Kumārajīva eclipsed the others, because of its fidelity to the original Sanskrit text, its clearness and elegant style, qualities that make it a masterpiece among the Chinese translations of Sanskrit Buddhist texts. The *Lotus Sūtra* was known in a great part of Asia – China, Korea, Japan – thanks to Kumārajīva's translation, and this is one of its major glorious titles. For more details about editions, commentaries, etc. of the *Lotus Sūtra*, see Akira Yuyama, *A Bibliography of the Sanskrit Texts of the Saddharmapuṇḍarīkasūtra*, Canberra: Australian National University Press, 1970, and Fernando Tola and Carmen Dragonetti, "El Sūtra del Loto (Saddharmapuṇḍarīka), su difusión, su influencia, su mensaje", in *Revista de Estudios Budistas* (REB) N° 2, México-Buenos Aires, 1991, pp. 69-115.

The Chinese version by Kumārajīva was translated into Japanese and English many times. Among the modern Japanese translations we point out that by Yukio Sakamoto and Yutaka Iwamoto, included in the *Iwanami Series* edited in Tokyo. We cannot omit mentioning the transcription in *kana* (Japanese syllable characters) contained in a manuscript from 1330 edited by the Reiyukai. See a review of this last one in this book. Among the English translatioms of the Chinese version by Kumārajīva we have those by Senchu Murano (1974, second edition: 1991), Bunnō Katō (1975, reprinted many times), Leon Hurvitz (1976). To the previous translations we add now that done by Dr.Tsugunari Kubo and Dr.Akira Yuyama, to which this review refers.

Kubo and Yuyama used for their translation the so-called "Kasuga edition" of the *Lotus Sūtra* of the year 1263, published in facsimile by Dr. Shōkō Kabutogi (Tokyo: The Reiyukai, 1979), instead of using the edition of Sūtra included in the *Taishō Shinshū Daizōkyō.* According to Dr. Kabutogi, who is a specialist in editions of the *Sūtra*, the Kasuga edition is superior to the other known editions. When they made their translation from the Chinese, Kubo and Yuyama also consulted the Sanskrit text of the *Sūtra*, specially the Manuscript of Kashgar (edited in Delhi, 1976, reprint: Tokyo: The Reiyukai, 1977), as well as the Tibetan translation of the *Sūtra.*

The translation by Kubo and Yuyama has been included in the Series *English Translation of the Sino-Japanese Buddhist Canon*, monumental project that the *Bukkyō Dendō Kyōkai* (Tokyo) is carrying on. This Series reunites English translations of the most important Buddhist texts from their Chinese versions. This inclusion marks the high quality of Kubo's and Yuyama's translation, as the *Bukkyō Dendō Kyōkai* applies strict criteria of excellence to the translations published in the mentioned Series.

The translation of Kubo and Yuyama is very valuable, because it has the qualities that every translation should have: it is faithful to the meaning of the original text as far as it is possible, and it is of an easy and pleasant reading, because of its fluency and elegance. We would dare to say that Kubo's and Yuyama's translation has surpassed all the previous English translations.

The Lotus Sūtra in Kana Characters. Kept in the Myōichi Memorial Hall of the Reiyukai of Tokyo, edited by Norio Nakada, 1988.

I. A facsimile edition, 2 volumes: *Myōichi Kinenkanbon*: *Kanagaki Hokkekyō*, of Norio Nakada (ed.), Tokyo: The Reiyukai, 1988. Part I: ix, 724 pages, 2 frontispieces in colour. Part II: 725-1346 pages.

II. Transcription, 1 volume: *Myōichi Kinenkanbon: Kanagaki Hokkeky²*, of Norio Nakada (ed.), Tokyo: The Reiyukai, 1989. iv, iii pages, 1341 columns.

III. Index, 1 volume: *Myōichi Kinenkanbon: Kanagaki Hokkekyō*, of Norio Nakada, Tokyo: The Reiyukai, 1980. vi, ix, iii, 615, xii pages.

In the first two volumes of this work, Professor Norio Nakada has given us a magnificent and complete *facsimile edition* of the eight *chüan* (*kan*) (*rolls, parts or volumes of a work*) of a manuscript of the year 1330 containing a translation into Japanese of the Chinese version of the *Lotus Sūtra* done by Kumārajīva. This manuscript is kept in the *Myiōchi Memorial Hall* of the *Reiyukai* in Tokyo. The translation is written in Japanese syllabary (*kana*), using eventually the Sino-japanese ideogrames (*kanji*) with interlinear indication of their Japanese pronunciation also by means of *kana*.

The second publication has the *typographical transcription* of the manuscript contained in the facsimile edition. The distribution of the typographical text follows exactly the distribution of the manuscript text (in the first two volumes of the facsimile edition) and for that reason makes its reading easier. Moreover Professor Nakada has eventually put between lines, besides the *kana* used by the manuscript, the corresponding *kanji,* taken from the Chinese translation of Kumārajiva. In this way, this second publication comes to complete the first one. The fact that the translation is basically in *kana* makes the text reading easier for those persons that know spoken Japanese and the Japanese syllabary (*kana*), but do not completely master the system of Sino-japanese ideograms (*kanji*).

The third volume is an excelent and complete Index of all the words contained in the Chinese translation of the *Sūtra*, in *kana* as well in *kanji.*

Besides its practical value, this publication will be useful for the study of the spread of the *Lotus Sūtra* in Japan.

The four volumes constitute a first class work, because of its excellent presentation. It should be emphasized in a special way the clarity of the facsimile edition.

This work is other valuable contribution of *The Reiyukai* to the studies of the *Lotus Sūtra* that enriches its previous publications:

Saddharmapuṇḍarīka Manuscripts Found in Gilgit, edited by Sōkō Watanabe, 1972-1975. Reprint: 1982;

Saddharma-Puṇḍarīka-Sūtra: Kashgar Manuscript, edited by Lokesh Chandra, with a foreword by Heinz Bechert. Second impression (1977). First published in New Delhi (1976);

The Kasuga Edition of the Lotus Sūtra, edited with an introduction by Shōkō Kabutogi, 1978;

Descriptive Catalogue of the Miao-fa-lien-hua-ching from Tunhuang collected by Aurel Stein and Paul Pelliot, by Shōkō Kabutogi with Forewords by K.B. Gardner and Bernard Frank, 1978;

A New Fragmentary Gilgit Manuscript of The Saddharmapuṇḍarīka, edited by Oskar von Hinüber (1982);

Index to the Saddharmapuṇḍarīkasūtra – Sanskrit, Tibetan, Chinese - edited by Yasunori Ejima and others, eleven fascicles, 1985-1993.

Seishi Karashima, A Glossary of Dharmaraksha's Translation of the Lotus Sutra, Tokyo: The International Research Institute for Advanced Buddhology, Soka University, 1998, 696 pp.

This is the first volume of the Series *Bibliotheca Philologica et Philosophica Buddhica*, created and directed by the prestigious Japanese Buddhologist Yūichi Kajiyama, and published by the *International Research Institute*, of the *Soka University*. It is an excellent glossary of the Chinese translation of the *Lotus Sūtra* done by Dharmaraksha. The translation of Dharmaraksha is included in the *Taishō Shinshū Daizōkyō*, the well-known Japanese edition of the Chinese Buddhist Canon, Volume IX, under the number 263.

Professor Seishi Karashima has chosen for this glossary around 4000 words of the translation of Dharmaraksha, excluding in principle the words, which occur with the same meaning in the Chinese classics before Dharmaraksha. Each word is accompanied with its *Pinyin* pronunciation, its English translation, volume, page and column numbers of the entry word in two well-known Chinese dictionaries: *Hanyudacidian* and *Dai- kanwajiten*, page, section and line numbers in Volume IX of the *Taishō* edition, in which the entry word occurs, the corresponding Sanskrit word, found in the Kern-Nanjio edition of the Sanskrit text of the *Lotus Sūtra*, and, finally, the corresponding Chinese word and its location in Kumārajīva's translation of the text, which is to be found in Volume IX of the *Taishō* edition.

Besides being a really valuable work from the philological point of view, and most necessary for the study of the Chinese translation of the *Lotus Sūtra* done by Dharmaraksha and for its comparison with the translation of the same text by Kumārajīva, this glossary is also extremely useful for the study and translation of any Chinese text because of the abundance of lexicographic material that it provides.

Professor Seishi Karashima announces in it his intention of preparing glossaries of other Chinese translations of Buddhist texts coming from India with the final aim of doing a Chinese Buddhist Dictionary. We eagerly expect the accomplishment of this project that would be of great help for the study of Chinese Buddhism.

P. S.: In the year 2005 Professor Seishi Karashima published *A Glossary of Kumārajīva's Translation of the Lotus Sutra*, Tokyo: The International Research Institute for Advanced Buddhology, Soka University, 2001, 528 pp. This publication follows the same method as used in the previous work of the *Glossary of Dharmaraksha's Translation of the Lotus Sutra.* The excellence and usefulness of both glossaries are the same. It is a new proof of the scholarly meticulousness and mastery of Sanskrit and Chinese languages of Professor Karashima. Together with this book other excellent publications concerning the *Lotus Sūtra* done by the *Soka Gakkai* in Japan must be mentioned:

Jiang Zhongxin edited (in facsimile and in transcription): *Sanskrit Lotus Sutra Fragments from the Lüshun Museum Colection*, Lüshun: Lüshun Museum – Soka Gakkai, 1997.

In cooperation with the *National Archives of Nepal*: *Saddharmapuṇḍarīkasūtram. Sanskrit Lotus Sutra Manuscript from the National Archives of Nepal (No.4-21) (Lotus Sutra Manuscript Series 2-1)*, 1998.

In the year 2000, Klaus Wille edited *Fragments of a Manuscript of the Saddharmapuṇḍarīkasūtra from Khādaliq.*

In the *Lotus Sutra Manuscripts Series 4*: *Saddharmapuṇḍarīkasūtram. Sanskrit Lotus Sutra Manuscripts from Cambridge University Library*, Facsimile Edition, 2002.

In the year 2003, Haruaki Kotsuki edited *Saddharmapuṇḍarīkasūtram. Sanskrit Lotus Sutra Manuscript from University of Tokyo General Library (No. 414). Romanized Text*, in the *Lotus Sutra Manuscript Series 5.*

The Lotus Sūtra, translated by Burton Watson, New York: Columbia University Press, 1993, xxix-359 pp.

Sūtra von der Lotosblume des wunderbaren Gesetzes, nach dem chinesischen Text von Kumārajīva ins Deutsche übersetzt und eingeleitet von Margareta von Borsig, Darmstadt: Wissenschaftliche Buchgesellchaft, 1993, 415 pp.

Le Sûtra du Lotus, suivi du Livre des sens innombrables et du Livre de la contemplation de Sage-Universel, traduit du chinois par Jean-Noël Robert, Paris: Fayard, 1997, 480 pp.

The *Lotus Sūtra* (*Saddharmapuṇḍarīkasūtra* in Sanskrit, *Miào fǎ lián huā jīng* in Chinese, *Hokkekyō* in Japanese) is not only one of the most important canonical texts but also one of the most accepted and appreciated Buddhist *Sūtras*, due – among other reasons – to its noble, generous and universal message, which promises all men without any difference the access to the Perfect Supreme Enlightenment that brings with itself the condition of *Buddha*, the Omniscience, and an almost infinite existence in a magnificent *World of Buddha* preaching the Doctrine and guiding other beings to Perfect Supreme Enlightenment.

The three translations, object of this review, are from the Chinese version done by Kumārajīva. Burton Watson's translation is accompanied with an introduction, a glossary of persons and places and of Sanskrit terms, and an Index; Margareta von Borsig's translation with an Introduction and a Bibliography on the *Lotus Sūtra*, and Jean-Noël Robert's translation with an Introduction and a Glossary of the most important terms used in the translation, and besides that the French translation also from Chinese of two *Sūtras* that Chinese and Japanese traditions consider to be as the introduction and the conclusion of the *Lotus Sūtra*: *The Sūtra of the Innumerable Meanings* and *The Sūtra of Meditation on the Bodhisattva Universal Virtue.*

The three translations are most valuable, of easy reading and faithful to the original. They will contribute to the spread of the knowledge of a Buddhist text that has had a remarkable influence in Eastern countries and is being now known and appreciated also in the West.

P. S.: Let us say that there is not a Spanish translation of the Chinese translation of the *Lotus Sūtra* done by Kumārajīva. We have done the translation of the *Lotus Sūtra* into Spanish from the Sanskrit original text, and of the *Sūtra of the Infinite Meanings* from the Chinese version done by the Indian monk Dharmajāṭayaśas who came to China in the year 481 A.D.

Our Spanish translation (with Introduction, Notes and several Indices) of the *Lotus Sūtra* has been published by *El Colegio de México-Asociación Latinoamericana de Estudios Budistas*, in Mexico, 1999, 555 pp.

Our Spanish translation of the *Sūtra of the Infinite Meanings*, containing also and Introduction, Notes, and several Indices, was printed in Spain (Bilbao), in 2000, by Desclée de Brouwer, S.A, 94 pp.

Dr. Flora Botton Beja, Professor in the *Centro de Estudios de Asia y Africa* (*CEAA*) of *El Colegio de México*, México, reviewed the Spanish translation by Tola and Dragonetti of the *Lotus Sūtra*, and published her review in the journal *Estudios de Asia y Africa*, Number 116, Mexico, September-December, 2001, pp. 569-574.

Dr. Rosalía C. Vofchuk, Professor of Sanskrit in the *University of Buenos Aires*, Argentina, published also a review on the Spanish translation of the *Lotus Sūtra* done by Tola and Dragonetti in the *Boletín de la Asociación Española de Orientalistas*, Año XXXIX – 2003, Madrid, pp. 285-286.

Very soon will appear in New Jersey, United States of America, published by Primordia Editors, the Portuguese translation of Tola's and Dragonetti's Spanish translation of the *Lotus Sūtra*, done by Dr. Carlos Alberto Da Fonseca Professor of Sanskrit in the *São Paulo University*, Brazil.

Young-ho Kim, A Study and Translation. Tao-sheng's Commentary on the Lotus Sūtra, Albany N.Y.: State University of New York Press, 1990, ix- 374 pp.

The present book is on the life, works and ideas of one of the greatest scholars of Chinese Buddhism, Chu Tao-sheng (*ca.* 360-434), whose original and creative thought had a very important influence in the following epochs of Buddhism.

Tao-sheng wrote commentaries, treatises, expositions, translations, etc. Unfortunately all his works have been lost except his important *Commentary* of the *Lotus Sūtra* (*Miao-fa lien-hua ching shu*) and some fragments and quotations of other works.

Besides a *Preface* and some previous remarks, the book has Three Parts.

Part I deals, in a detailed way, with the state of Buddhist Studies in China before Tao-sheng; the biography of Tao-sheng (it is important to point out that he studied with Kumārajīva, the famous translator to Chinese of the original Sanskrit text of the *Lotus Sūtra*); his works, his doctrines (concerning the Instantaneous Enlightenment, the *Buddha*'s Nature, the *Dharmakāya*, etc.) and finally the influence he exerted on his contemporaries and the Buddhists of the later generations.

Part II contains a critical study of Tao-sheng's *Commentary* on the *Lotus Sūtra* from a literary and doctrinaire point of view, pointing out the central ideas of the *Commentary.*

Finally *Part III* is constituted by a translation from Chinese into English of the Commentary.

The work is profusely provided with learned and explanatory notes, includes a *Glossary* of the Chinese characters (pp. 341-349) and a rich *Bibliography* (pp. 351-363).

The present book of Young-ho Kim, Assistant Professor of Philosophy at *Inha University* in Korea, is based on a solid knowledge of the texts and on the studies related to its subject in Chinese, Japanese and Western languages; it is remarkable for its profound insight of Tao-sheng's thought and for its great critical sense, and its clear and concise exposition.

This work is the best study up to the moment, at least in Western language, on Tao-sheng; and in many places rectifies, fixes or makes clearer the works of Walter Liebenthal on the same subject, published in *Monumenta Nipponica* 11, 3 (1955), pp. 64-96, and 12, 1-2 (1956), pp. 65-103, and 12, 3-4 (1956), pp. 73-100.

The translation of Tao-sheng's commentary is faithful and precise. This book is an essential contribution to the bibliography and knowledge not only of *Lotus Sūtra* but also of Chinese Buddhism.